Grammar
Form and Function 1

Second Edition

Milada Broukal

D1616758

Grammar Form and Function 1, Second Edition

Published by McGraw-Hill ESL/ELT, a business unit of The McGraw-Hill Companies, Inc., 1221 Avenue of the Americas, New York, NY 10020. Copyright © 2010 by The McGraw-Hill Companies, Inc. All rights reserved. No part of this publication may be reproduced or distributed in any form or by any means, or stored in a database or retrieval system, without the prior written consent of The McGraw-Hill Companies, Inc., including, but not limited to, in any network or other electronic storage or transmissions, or broadcast for distance learning.

5 6 7 8 9 10 11 12 DOW/DOW 13 12

ISBN   0-07-338462-3 (Student Book)

Developmental Editor: Nan Clarke
Contributing Writer: Joe Loree
Project Manager: Jenny Hopkins
Publishing Management: Hyphen – Engineering Education
Cover Design: Page2, LLC
Interior Design: Hyphen – Engineering Education

The credits section for this book begins on page 428 and is considered an extension of the copyright page.
Cover photo: Sailing boat, British Columbia (Canada); © iStockphoto.com/laughingmango

www.esl.mcgraw-hill.com

The **McGraw-Hill** Companies

Acknowledgements

The publisher and author would like to thank the following educational professionals whose comments, reviews, and assistance were instrumental in the development of the Grammar Form and Function series.

- Mary Ahlman, *Coastline Community College*, Fountain Valley, CA
- Tony Albert, *Jewish Vocational Services*, San Francisco, CA
- Carlos Alcazar, *Newport Mesa Adult School*, Costa Mesa, CA
- Ted Andersen, *INTRAX International Institute*, San Francisco, CA
- Leslie A. Biaggi, *Miami-Dade Community College*, Miami, FL
- Sharon Bidaure, *INTRAX International Institute*, San Francisco, CA
- Grace Low Bishop, *Houston Community College*, Houston, TX
- Taylor Blakely, *Newport Mesa Adult School*, Costa Mesa, CA
- Gerry Boyd, *Northern Virginia Community College*, Annandale, VA
- Marcia Captan, *Miami-Dade Community College*, Miami, FL
- Sue Chase, *Coastline Community College*, Fountain Valley, CA
- Yongjae Paul Choe, *Dongguk University*, Seoul, Korea
- Mei Cooley, *INTRAX International Institute*, San Francisco, CA
- Laurie Donovan, *Houston Baptist University*, Houston, TX
- Elinore Eaton, *INTRAX International Institute*, San Francisco, CA
- Emma Fuentes, *INTRAX International Institute*, San Francisco, CA
- Sally Gearhart, *Santa Rosa Junior College*, Santa Rosa, CA
- Betty Gilfillan, *Houston Community College*, Houston, TX
- Frank Grandits, *City College of San Francisco*, San Francisco, CA
- Mary Gross, *Miramar College*, San Diego, CA
- Martin Guerin, *Miami-Dade Community College*, Miami, FL
- Earl Hayes, *City College of San Francisco*, San Francisco, CA
- Patty Heiser, *University of Washington*, Seattle, WA
- Lillian Johnston, *Houston Baptist University*, Houston, TX
- Susan Kasten, *University of North Texas*, Denton, TX
- Sarah Kegley, *Georgia State University*, Atlanta, GA
- Kelly Kennedy-Isern, *Miami-Dade Community College*, Miami, FL
- Elisabeth Lindgren, *INTRAX International Institute*, San Francisco, CA
- Wayne Loshusan, *INTRAX International Institute*, San Francisco, CA
- Irene Maksymjuk, *Boston University*, Boston, MA
- Linda Maynard, *Coastline College*, Garden Grove, CA
- Gisele Medina, *Houston Community College*, Houston, TX
- Christina Michaud, *Bunker Hill Community College*, Boston, MA
- Mike Missiaen, *INTRAX International Institute*, San Francisco, CA
- Cristi Mitchell, *Miami-Dade Community College-Kendall Campus*, Miami, FL
- Ilene Mountain, *Newport Mesa Adult School*, Costa Mesa, CA
- Susan Niemeyer, *Los Angeles City College*, Los Angeles, CA
- Carol Piñeiro, *Boston University*, Boston, MA
- Michelle Remaud, *Roxbury Community College*, Boston, MA
- Diana Renn, *Wentworth Institute of Technology*, Boston, MA
- Corinne Rennie, *Newport Mesa Adult School*, Costa Mesa, CA
- Jane Rinaldi, *Cal Poly English Language Institute*, Pomona, CA
- Alice Savage, *North Harris College*, Houston, TX
- Sharon Seymour, *City College of San Francisco*, San Francisco, CA
- Larry Sims, *University of California-Irvine*, Irvine, CA
- Karen Stanley, *Central Piedmont Community College*, Charlotte, NC
- Roberta Steinberg, *Mt. Ida College*, Newton, MA
- Margo Trevino, *Houston Baptist University*, Houston, TX
- Duane Wong, *Newport Mesa Adult School*, Costa Mesa, CA

Contents

Appendices

WELCOME TO

GRAMMAR FORM AND FUNCTION, SECOND EDITION!

Memorable photos bring grammar to life.

8H — The Simple Present with Time Clauses and *If* Clauses

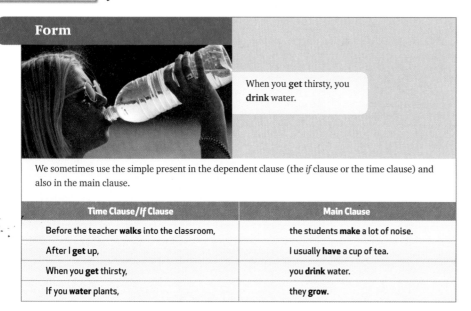

Form

When you **get** thirsty, you **drink** water.

We sometimes use the simple present in the dependent clause (the *if* clause or the time clause) and also in the main clause.

Time Clause/*If* Clause	Main Clause
Before the teacher **walks** into the classroom,	the students **make** a lot of noise.
After I **get** up,	I usually **have** a cup of tea.
When you **get** thirsty,	you **drink** water.
If you **water** plants,	they **grow**.

FORM presentations teach grammar structures through clear comprehensive charts, each of which is accompanied by **a full-color photo** that facilitates students' recall of the target grammar structure.

FUNCTION explanations clarify how and when to use grammar structures.

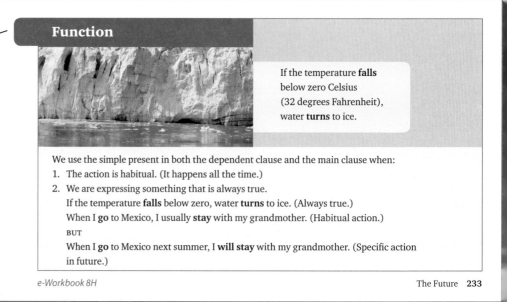

Function

If the temperature **falls** below zero Celsius (32 degrees Fahrenheit), water **turns** to ice.

We use the simple present in both the dependent clause and the main clause when:
1. The action is habitual. (It happens all the time.)
2. We are expressing something that is always true.
    If the temperature **falls** below zero, water **turns** to ice. (Always true.)
    When I **go** to Mexico, I usually **stay** with my grandmother. (Habitual action.)
    BUT
    When I **go** to Mexico next summer, I **will stay** with my grandmother. (Specific action in future.)

e-Workbook 8H

PRACTICE activities guide students from accurate production to fluent use of the grammar.

3 Practice

A Read the sentences about Mario's Restaurant. Underline the correct verb.

1. All of the food (<u>is</u>/are) delicious.
2. All of the dishes (come/comes) with a salad.
3. Most of the wines (is/are) Italian.
4. None of the dishes (is/are) expensive.
5. Almost all of the dishes (have/has) pasta with them.
6. Some of the servers (is/are) Italian.
7. All of the music (is/are) Italian.
8. Almost all of the furniture (is/are) Italian.
9. All of the fish (is/are) very fresh.
10. Some of the pizzas (is/are) wonderful.

B Listen and check your answers. Then listen again and repeat each sentence.

AUDIO
DOWNLOAD
CD4, 20, 21
246 Unit 9

NEW! LISTENING activities highlight the aural/oral dimension of grammar, further increasing students' ability to use and understand spoken English.

Writing: Describe Objects

Write a descriptive paragraph.

STEP 1   Work with a partner. Ask and answer questions about what is on the table. Use *how much, how many, a/an, the, a little, a lot, a few, some, any, no,* and so forth.

Example
YOU: How many eggs are there?
YOUR PARTNER: There are two eggs.

STEP 2   Write a paragraph about what is on the table. Write one sentence in your paragraph that has three or more nouns together. Be sure to put a comma between each noun and before the word *and*.

> *There is a lot of food on the table. There is some bread, some cheese, and some fruit on the table.*

STEP 3   Work with a partner to edit your paragraph. Check spelling, punctuation, vocabulary, and grammar. Then write your final copy.

144 Unit 5

WRITING assignments guide students to develop writing and composition skills through step-by-step tasks.

ALL-NEW TECHNOLOGY ENHANCEMENTS!

NEW! e-WORKBOOK frees teachers from homework correction and provides students with a wealth of interactive practice, anytime—anywhere.

Add instructional hours to the course, provide homework and additional standardized test-taking exercises, and help learners practice the form and function of each grammar point. Audio segments, photos, and video clips enhance many activities.

To purchase e-Workbooks online, visit: http://books.quia.com/books.

NEW! AUDIO DOWNLOAD CENTER offers students the ability to access DOWNLOAD and download MP3 files for all of the listening activities in the Student Book. All Audio Download Center content can be found by visiting **www.esl.mcgraw-hill.com/audio**. To navigate the MP3 files, search for your: Unit Number>Page Number>Activity.

NEW! EZ® Test CD-ROM Test Generator and EZ Test Online enables instructors to access a wealth of grammar items that they can use to create customized tests for each unit. Assessment content is also available at **www.eztestonline.com**.

All-new Internet Activity Worksheets in the Teacher's Manual encourage students to access the Internet to read, research, and analyze information, developing necessary academic skills.

NEW SPECIAL FEATURES

NEW! LISTENING PUZZLES provide audio-based challenges for students to practice new grammar concepts.

NEW! ACADEMIC READING CHALLENGES recycle key vocabulary and grammar in longer contexts, prompting students to integrate their language and critical thinking skill development.

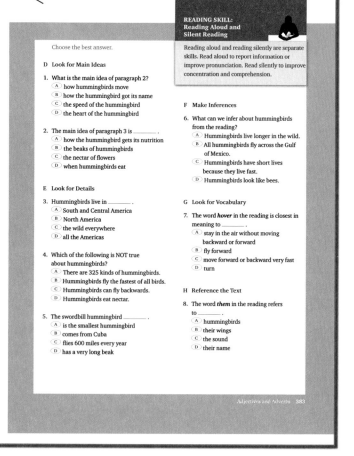

To the Instructor

Series Overview

Form is the structure of a grammar point and what it looks like. Practice of the form builds students' accuracy and helps them recognize the grammar point in authentic situations so they are better prepared to understand what they are reading or what other people are saying.

Function is when and how we use a grammar point. Practice of the function builds students' fluency and helps them apply the grammar point in their real lives.

Mastery of grammar relies on students knowing the rules of English (form) and correctly understanding how to apply them (function). Providing abundant practice in both form and function is key to student success.

Grammar Form and Function, Second Edition is a three-level, communicative grammar series that helps students successfully learn the rules of essential English grammar (form) and when to apply them and what they mean (function). This new full-color edition ensures academic success and a greater ability to comprehend and communicate with ease through the addition of a robust listening program, new academic readings, new communicative activities, and more opportunities for practice with the e-Workbook.

Components and Unit Organization

Each level of Grammar Form and Function, Second Edition includes:

a **Student Book** with 14 units to present and reinforce the grammar. For each grammar point, the Grammar Form and Function, Second Edition Student Book follows a consistent format:

- **Presentation of Form**. The Student Book presents the complete form, or formal rule, along with several examples for students to clearly see the model. There are also relevant, full-color photos to help illustrate the grammar point.
- **Presentation of Function**. The text explains the function of the grammar point, or how it is used, along with additional examples for reinforcement.
- **Practice**. Diverse exercises practice the form and function together.
- **Application**. Students apply the grammar point in open-ended, communicative activities that integrate all language skills.

- All-new **Listening** and **Listening Puzzle** activities provide students with numerous opportunities to develop their oral/aural and discrimination skills.

- **Pair Up and Talk** encourages students to practice conversation and grammar structures with a partner.
- **Your Turn** invites students to personalize the grammar and language.

- **Read** and **Reading Challenge** activities develop reading and thinking skills.
- **Writing** tasks develop writing and composition skills.
- **Self-Test**. Students take a quiz to see what they learned and what they still need to work on and practice.

an **e-Workbook** that extends learning, practice, and testing opportunities.

a **Complete Audio CD Program** for teachers that contains all of the listening activities. Each listening activity will include an audio icon with CD and tracking information. The complete audio files are also available for students as 🎵 **MP3 downloads**.

an **EZ Test ® Test Generator** that includes 560 additional testing items that teachers can use and customize to create tests.

a **Teacher's Manual** to make preparation quick. Each unit of this Teacher's Manual includes:
- an overview of each unit to summarize the contents
- **Notes on the Photos** to describe the photos in the Form and Function sections and give background and cultural information
- **Warm-Up Activities** to engage students in the topic and activate the target grammar
- Useful teaching tips and techniques for both new and experienced instructors to provide students with the information they need
- multiple expansion ideas, games, and writing activities to extend and personalize learning
- **Notes on Culture, Notes on Usage, and Notes on Vocabulary** to help instructors clarify, explain, and present the information with ease
- answers to **Frequently Asked Questions** (FAQs) to provide the instructor and students with a deeper understanding of the structure
- answer keys for the exercises and Self-Tests
- **Unit Tests** in a standardized test format and test answer keys to assess understanding and mastery of the unit
- new **EZ Test ®CD-ROM Test Generator**
- the **Complete Audio CD Program**

Teaching With *Grammar Form and Function, Section Edition*

Leveling and Use

While classes and instructors differ, the Grammar Form and Function, Second Edition Student Books are designed to be used in the following levels:

> *Grammar Form and Function 1, Second Edition*: beginning
>
> *Grammar Form and Function 2, Second Edition*: intermediate
>
> *Grammar Form and Function 3, Second Edition*: high-intermediate to advanced

Grammar Form and Function, Second Edition is a flexible series, and instructional hours can vary depending on the needs of the learners. Instructors can greatly expand their instruction and increase their students' exposure to and practice with the language by using all of the activities in the Student Book, in the e-Workbook, and the additional suggestions and resources provided in the Teacher's Manual.

Assessment

Students and instructors of the Grammar Form and Function, Second Edition series have numerous opportunities to assess progress. There are two **Self-Tests** for each unit—one at the end of each Student Book unit and another at the end of each e-Workbook unit. The Self-Tests build student confidence, encourage student independence as learners, and increase student competence in following standardized test formats.

The Teacher's Manual also includes comprehensive **Tests**. They serve as important tools for the teacher in measuring student mastery of grammar structures. In addition, Grammar Form and Function, Second Edition includes the **EZ Test® CD-ROM Test Generator**. This tool enables instructors to access a wealth of grammar items that they can use and customize to create tests for each unit.

Technology Resources

Grammar Form and Function, Second Edition includes an all-new e-**Workbook**. The e-Workbook can be used to add instructional hours to the course, to provide homework practice and additional standardized testing practice, and to help learners practice the form and function of each grammar point. Color photos, audio segments, and video clips enhance many activities. Students can access the e-Workbook at **http://books.quia.com/books**.

Grammar Form and Function, Second Edition includes reproducible Internet Activity Worksheets that will help students expand their online learning and research skills.

Grammar Form and Function, Second Edition has a wealth of listening activities to encourage communicative competence. The audio icon in the Student book indicates when audio activities are available and the CD or MP3 tracking number. All of the listening activities are available for the instructors on the Complete Audio CD Program that is packaged with the Teacher's Manual. Students can also access and download the **MP3 files** for these activities at the Grammar Form and Function **Audio Download Center** at **www.esl.mcgraw-hill.com/audio**. Select *Grammar Form and Function, 2nd Edition, Level 1*, and download the audio files.

Unit 1

The Present of *Be*

We're from India.

1A	Nouns: Singular **(a book)**
1B	Nouns: Plural **(books)**
1C	Subject Pronouns **(I, you, he, she, it, we, they)**
1D	Subject Pronoun + Present of *Be* **(I am, I'm)**
1E	Negative of *Be* **(I am not. I'm not.)**
1F	*Be* + Adjective **(I'm happy.)**
1G	Possessive Adjectives **(my, your, his, her, its, our, their)**
1H	Demonstratives: *This*, *That*, *These*, and *Those* **(This is my book. These are your books.)**
1I	*Yes/No* Questions with *Be* **(Are you a student? Is she a student?)**
1J	Questions with *What*, *Where*, and *Who* **(What is your name?)**
1K	Prepositions of Place **(in, on, under, above, between)**
✦	Listening Puzzle: Countries
✦	Reading Challenge: Uluru
✦	Writing: Describe Yourself
✦	Self-Test

1A Nouns: Singular

Form/Function

| dog | apple | boy |

Nouns name people, places, animals, and things. Nouns can be singular (one) or plural (more than one). We put *a* or *an* in front of many singular nouns. *A* and *an* have the same meaning. They mean *one* (1).

1. We use *an* when a word begins with the vowels *a, e, i,* and *o.*

    an apple   **an** egg   **an** ice cream   **an** orange

    We use *an* when a word begins with *u* and has a vowel sound.

    an umbrella   **an** uncle

    We use *a* when a word begins with a vowel that sounds like *y.*

    a university   **a** united country   **a** unit   **a** European

2. We also use *an* when a word begins with a silent *h.*

    an hour   **an** honest man   **an** honorable person

    But we use *a* when the *h* is not silent.

    a house   **a** horse   **a** hat

3. We use *a* when a word begins with a consonant sound: *b, c, d, f, g, h, j, k, l, m, n, p, q, r, s, t, v, w, y,* and *z.*

    a book   **a** teacher   **a** country   **a** cat   **a** flower

1 Practice

A Write *a* or *an* before the word.

1. _____*a*_____ table
2. _____ ear
3. _____ animal
4. _____ hotel
5. _____ eye
6. _____ armchair
7. _____ question
8. _____ uncle

9. _____ city
10. _____ house
11. _____ bed
12. _____ exercise
13. _____ university
14. _____ elephant
15. _____ office
16. _____ hourglass

B Listen and check your answers. Then listen again and repeat each phrase.

AUDIO

DOWNLOAD

CD1, 2, 3

1B Nouns: Plural

Form

| a boy | boys | a man | men |

Regular Plurals			
Noun Ending	Spelling Rule	Singular (1)	Plural (+1)
Most consonants	Add -s.	a book a car a teacher	books* cars teachers
The consonants **s**, **ss**, **sh**, **ch**, **x**	Add -es.	a bus a dress a dish a watch a box	buses dresses dishes watches boxes
Consonant + **y**	Drop *y* and add -*ies*.	a baby a country	babies countries
Vowel + **y**	Add -s.	a boy	boys
f or **fe**	Change to -*ves*.	a leaf a life	leaves lives
Irregular Plurals			
Singular (1)		Plural (+1)	
a man		men	
a woman		women	
a child		child**ren**	
a tooth		te**e**th	
a foot		f**ee**t	
a mouse		m**i**ce	
a sheep		**sheep**	
a fish		**fish**	

*We do not use **a/an** with plurals.

2 Practice
Write the plural.

1. key   _____keys_____
2. child   _____
3. city   _____
4. wife   _____
5. woman   _____
6. pen   _____

7. leaf	_____	12. lemon	_____
8. mouse	_____	13. house	_____
9. fish	_____	14. sandwich	_____
10. story	_____	15. brush	_____
11. foot	_____	16. match	_____

3 Practice
Read the words. Write the plural forms in the correct columns.

beach	class	lady	pen	wife
chair	fish	library	shelf	wolf
child	glass	party	street	woman

-s	-es	-ies	-ves	irregular
chairs	classes	ladies	wolves	children

1c Subject Pronouns

Form		
Singular		**Plural**
I		we
you		you
he/she/it		they

1. We use *he* for a man or a boy.

2. We use *she* for a woman or a girl.

3. We use *it* for an animal or a thing.

4. We use *they* for the plural. We use *they* for people, animals, and things.

4 Practice

Write *he*, *she*, *it*, or *they* under the pictures.

1. _____they_____

2. _____

3. _____

4. _____

5. _____

6. _____

7. _____

8. _____

9. _____

5 Practice

Write *he*, *she*, *it*, *we*, *you*, or *they*.

1. man _____he_____
2. woman _____
3. girls _____
4. chairs _____
5. dictionary _____
6. Tony and Ed _____

7. pen _____
8. cats _____
9. book _____
10. Susan and I _____
11. Tony and you _____
12. Susan _____

Form

> She's Sang Hee. He's Shin.
> They are students.
> They are Korean.

Pronoun + *Be*	Contractions
I **am** a student.	**I'm** a student.
You **are** a student.	**You 're** a student.
He **is** Shin.	**He's** Shin.
She **is** Sang Hee.	**She's** Sang Hee.
It **is** a book.	**It's** a book.
We **are** students.	**We're** students.
You **are** friends.	**You're** friends.
They **are** Korean.	**They're** Korean.

Function

We use *am*, *is*, and *are*:
1. To say who we are or who someone else is.
   I **am** Annie.   He**'s** Eddie.
2. To say what we are or what someone else is.
   We **are** students.   They **are** teachers.
3. To talk about nationality.
   I**'m** Turkish.   They**'re** Brazilian.
4. To describe people, things, or places.
   He**'s** hungry.   She**'s** beautiful.

6 Practice

Complete the sentences. Use *am*, *is*, or *are*.

1. I _____*am*_____ a student.
2. You _____ a student, too.
3. We _____ students.
4. He _____ a teacher.
5. Mr. Long and Mr. Black _____ teachers.
6. Annie _____ from Brazil.
7. Eddy _____ 16.
8. They _____ students.
9. You two _____ American.
10. She _____ from Singapore.

7 Practice

A Complete the sentences with contractions of *am*, *is*, or *are*.

1. It _'s_____ a passport.
2. They _____ keys.
3. We _____ from Canada.
4. He _____ a doctor.
5. She _____ a teacher.
6. I _____ Italian.
7. You _____ late.
8. We _____ from Brazil.
9. It _____ a book.
10. He _____ from Spain.

B Listen and check your answers. Then listen again and repeat each sentence.

CD1, 4, 5

Form/Function

She **isn't** a student.
She'**s** a teacher.

Subject	Be + Not		Contractions with Subject	Contractions with *Not*
I	**am not**	a teacher.	**I'm** not a teacher.	*
You	**are not**	from Mexico.	**You're** not from Mexico.	you **aren't**
He She It	**is not**	a student. 21. good.	**He's** not a student. **She's** not 21. **It's** not good.	he **isn't** she **isn't** it **isn't**
We You They	**are not**	Americans. teachers. from Japan.	**We're** not Americans. **You're** not teachers. **They're** not from Japan.	we **aren't** you **aren't** they **aren't**

*There is no contraction for *am not*. We do not use *I'm* at the end of a sentence.
CORRECT: Yes, I am.
INCORRECT: ~~Yes, I'm.~~

8 Practice
Complete the negative sentences. Use *am not, is not,* or *are not.*

1. Mexico _____is not_____ a city. It's a country.

2. I _____ Spanish. I'm Italian.

3. You _____ Spanish. You're Brazilian.

4. He _____ from China. He's from Korea.

5. We _____ from Hong Kong. We're from Singapore.

6. They _____ from England. They're from Australia.

7. It _____ from China. It's from Japan.

8. The teacher _____ from the United States. He's from Canada.

9 Practice

A Complete the sentences. Use *'m not, 's not, isn't, 're not,* or *aren't.*

1. I _____'m not_____ in class 1A. I'm in class 2A.

2. The class _____ at 10:00. It's at 9:00.

3. The students _____ in the classroom. They're outside.

4. The book _____ black. It's white.

5. The exercises _____ long. They're short.

6. The questions _____ difficult. They're easy.

7. She _____ in class today. She's sick.

8. The food in the cafeteria _____ bad. It's good.

9. I _____ ready. Please wait.

10. We're students. We _____ teachers.

B Listen and check your answers. Then listen again and repeat each sentence.

CD1, 6, 7

C Listen again. Where is the speaker? Circle the letter of the correct answer.

CD1, 8

A   in a store
B   at a school

C   at a hospital
D   in an office

10 Practice

Look at the chart below. Complete the sentences on page 12 with *is/isn't* or *are/aren't.*

Name	Country	Age	Occupation
Mei	China	28	teacher
Rengin	Turkey	26	student
Eduardo	Mexico	30	doctor
Nuri	Turkey	24	student

The Present of *Be* **11**

1. Mei _____is_____ from China. She _____isn't_____ from Turkey.

2. Mei _____ 28 years old. She _____ a teacher.

3. Rengin _____ from Turkey. She _____ a doctor.

4. Eduardo _____ from Italy. He _____ from Mexico.

5. Rengin and Nuri _____ from Turkey. They _____ students.

6. They _____ teachers. They _____ doctors.

1F | *Be* + Adjective

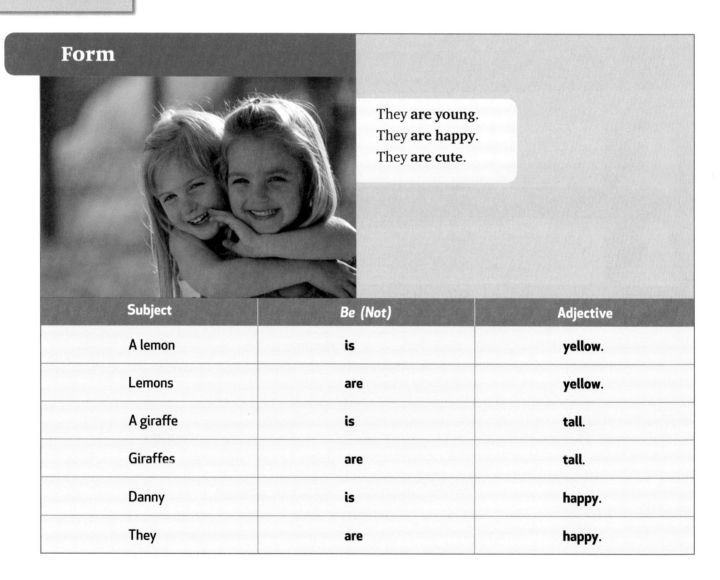

They **are young**.
They **are happy**.
They **are cute**.

Subject	Be (Not)	Adjective
A lemon	is	yellow.
Lemons	are	yellow.
A giraffe	is	tall.
Giraffes	are	tall.
Danny	is	happy.
They	are	happy.

Function

1. Adjectives describe nouns: people, places, animals, or things.

   a **cute** kitten   a **small** skirt   a **young** woman

   a **rich** family   a **cheap** ticket   an **old** city

2. Adjectives do not change for singular or plural.

   He is **a good man**. They are **three good women**.

3. We can put an adjective after *be*.

   They are **hungry**.   We are **thirsty**.

4. We usually make adjectives of nationality from the name of the country.

   We write the country and the adjective with a capital letter.

   He is from **Turkey**.   He is **Turkish**.

Country	Adjective
Brazil	Brazilian
Chile	Chilean
China	Chinese
England	English
France	French
Iran	Iranian
Japan	Japanese
Korea	Korean
Mexico	Mexican
Norway	Norwegian
Peru	Peruvian
Poland	Polish
Portugal	Portuguese
Singapore	Singaporean
Sudan	Sudanese
Sweden	Swedish
Thailand	Thai
United States of America	American

11 Practice

Write sentences about the photos. Use *he*, *she*, *they*, the present form of *be*, and the adjectives.

angry   happy   old   sad   strong   young

1. _She is sad_ .

2. _____ .

3. _____ .

4. _____ .

5. _____ .

6. _____ .

12 Practice

Complete these sentences with the correct nationalities.

1. Song is from Korea. She's _Korean_ .

2. Angel is from Peru. He's _____ .

3. Karin is from Sweden. She's _____ .

4. Ev is from Sudan. He's _____ .

5. Anna is from Poland. She's _____ .

6. Louis is from France. He's _____ .

13 **Practice**

Complete the sentences. Use *is* or *are* and one of these adjectives. More than one answer is possible.

brown	cold	fresh	hard	hot	red	sour
chewy	crunchy	green	heavy	orange	salty	sweet

1. A lemon _____is sour_____ .

2. Tomatoes _____ .

3. Potato chips _____ .

4. A watermelon _____ .

5. An ice cube _____ .

6. An apple _____ .

7. Sugar _____ .

8. Cakes _____ .

9. Soup _____ .

10. Carrot sticks _____ .

11. Chocolate _____ .

12. Bubble gum _____ .

14 **Practice**

Complete the sentences with an affirmative or negative contraction of *be* and the adjectives.

happy	thin	lazy	rich	short	shy	sick	single

1. Ted isn't poor. He _'s rich_____ .

2. Ted isn't tall. He _____ .

3. Ted isn't sad. He _____ .

4. Ted is friendly. He _____ .

5. Ted is healthy. He _____ .

6. Ted isn't married. He _____ .

7. Ted isn't hardworking. He _____ .

8. Ted isn't heavy. He _____ .

The Present of *Be* **15**

15 Practice

A Look at the picture of Ann. Write sentences. Use *is/isn't* or *are/aren't* and one of the adjectives in parentheses.

Ann

Name:	Ann Greene	Occupation:	University student
Nationality:	American	Height:	6 feet (1.8 meters)
Marital Status:	Single	Weight:	143 pounds (65 kilos)

1. (Chinese/American) *She isn't Chinese. She's American* _____ .
2. (short/tall) _____ .
3. (lazy/hardworking) _____ .
4. (heavy/thin) _____ .
5. (old/young) _____ .
6. (married/single) _____ .

B Listen and check your answers. Then listen again and repeat each sentence.

CD1, 9, 10

16 Your Turn

Write about yourself. Use five of the adjectives.

friendly/shy   hardworking/lazy   married/single   tall/short   young/old

Example
I'm Elsie Gonzales. I'm hardworking. I'm not lazy. I'm not shy. I'm friendly.

1G Possessive Adjectives

Form

> That's **my** teacher.
> **Her** name is Ms. Bell.

Pronouns	Possessive Adjectives
I	**my**
you	**your**
he	**his**
she	**her**
it	**its**
we	**our**
they	**their**

Function

1. We call *my, your, his, her, its, our,* and *their* possessive adjectives. We use possessive adjectives before nouns.

   my book   **his** name   **our** house

2. We use possessive adjectives to show that something belongs to someone.

   My car is red.   **Her** car is blue.

17 Practice

Anita is talking about her family. Complete the sentences with *my*, *your*, *his*, *her*, *its*, *our*, or *their*.

_____My_____ name is Anita. I'm 20 years old. I am a student. _____
  1   **2**

brother is a student, too. _____ name is Andrew. He is _____ favorite
                                        3   **4**

brother. I have a mother and a father. They are in Los Angeles. _____
                                                                                          5

last name is Armstrong. _____ father is 53 years old. _____
                                        6   **7**

name is Robert. _____ mother is 48 years old. _____ name is Olivia.
                            8   **9**

They have a house. _____ house is small. They also have a cat.
                                10

_____ name is Spot. I have four brothers and two sisters. _____ family is big
      11   **12**

and happy!

18 Pair Up and Talk

A Practice the conversation with a partner.

A: Look at Anita. Her favorite music is rock.

B: Her favorite sport is tennis.

A: Her favorite food is chocolate.

B Look at the chart. Talk about Anita, Andrew, their parents, and yourself. Use *his*, *her*, *their*, *my*, and words from the chart.

	Music	Sports	Food
Anita	rock	tennis	chocolate
Andrew	rock	football	fries
Their parents	opera	ice-skating	pasta
You	*jazz*		

1H Demonstratives: *This, That, These,* and *Those*

Form

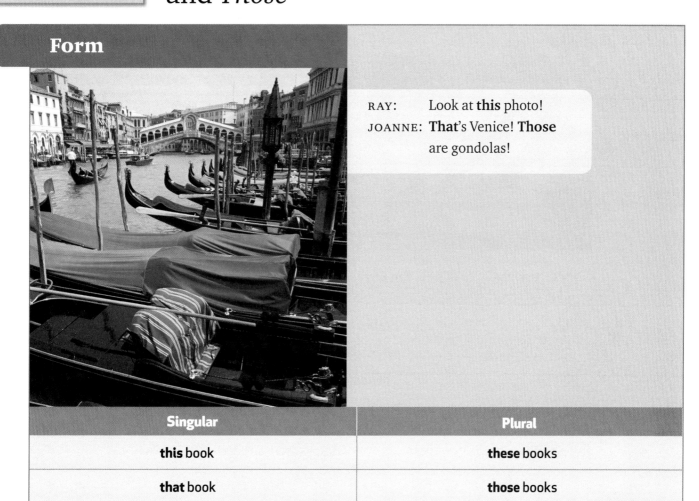

RAY: Look at **this** photo!
JOANNE: **That**'s Venice! **Those** are gondolas!

Singular	Plural
this book	**these** books
that book	**those** books

Function

We use *this* and *these* for people and things that are near to us. We use *that* and *those* for people and things that are not near.

This is my book. (The book is near me.)
That is your book. (The book is not near me.)

19 Practice

A Mrs. Cooper has a visitor. Her name is Berta. Berta wants to practice her English. Complete Berta's answers with *this is, that is, these are,* or *those are.*

MRS. COOPER: Give me the English names for the things you can see.

BERTA:

1. _____*This is*_____ a table.

2. _____ a newspaper.

3. _____ a dictionary.

4. _____ a pen.

5. _____ a cup.

6. _____ sandwiches.

7. _____ a napkin.

8. _____ my books.

B Listen and check your answers. Then listen again and repeat each sentence.

CD1, 11, 12

20 Pair Up and Talk

A Practice the conversation with a partner.

A: This is my jacket.

B: That is his chair.

B Now point to or touch things or people in the classroom. Use *this* or *that* and words from the list.

| blackboard | classmate | jacket | sweater | textbook |
| chair | dictionary | notebook | teacher | watch |

1I | *Yes/No* Questions with *Be*

Form

Are you from Indonesia?
No, we're not.
We're from India.

Yes/No Questions			Short Answers	
Be	**Subject**		**Affirmative**	**Negative**
Am	I		**Yes,** you **are.**	**No,** you**'re not**/you **aren't.**
Are	you		I **am.**	I**'m not.**
Is	he she it	from India?	he **is.** she **is.** it **is.**	he**'s not**/he **isn't.** she**'s not**/she **isn't.** it**'s not**/it **isn't.**
Are	you we they		we **are.** you **are.** they **are.**	we**'re not**/we **aren't.** you**'re not**/you **aren't.** they**'re not**/they **aren't.**

Function

1. *Yes/No* questions begin with *am*, *is*, or *are*. In short answers, we only use *yes* or *no*, the subject pronoun, and the verb. We add *not* if the answer is negative.
   Are you a student? **Yes, I am./No, I'm not.**
2. After *yes*, we do not contract forms of *be*. After *no*, there are two possible contractions. There is no difference in meaning.
   It isn't here. OR **It's not** here.
   CORRECT: Yes, **I am.**/Yes, **she is.**
   INCORRECT: Yes, I'm./Yes, she's.

21 Practice

A Read the information about the two people below. Then complete the questions and answers.

Name:	Patricia Carlos		Name:	Dave Fan
Age:	18		Age:	18
Job:	Student		Job:	Student
Nationality:	Colombian		Nationality:	Malaysian
Marital status:	Single		Marital status:	Single

1. _____*Is she*_____ a teacher?   No, she isn't.

2. Is she young?   Yes, _____*she is*_____ .

3. Is she Brazilian?   No, _____ .

4. _____ Colombian?   Yes, she is.

5. _____ 18 years old?   Yes, she is.

6. Is she a student?   Yes, _____ .

7. _____ 19 years old?   No, he isn't.

8. _____ Malaysian?   Yes, he is.

9. Is he a doctor?   No, _____ .

10. _____ single?   Yes, he is.

11. _____ students?   Yes, they are.

12. _____ young?   Yes, they are.

13. Are they single?   Yes, _____ .

14. _____ American?   No, they aren't.

B Listen and check your answers. Then work with a partner. Listen again and repeat the questions and answers.

  CD1, 13, 14

22 Practice

Work with a partner. Ask and answer questions.

1. _Is she_ _____ a teacher?

   No, she isn't _____ .

   She's a doctor _____ .

2. _Are they_ _____ flowers?

   Yes, they are _____ .

   _____ .

3. _____ a dog?

   _____ .

   _____ .

4. _____ a camera?

   _____ .

   _____ .

5. _____ books?

   _____ .

   _____ .

6. _____ glasses?

   _____ .

   _____ .

7. _____ peppers?

   _____ .

   _____ .

8. _____ the Statue of Liberty?

   _____ .

   _____ .

1J | Questions with *What*, *Where*, and *Who*

Form

JOHN: **Who** is she?
SUE: She is a student.
JOHN: **What**'s her name?
SUE: Her name is Maria Verdi.
JOHN: **Where**'s she from?
SUE: She's from Italy.

Questions			Answers
Wh- Word	*Be*	Subject	
What	is	your name?	My name is Kelly.
What	are	these?	They're pens.
Where	is	Joe?	He's at home.
Where	are	you from?	I'm from Mexico.
Who	is	he?	He's my brother.
Who	are	they?	They're visitors.

Contractions	
what is	**what's**
where is	**where's**
who is	**who's**

Function

We use question words such as *what*, *where*, and *who* to ask for information.

1. We use *what* to ask questions about things.

    QUESTION: **What** is that?

    ANSWER: It's a pen.

2. We use *where* to ask questions about location.

    QUESTION: **Where** is Silvia?

    ANSWER: She's at school.

3. We use *who* to ask questions about people.

    QUESTION: **Who** is he?

    ANSWER: He's my teacher.

23 Practice

Look at the photos and the information about the people. Write questions with *who*, *what*, and *where*.

1. <u>Who is she</u>   ?

   She is Sarah Jones.

2. _____ ?

   She's an actress.

3. _____ ?

   She is from New York.

4. _____ ?

   He's Paul Estrada.

5. _____ ?

   He is from Peru.

6. _____ ?

   He is a student.

7. _____ ?

   I'm Ben Thomas.

8. _____ ?

   I'm from Canada.

9. _____ ?

   I'm a teacher.

Function

We use prepositions of place to say where people or things are.
Here are some prepositions of place.

1. The mouse is **in** the box.

2. The mouse is **on** the box.

3. The mouse is **under** the box.

4. The mouse is **behind** the box.

5. The mouse is **above** the box.

6. The mouse is **in front of** the box.

7. The mouse is **between** the boxes.

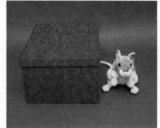

8. The mouse is **next to** the box.

We also say:
at school, **at** the office, **at** the airport, **in** my apartment, **in** the classroom
on the second floor, **on** the third floor, **on** the tenth floor

24 Practice
Complete the paragraph with the prepositions.

above   at   behind   in   in front of   next to   on   under

Ricky isn't _____*in*_____ his bedroom. He is _____ school right now.
                    1   **2**

His room is _____ the second floor of his house. Look at his room.
                       3

A glass is _____ the chair. A clock is _____ the desk. His lamp is
                     4   **5**

_____ the computer. Books are _____ the desk. A book is _____
        6   **7**   **8**

the computer. His red jacket is _____ the chair. The backpack is
                                          9

_____ the desk. A notebook is _____ the backpack.
        10   **11**

25 Pair Up and Talk
A   Practice the conversation with a partner.

A: **Where** is your pen?
B: My pen is **on** the desk.

B   Ask and answer questions with *where* and these phrases.

the board   the door   your backpack   your dictionary
the clock   the teacher   your book   your pen

26 Read
Read the story. Then write answers to the questions.

HAPPY OR NOT?

There is a man with two children. His name is Alfred. His daughter is Emma. His son is Bert. Emma is a gardener. Bert is a brickmaker. One day, the father asks Emma, "Are you happy?" Emma says, "Yes, I am father. There is a lot of rain for my plants." Then the father asks Bert, "Are you happy?" Bert says, "No, father, I'm not. There is a lot of rain, and my bricks aren't dry." The father is confused. He says, "My daughter is happy, but my son is unhappy. Now what am I?"

1. Who are Emma and Bert?

   _____ .

2. Who is Alfrcd?

   _____ .

3. What is Emma?

   _____ .

4. What is Bert?

   _____ .

5. Are Emma and Bert happy?

   _____ .

6. Is there rain for the plants?

   _____ .

7. Why aren't the bricks dry?

   _____ .

8. Is the father happy?

   _____ .

Listening Puzzle

AUDIO DOWNLOAD   CD1, 15

A Listen and check the correct answer.

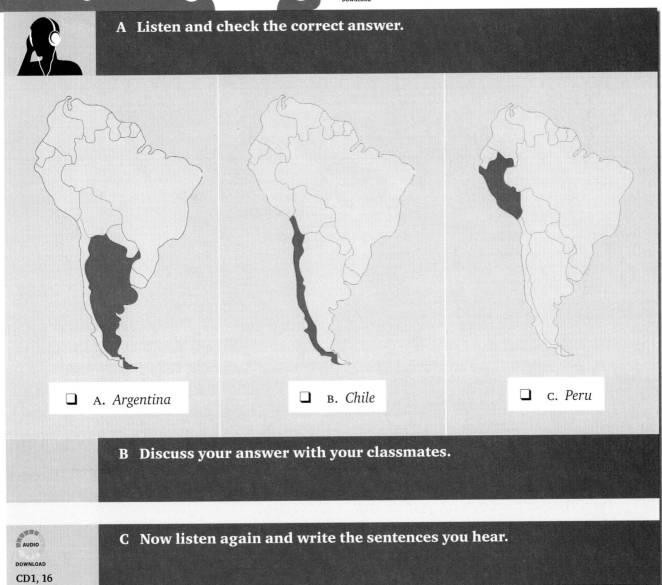

☐ A. *Argentina* ☐ B. *Chile* ☐ C. *Peru*

B Discuss your answer with your classmates.

AUDIO DOWNLOAD CD1, 16

C Now listen again and write the sentences you hear.

A Before You Read

Answer the questions.

1. Where is Australia?
2. What is Australia famous for?

B Read

ULURU

DID YOU KNOW ... ?
Uluru is millions of years old.

The center of Australia is desert. For Australians, this desert is the "Outback." Here in the desert, there is a very big stone. It is 1,143 feet (348 5 meters) high, two miles (3.2 kilometers) long, and ½ mile (804 meters) wide. This is "Uluru," or Ayers Rock.

The rock is famous for its colors in the day. 10 In the morning it is pink, but at sunset it is orange. The color of the rock is different with the weather, too. After rain, the rock looks different. There are stripes of silver. There are waterfalls, too. These are about 700 feet (213 15 meters) high.

Over 400,000 visitors come to the Outback every year. They come to see Uluru. Uluru is a special place for the native Australians, or Aborigines. It is a sacred, or religious, place 20 for them.

C Notice the Grammar

Underline all forms of the verb *be* and all pronouns.

Choose the best answer.

D Look for Main Ideas

1. What is Uluru?
   - (A) It is a desert.
   - (B) It is a stone.
   - (C) It is the Outback.

2. Where is Uluru?
   - (A) It is in Ayers Rock.
   - (B) It is in the Outback.
   - (C) It is in the center of the stone.

3. What color is Uluru in the morning?
   - (A) silver
   - (B) orange
   - (C) pink

4. What is Uluru famous for?
   - (A) its size
   - (B) its colors
   - (C) its Aborigines

5. For the Aborigines, Uluru is _____ .
   - (A) a place for visitors
   - (B) a place for rain
   - (C) a sacred place

READING SKILL:
Pre-Reading Questions

Pre-reading questions help you use what you know about a subject. These questions help you to understand the reading.

Writing: Describe Yourself

Write four sentences about yourself.

STEP 1   Read the information about the person below. Then complete the sentences.

Name: Engin Almas
Age: 20
Job: Student
Nationality: Turkish

His name _____*is*_____ Engin Almas. He _____ 20 years old. He is a _____ .
He _____ Turkish.

STEP 2   Complete the information about yourself.

Name: _____
Age: _____
Job: _____
Nationality: _____

STEP 3   Write about yourself. Follow the model. Remember to use capital letters for names.

My name is Engin Almas. I am 20 years old.

A Choose the best answer, A, B, C, or D, to complete the sentence. Darken the oval with the same letter.

1. Eggs _____ black.

   A. are not   Ⓐ Ⓑ Ⓒ Ⓓ
   B. isn't
   C. no are
   D. no is

2. A: Are you a student?
   B: Yes, _____ .

   A. I'm   Ⓐ Ⓑ Ⓒ Ⓓ
   B. I am
   C. I'm not
   D. I'm student

3. _____ my grammar book?

   A. Is   Ⓐ Ⓑ Ⓒ Ⓓ
   B. When's
   C. Who's
   D. Where's

4. _____ the capital of Mexico?

   A. Who's   Ⓐ Ⓑ Ⓒ Ⓓ
   B. Is
   C. Where
   D. What's

5. The teacher is _____ the classroom.

   A. on   Ⓐ Ⓑ Ⓒ Ⓓ
   B. in
   C. at
   D. from

6. _____ are doctors.

   A. This woman   Ⓐ Ⓑ Ⓒ Ⓓ
   B. These woman
   C. These women
   D. These womans

7. They are _____ .

   A. good childs   Ⓐ Ⓑ Ⓒ Ⓓ
   B. goods children
   C. good childrens
   D. good children

8. A: _____ that man?
   B: That's my father.

   A. Who   Ⓐ Ⓑ Ⓒ Ⓓ
   B. What's
   C. Who's
   D. What

9. _____ airplanes are big.

   A. Those   Ⓐ Ⓑ Ⓒ Ⓓ
   B. This
   C. They
   D. It

10. A: _____ at school today?
    B: Yes, he is.

    A. Is Ken   Ⓐ Ⓑ Ⓒ Ⓓ
    B. Ken
    C. Ken he is
    D. Ken is

1. How old is the pyramids in Egypt?
   A   B   C   D

   Ⓐ   Ⓑ   Ⓒ   Ⓓ

2. What are the name of the
   A   B   C

   seven continents?
   D

   Ⓐ   Ⓑ   Ⓒ   Ⓓ

3. My brother is a student in an university in
   A   B   C   D

   my country.

   Ⓐ   Ⓑ   Ⓒ   Ⓓ

4. Watches from Switzerland are expensives.
   A   B   C   D

   Ⓐ   Ⓑ   Ⓒ   Ⓓ

5. That's my teacher in front the classroom.
   A   B   C   D

   Ⓐ   Ⓑ   Ⓒ   Ⓓ

6. They're visitor from Guatemala
   A   B   C

   in Central America.
   D

   Ⓐ   Ⓑ   Ⓒ   Ⓓ

7. Good doctors are important in an hospital.
   A   B   C   D

   Ⓐ   Ⓑ   Ⓒ   Ⓓ

8. An horse is an intelligent animal.
   A   B   C   D

   Ⓐ   Ⓑ   Ⓒ   Ⓓ

9. That man are a famous actor in my country.
   A   B   C   D

   Ⓐ   Ⓑ   Ⓒ   Ⓓ

10. Puerto Rico is a island and a country
    A   B   C

    in the Atlantic Ocean.
    D

    Ⓐ   Ⓑ   Ⓒ   Ⓓ

Unit 2

Be: *It*, *There*, and the Simple Past of *Be*

There's a woman at
the desk.

Form/Function

It's hot.
It's sunny.
It's 90 degrees Fahrenheit/32 degrees Celsius.
Cindy is in the swimming pool.

We use *it* to talk about the weather.

It's sunny.

Questions	Answers
How's the weather in Los Angeles? What's the weather like today?	It's sunny. It's hot/cold. It's rainy. It's windy. It's not cold.
What's the temperature like today?	It's 90 degrees Fahrenheit/32 degrees Celsius.

1 Practice

A Write the answers to the questions.

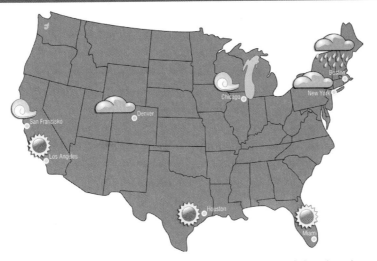

1. What's the weather like in New York City? _It's cloudy_____ .

2. How's the weather in Houston? _____ .

3. What's the weather like in Los Angeles? _____ .

4. Is it rainy or windy in Chicago today? _____ .

5. Is it hot or cold in Miami? _____ .

6. What's the weather like in Boston? _____ .

7. How's the weather in San Francisco? _____ .

8. Is it cloudy or windy in Denver? _____ .

B **Listen and check your answers. Work with a partner. Then listen again and repeat the questions and answers.**

CD1, 17, 18

2 Pair Up and Talk

Work with a partner. Ask your partner about the weather today. Ask about the weather map.

A: What's the weather like today?

B: It's cool and cloudy.

2B | *It* to Tell the Time

Form/Function

A: What time is **it**?
B: **It's** eleven past 10:00.

1. We use *it* to talk about time, including days, dates, months, and years.

Time		Days, Dates, Months, Years	
Question	**Answers**	**Questions**	**Answers**
		What day is **it**?	**It's** Wednesday.
	It's two.	What month is **it**?	**It's** July.
What time is **it**?	**It's** two o'clock.		
	It's two P.M.	What year is **it**?	**It's** 2008.
		What's the date today?	**It's** July 6th.

2. We can express the time in different ways.

   2:15   **It's** two fifteen.   OR   **It's** a quarter past two.

   10:35   **It's** ten thirty-five.   OR   **It's** twenty-five to eleven.

3. When we say 12 A.M., it's midnight.

4. When we say 12 P.M., it's noon, or midday.

   *A.M. = morning (before noon)

   *P.M. = after noon (between noon and midnight)

3 Practice
A Say these times.

1.

2.

3.

4.

5.

6.

B   Listen and check your answers. Then listen again and repeat each time.

AUDIO

DOWNLOAD

CD1, 19, 20

4 Practice
Match the questions with the answers.

A		B
_e_	1. What time is it?	a. It's Monday.
_____	2. What month is it?	b. It's 2003.
_____	3. What year is it?	c. It's September.
_____	4. What day is it?	d. It's September 10th.
_____	5. What's the date today?	e. It's 2:30.

5 Pair Up and Talk
Work with a partner. Ask and answer the questions from Practice 4.

Form

When is Timmy's birthday?
It's **on** September 10th.
It's **on** Sunday.

When

Question			Answers
When	*Verb*		
When	is	your birthday?	It's on September 10th. On September 10th. September 10th.

What

Questions				Answers
What	*Noun*	*Verb*	*Object*	
What **What**	day time	is	the party?	It's on Sunday. On Sunday. It's at 8:00. At 8:00. 8:00.

Function

1. We use *when* or *what* for questions about time.

   When is your birthday?   It's on Sunday.

   What day is the party?   It's on Sunday.

   What time is the party?   It's at 8:00.

2. When we talk about time, we usually use the prepositions *in, on,* or *at.*

   a. We use *in* for parts of the day and with months, seasons, and years:

      in the morning, **in** the afternoon, **in** the evening

      in July, **in** August, **in** September

      in the spring, **in** the summer, **in** the winter, **in** the fall

      in 1746, **in** 1942, **in** 2008

   b. We use *at* with *night*: **at** night

   c. We use *on* with days and dates:

      on Monday, **on** Tuesday morning

      on September 12th OR **on** the 12th of September

   d. We use *at* for times of the day:

      at 2 o'clock, **at** 5:15

3. We use *from … to* for the start and finish of something:

   from 9 **to** 10, **from** 7:30 **to** 11:15

6 Practice

Complete the sentences with the prepositions of time *in, on, at,* or *from … to.*

1. I was born _____*in*_____ August.

2. I was born _____ 1985.

3. I was born _____ August 20, 1985.

4. I get up _____ seven o'clock.

5. My class is _____ 9:15.

6. I have class _____ Mondays and Wednesdays.

7. I have class _____ the morning.

8. I work _____ Tuesday _____ Thursday.

9. I study _____ night.

10. I go to bed _____ 11:30.

7 Practice

Work with a partner. Ask and answer questions about holidays. Then write the answers.

January

S	M	T	W	T	F	S
			1 *New Year's Day*	2	3	4
5	6	7	8	9	10	11
12	13	14	15	16	17	18
19	20	21	22	23	24	25
26	27	28	29	30	31	

February

S	M	T	W	T	F	S
						1
2	3	4	5	6	7	8
9	10	11	12	13	14 *Valentine's Day*	15
16	17	18	19	20	21	22
23	24	25	26	27	28	

May

S	M	T	W	T	F	S
		1	2	3	4	5
6	7	8	9	10	11	12
13 *Mother's Day*	14	15	16	17	18	19
20	21	22	23	24	25	26
27	28	29	30	31		

November

S	M	T	W	T	F	S
1	2	3	4	5	6	7
8	9	10	11	12	13	14
15	16	17	18	19	20	21
22	23	24	25	26 *Thanksgiving*	27	28
29	30					

1. When is New Year's Day? *It's on January 1st* .

2. What day is New Year's Day? _____ .

3. When is Mother's Day? _____ .

4. What day is Mother's Day? _____ .

5. When and what day is Valentine's Day? _____ .

6. When and what day is Thanksgiving? _____ .

8 Pair Up and Talk

A Practice the conversation with a partner.

A: When is the last day of class?

B: It's on December 17th.

B Now practice the conversation with your partner again. Use these phrases.

the last day of class	the next test	your birthday
the next school holiday	Valentine's Day	

2D Statements with *There + Be*

Form

There is a table.
There are two cups on the table.
There isn't a glass of water.
There aren't four hands.

Affirmative

	There	Be	Subject	Location
Singular	There	is	a woman	at the table.
Plural	There	are	two cups	on the table.

Negative

	There	Be + Not	Subject	Location
Singular	There	isn't	a glass	on the table.
Plural	There	aren't	any* glasses	on the table.

Contractions

there is	there's
there is not	there isn't there's not
there are not	there aren't

*We use *any* before plural nouns that follow negative verbs and in *yes/no* questions.
Are there **any** cookies on the table? (*yes/no* question) No, there aren't **any** cookies on the table. (negative verb)

Function

1. We use *there is/there's* or *there are* to say something exists.

   There's a computer in the room.

   There are books on the desk.

2. We use *there isn't/there aren't* to say something doesn't exist.

   There isn't a waiter in the picture.

   There aren't any glasses on the table.

9 Practice

A Look at Ted's kitchen. Complete the sentences with *there is* or *there are*.

1. ___There is___ a table in the kitchen. _____ two chairs.

2. _____ plates and pots on the table.

3. _____ cups on the floor. _____ a telephone on the floor, too.

4. _____ a pot on the stove.

5. _____ pots and dishes in the sink.

6. _____ a backpack under the table. _____ a jacket on the floor.

B Listen and check your answers. Then listen again and repeat each sentence.

CD1, 21, 22

44 Unit 2

10 Practice

Look at the photo. Complete the sentences with *there's/there are* or *there isn't/there aren't*.

1. ____There's____ a woman at the desk.

2. _____ a desk.

3. _____ a laptop.

4. _____ a telephone.

5. _____ flowers.

6. _____ any books.

7. _____ a clock.

8. _____ papers.

9. _____ pens.

10. _____ any bottles of water.

11 Your Turn

Write sentences about things that are and are not in your classroom.

Things in the classroom

1. *There are desks* .
2. _____ .
3. _____ .
4. _____ .
5. _____ .

Things not in the classroom

6. _____ .
7. _____ .
8. _____ .
9. _____ .
10. _____ .

Questions with *There + Be*

Form

A: **Is there** a big hotel near the lake?
B: No, **there isn't.**

Questions with *Is There / Are There*				Short Answers	
Be	**There**	**Subject**	**Location**	**Affirmative**	**Negative**
Is	**there**	a bank	in the town?	**Yes,** there **is.**	**No,** there **isn't.**
Are	**there**	any shops		there **are.**	there **aren't.**

Questions with *How Many*			Answers
How Many	**Plural Noun**	*Be + There*	*There + Be + Number + Noun*
How many	restaurants	**are there?**	**There is** one restaurant.
			There are two restaurants.

12 Practice

A Read the brochure for a hotel resort.

BLUE LAKE HOTEL

WELCOME TO THE BLUE LAKE HOTEL!

This is the view from the hotel. You are in the mountains in just five minutes.

There are 250 rooms in the hotel. There are three restaurants and over 20 shops. There is an exercise center, and there are two swimming pools. There is a movie theater, too.

There is an underground parking lot. There is also a train near the hotel. The train takes you to the town of Gertan in 20 minutes.

Come and relax in the mountains.

B Complete the questions and answers with *there is, there isn't, there are, there aren't, is there,* or *are there.* Use *how many* when necessary. Use *yes* and *no* as necessary.

1. Is there a view from the hotel? <u>Yes, there is</u> .

2. _____ mountains near the hotel? Yes, _____ .

3. _____ an exercise center? _____ .

4. _____ train service to the town? _____ .

5. _____ an underground parking lot? _____ .

6. _____ a town near the hotel? _____ .

7. _____ a movie theater? _____ .

8. How many swimming pools _____ ? _____ .

9. How many restaurants _____ ? _____ .

10. _____ shops _____ ? _____ .

C Listen and check your answers. Then work with a partner. Listen again and repeat the questions and answers.

AUDIO
DOWNLOAD
CD1, 23, 24

13   Pair Up and Talk

A   Practice the conversation with a partner.

A: How many minutes are there in an hour?

B: There are 60.

B   Now practice the conversation with your partner again. Use these words and phrases.

centimeters/a meter   days/a year   hours/day   minutes/an hour

days/a week   hours/a week   inches/a foot   weeks/a year

14   Practice

Work with a partner or group. Think of a word. Your partner or the group guesses the word. Ask and answer questions with *is there, are there, there is,* or *there are.*

Example

QUESTION: How many letters are there in the word?

ANSWER: There are eight letters.

QUESTION: Is there an *e* in it?

ANSWER: Yes, there is. (Continue until someone guesses the word.)

15   Practice

Work in pairs or groups. Ask and answer questions about your hometowns. Use *it* and *there + be.* Use these ideas or your own.

beach   parks   shopping malls   tourists

mountains   river   subway   weather

Example

1.   What's the weather like in the summer? It's very hot.

2.   Is it rainy in the winter? Yes, it is.

3.   Is there a beach near your hometown? No, there isn't.

4.   Are there any parks in your hometown? Yes, there are.

Form

John is working, **but** he is not in the office.

1. We use a comma before the conjunctions *and*, *but*, and *or* when we connect two sentences.
   The food at this restaurant is delicious, **and** it's cheap.
   The food is cheap, **but** it's not good.
   We can go to an Italian restaurant, **or** we can go to a Chinese restaurant.

2. We do not use a comma when the conjunction separates two adjectives.
   The food is good **and** cheap.
   She is tired **but** happy.
   It's good **or** bad.

3. We do not use a comma when the conjunction separates two nouns or prepositional phrases.
   There are closets **and** windows in my apartment.
   Are you busy Saturday **or** Sunday?
   There are oranges in the refrigerator **and** on the table.

Function

We use *and*, *but*, and *or* to join two sentences.

Conjunction	Function	Example
and	adds information	The coat is beautiful. The coat is beautiful **and** warm.
but	gives a contrasting idea	I want to go skiing. I don't have the money. I want to go skiing, **but** I don't have the money.
or	gives a choice	We go. We stay. We go, **or** we stay.

16 Practice

A Complete the sentences with *and*, *but*, or *or*.

1. Our school is old, _____ *but* _____ it is clean.

2. The classrooms are sunny _____ bright.

3. There are old tables _____ chairs in our classroom.

4. The chairs are old, _____ they are strong.

5. There are two cafeterias. There is a cafeteria for the students, _____ there is a cafeteria for the teachers.

6. We sell two kinds of food: hot food like pizza _____ cold food like sandwiches.

7. In my class, there are students from Mexico, _____ there are students from Japan.

8. Is your teacher funny _____ serious?

9. My English class is great, _____ I have a lot of homework.

10. Is your book blue, _____ is it green?

B Listen and check your answers. Then listen again and repeat each sentence.

AUDIO
DOWNLOAD
CD1, 25, 26

C Listen again. Read the sentences. Circle *True* or *False*.

AUDIO
DOWNLOAD
CD1, 27

		True	False
1.	Students and teachers eat together.	True	False
2.	The students are from different countries.	True	False
3.	The speaker does not like his/her English class.	True	False

Your Turn
Write four things about where you live.

1. _____ .

2. _____ .

3. _____ .

4. _____ .

18 **Practice**
Match the ideas in A and B. Then write sentences with *and*, *but*, and *or*. Use commas and capital letters correctly.

	A		**B**
_c_ **1.**	He's not rich	**a.**	it's warm today.
2.	It's winter	**b.**	afternoon?
3.	What's the best time for you? Morning	**c.**	he has an expensive car.
4.	It's late	**d.**	Italian.
5.	Is a tomato a fruit	**e.**	bad?
6.	Is this milk good	**f.**	a vegetable?
7.	She speaks Spanish, French,	**g.**	the food is very good.
8.	The restaurant is clean	**h.**	I'm tired. Let's go home.

1. _He's not rich, but he has an expensive car_ .

2. _____ .

3. _____ .

4. _____ .

5. _____ .

6. _____ .

7. _____ .

8. _____ .

The Simple Past of *Be*: Affirmative and Negative Statements

Form

Bertie and Brenda 50 years ago
Brenda **was** 25 years old in the photo.
Brenda is 75 years old today.

Bertie and Brenda today
Bertie and Brenda are happy today.
They **were** happy 50 years ago.

Subject	Be (Not)		Time Expressions
I	was (not)		yesterday.
You	were (not)		two hours ago.
He/She/It	was (not)		three weeks ago.
We	were (not)	here	four months ago.
They	were (not)		last night/week/month/year.
			in 1980.

Contractions	
was not	wasn't
were not	weren't

Function

We use *was* and *were* to talk about the past. For this reason, we often use time expressions like *yesterday, four hours ago, last week, 20 years ago,* and *in 1995* with *was* and *were*.

It **was** cold **yesterday**.
We **weren't** in New York **in 1998**.

---

19 Practice

A Complete the sentences with *is, was, are,* or *were*.

1. Today, Bertie _____*is*_____ 80 years old.

2. Fifty years ago, Bertie _____ an engineer.

3. Brenda _____ a secretary 50 years ago.

4. Brenda _____ 75 years old today.

5. Fifty years ago, they _____ in the city most of the time.

6. Today, they _____ on their farm.

7. Bertie and Brenda _____ happy 50 years ago.

8. Bertie and Brenda _____ happy today.

B Listen and check your answers. Then listen again and repeat each sentence.

AUDIO
DOWNLOAD
CD1, 28, 29

C Listen again. What is Brenda's age now? Circle the letter of the correct answer.

AUDIO
DOWNLOAD
CD1, 30

A 80
B 50
C 75

Be: It, There, and the Simple Past of *Be* 53

20 Practice

Complete the sentences about Michelangelo and Leonardo da Vinci with *was, were, wasn't,* or *weren't.*

Michelangelo

Italian

painter

young (when in Florence)

architect

single

Leonardo da Vinci

Italian

painter

old (when in Florence)

architect, inventor, and engineer

single

Leonardo da Vinci and Michelangelo ____*were*____ Italians. They both _____
　　　　　　　　　　　　　　　　　　　　　　1　　　　　　　　　　　　　　　　2

in Florence, Italy at the same time. Leonardo _____ young, but Michelangelo
　　　　　　　　　　　　　　　　　　　　　　　　　　　3

_____ young. Leonardo and Michelangelo _____ both architects. Leonardo
　　4　　　　　　　　　　　　　　　　　　　　　　　　5

_____ an inventor, but Michelangelo _____ an inventor. Leonardo
　　6　　　　　　　　　　　　　　　　　　7

_____ an engineer, but Michelangelo _____ an engineer. Leonardo
　　8　　　　　　　　　　　　　　　　　　9

_____ single, and Michelangelo _____ single. Both Leonardo and
　　10　　　　　　　　　　　　　　　　　11

Michelangelo _____ married.
　　　　　　　　　12

2H | The Simple Past of *Be*: Questions

Form

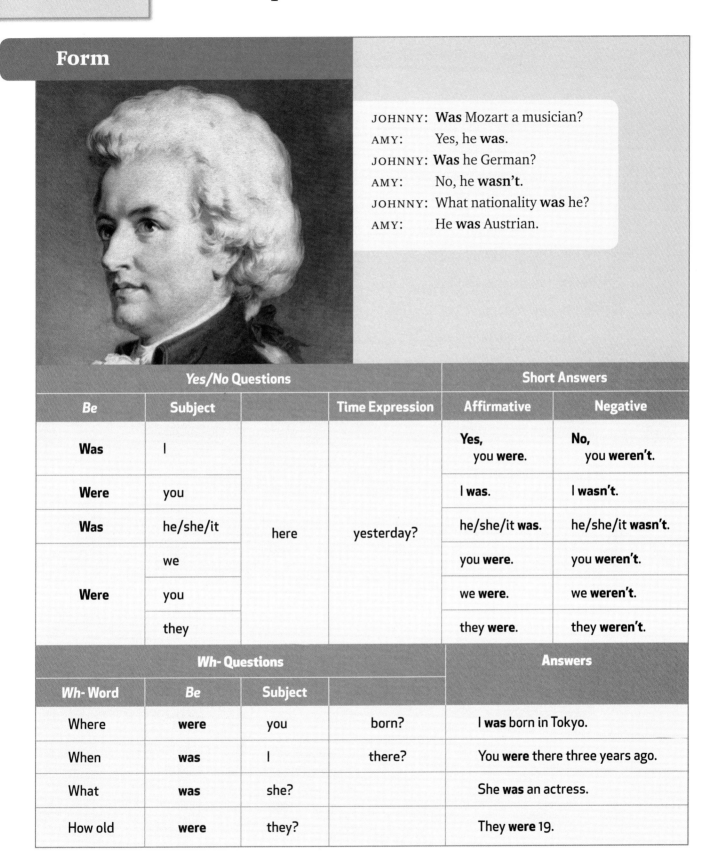

JOHNNY: **Was** Mozart a musician?
AMY: Yes, he **was**.
JOHNNY: **Was** he German?
AMY: No, he **wasn't**.
JOHNNY: What nationality **was** he?
AMY: He **was** Austrian.

Yes/No Questions				Short Answers	
Be	**Subject**		**Time Expression**	**Affirmative**	**Negative**
Was	I			**Yes,** you **were**.	**No,** you **weren't**.
Were	you			I **was**.	I **wasn't**.
Was	he/she/it	here	yesterday?	he/she/it **was**.	he/she/it **wasn't**.
	we			you **were**.	you **weren't**.
Were	you			we **were**.	we **weren't**.
	they			they **were**.	they **weren't**.

Wh- Questions				Answers
Wh- Word	**Be**	**Subject**		
Where	**were**	you	born?	I **was** born in Tokyo.
When	**was**	I	there?	You **were** there three years ago.
What	**was**	she?		She **was** an actress.
How old	**were**	they?		They **were** 19.

21 Practice

A Write questions about a new restaurant. Use the words and expressions.

1. the food/good _Was the food good_ ?
2. the food/expensive _____ ?
3. the servers/polite _____ ?
4. the restaurant/clean _____ ?
5. the place/busy _____ ?
6. the restaurant/convenient _____ ?
7. the plates/full _____ ?
8. the service/good _____ ?
9. the restaurant/big _____ ?
10. the food/tasty _____ ?

B Listen and check your answers. Then listen again and repeat the questions.

AUDIO

DOWNLOAD

CD1, 31, 32

22 Pair Up and Talk

A Practice the conversation with a partner.

A: Was Napoleon a musician?

B: No, he wasn't. He was a politician.

B Now practice the conversation with your partner again. Use these words and phrases.

Napoleon/a musician	Marilyn Monroe/Chinese	Princess Diana/American
Mozart/a painter	The Beatles/French	Cleopatra/Egyptian
Elvis Presley/a singer	Picasso/a politician	Mozart and Beethoven/ musicians
George Washington and John F. Kennedy/presidents of the United States		

23 Practice

Match the questions and answers.

		Questions		Answers
_c_	**1.**	When were your grandparents married?	**a.**	He was a bank manager.
			b.	It was in Boston.
____	**2.**	How old was your grandfather?		
			c.	In 1932.
____	**3.**	What was your grandfather?	**d.**	He was 30 years old.
____	**4.**	How old was your grandmother?		
			e.	Yes, it was.
____	**5.**	Where was the wedding?	**f.**	She was 22.
____	**6.**	Was it a big wedding?		

24 Your Turn

Answer the six questions in Practice 23 about your own grandparents or other people you know. Then write two more sentences about them.

1. _My grandparents were married in 1954_____ .

2. _____ .

3. _____ .

4. _____ .

5. _____ .

6. _____ .

7. _____ .

8. _____ .

9. _____ .

25 Pair Up and Talk
A   Practice the conversation with a partner.

A: Where were you born?
B: I was born in Hong Kong.

B   Now practice the conversation with your partner again. Use these words and phrases.

how many people/at your party   where/you born
how old/you   where/you on your birthday
when/your last birthday   who/at the party

26 Read
Read the story. Then write answers to the questions.

THE MULE

A mule is the child of a horse and a donkey. Once there was a mule. One day, the mule was very happy. It was very energetic.
"I am a very fast animal. My mother is a racehorse. So I am fast like a racehorse."

The mule was here one minute and there another minute. After an hour or so, the mule was very, very tired. Then the mule said, "Oh, yes, my father was a donkey."

1. What is a mule?

   _____ .

2. Why was the mule happy?

   _____ .

3. What was the mule's mother?

   _____ .

4. How was the mule after an hour or so?

   _____ .

5. What was the mule's father?

   _____ .

Listening Puzzle

AUDIO DOWNLOAD CD1, 33

A Listen and check the correct answer.

❑ A. *Boston*   ❑ B. *New York City*   ❑ C. *San Francisco*

B Discuss your answer with your classmates.

AUDIO DOWNLOAD CD1, 34

C Now listen again and write the sentences you hear.

A Before You Read

Answer the questions.

1. Where is Hawaii?
2. How many islands are there in Hawaii?

B Read

HAWAII

DID YOU KNOW ... ?
Hawaii became the
50th state of the USA
in 1959.

There are 132 islands in the state of Hawaii.
There are people on eight of the islands. There
are four main Hawaiian Islands. These are Maui, 15
Oahu, Kauai, and the Big
5 Island. Hawaii is about 2,000
miles (3,219 kilometers) from
California. It is in the
Pacific Ocean.

The first people in Hawaii
10 were from islands in the
South Pacific. Today, the people of Hawaii are
from different countries. There are Asians,

Americans, and Europeans. About one percent
of them are pure Hawaiian.

The Hawaiian language is important for
Hawaiians. It has 18 letters. There are ten vowels
and eight consonants. The word *aloha* is hello
or good-bye or love. The word *mahalo* is thank
you. Hawaiians also speak English. It is the
20 language of the state.

Hawaii is famous for surfing and pineapples.
Of course, many people go there for
vacations, too.

C Notice the Grammar

Underline all forms of the verb *be*.

Choose the best answer.

D Look for Main Ideas

1. How many islands are there in Hawaii?
   - (A) 8
   - (B) 132
   - (C) 5

2. Pure Hawaiians are from _____ .
   - (A) China
   - (B) Japan
   - (C) the South Pacific

3. Hawaii is _____ .
   - (A) near California
   - (B) a U.S. state
   - (C) a country

4. In the Hawaiian language, there are _____ .
   - (A) 18 vowels
   - (B) 18 letters
   - (C) 10 consonants

5. The official language of Hawaii is _____ .
   - (A) English
   - (B) Hawaiian
   - (C) Chinese

6. The word *mahalo* in Hawaiian is _____ .
   - (A) good-bye
   - (B) hello
   - (C) thank you

Writing: Describe a Place

Write a postcard about your vacation.

STEP 1   Work with a partner. You are on vacation. Use the words and phrases. Ask and answer questions about your hotel.

Example

name

A: What's the name of the hotel?

B: The name of the hotel is Paradise Hotel.

a view	is there/are there	restaurant	the weather
gym	many tourists	stores	what
how old	name	swimming pool	your room

STEP 2   Write the answers to the questions from Step 1.

STEP 3   Read this postcard.

Dear Lin,
    I am at the Palace Hotel on the beach in Hawaii. It is sunny and hot today. The temperature is about 90 degrees (32 C), but it's nice. The hotel is wonderful. There is a swimming pool, and there is a gym. There are restaurants and stores in the hotel. There are tourists from many countries here. The view from my room is wonderful. I love Hawaii.
Love,
Julie

STEP 4   Write a postcard like the one above, but use your answers from Step 2. Use *but* or *and* in one sentence. Be sure to use commas correctly.

STEP 5   Work with a partner to edit your postcard. Check spelling, punctuation, vocabulary, and grammar.

STEP 6   Write your final postcard.

Self-Test

A   Choose the best answer, A, B, C, or D, to complete the sentence. Darken the oval with the same letter.

1. How many states _____ in the United States?

   A. there is   Ⓐ Ⓑ Ⓒ Ⓓ
   B. is there
   C. are there
   D. there are

2. _____ any mountains in Mexico?

   A. There is   Ⓐ Ⓑ Ⓒ Ⓓ
   B. Is there
   C. Are there
   D. There are

3. Thomas Edison was born _____ 1847.

   A. on   Ⓐ Ⓑ Ⓒ Ⓓ
   B. in
   C. at
   D. by

4. _____ cold at the South Pole.

   A. It is   Ⓐ Ⓑ Ⓒ Ⓓ
   B. There is
   C. Is it
   D. It has

5. Is a tomato a fruit, _____ is it a vegetable?

   A. and   Ⓐ Ⓑ Ⓒ Ⓓ
   B. but
   C. or
   D. there

6. _____ 13 million people in Tokyo, Japan.

   A. Are there   Ⓐ Ⓑ Ⓒ Ⓓ
   B. There are
   C. It is
   D. There is

7. The airport is open _____ night.

   A. in   Ⓐ Ⓑ Ⓒ Ⓓ
   B. from
   C. on
   D. at

8. Elvis Presley died _____ August, 1977.

   A. in   Ⓐ Ⓑ Ⓒ Ⓓ
   B. at
   C. on
   D. from

9. Princess Diana died _____ August 31, 1997.

   A. in   Ⓐ Ⓑ Ⓒ Ⓓ
   B. at
   C. on
   D. over

10. Days are short _____ winter.

    A. at   Ⓐ Ⓑ Ⓒ Ⓓ
    B. in
    C. on
    D. the

1. There is nine-fifteen in Los Angeles, but it is
   A   B   C
   six-fifteen in New York.
   D

   Ⓐ Ⓑ Ⓒ Ⓓ

2. Canada but the United States are in
   A   B   C D
   North America.

   Ⓐ Ⓑ Ⓒ Ⓓ

3. Marie Curie were a French scientist, but she was
              A   B   C
   born in Poland in 1859.
        D

   Ⓐ Ⓑ Ⓒ Ⓓ

4. The Chinese New Year is on January
                   A   B C
   or February.
   D

   Ⓐ Ⓑ Ⓒ Ⓓ

5. It is winter in Canada, or it is summer
   A   B C
   in Argentina.
   D

   Ⓐ Ⓑ Ⓒ Ⓓ

6. Valentine's Day is in February 14, but it is not
                    A   B   C
   a holiday.
   D

   Ⓐ Ⓑ Ⓒ Ⓓ

7. There aren't any trees in Antarctica because
   A   B   C
   there is very cold there.
   D

   Ⓐ Ⓑ Ⓒ Ⓓ

8. Thanksgiving Day in the United States is
                   A   B   C
   always in a Thursday.
         D

   Ⓐ Ⓑ Ⓒ Ⓓ

9. There is one hundred centimeters in one meter.
   A   B   C   D

   Ⓐ Ⓑ Ⓒ Ⓓ

10. George Washington and John F. Kennedy was
                       A   B
    American presidents.
    C   D

    Ⓐ Ⓑ Ⓒ Ⓓ

Unit 3

The Simple Present

Brenda **always** walks home from school.

3A | The Simple Present

Form

Janet **works** in an office.
She **sits** at her desk and **types** on a computer.

Subject	Verb	Subject	Verb
I		He	
You	work.	She	works.
We		It	
They			

Function

She **speaks** on the telephone and **types** on her computer.

We use the simple present when we talk about what people do all the time, or again and again.

1 Practice

A Read the sentences about a typical day for Janet. Underline the correct form of the verb.

1. The alarm clock (ring/<u>rings</u>) at 7:00 every morning.
2. She (get/gets) up.
3. She (take/takes) a shower.
4. Janet says, "I (brush/brushes) my teeth every morning."
5. She (put/puts) on her clothes.
6. Janet (eat/eats) breakfast with her sister Meg.
7. They (watch/watches) the news on television.
8. Meg (stay/stays) home.
9. They (say/says) good-bye.
10. Janet (lock/locks) the door.
11. She (wait/waits) for the bus.
12. She (get/gets) on the bus.

B Listen and check your answers. Then listen again and repeat each sentence.

AUDIO

DOWNLOAD

CD1, 35, 36

2 Your Turn

Write four things you do every day. Then work with a partner. Write things he or she does every day.

1. _I get up at 7:30_ .
2. _____ .
3. _____ .
4. _____ .
5. _____ .

6. _Liu gets up at 8:00_ .
7. _____ .
8. _____ .
9. _____ .
10. _____ .

Form

Penguins **never** fly.
Penguins **usually** eat fish.
Penguins **often** swim.

1. *Always, usually, often, sometimes, rarely,* and *never* are adverbs of frequency. We often use them with simple present verbs. They come between the subject and the verb.

Subject	Adverb of Frequency	Simple Present	
I	**always**	do	my homework.
You	**usually**	get up	early.
Tony	**often**	listens	to the radio.
She	**sometimes**	drinks	tea.
We	**rarely**	go	to the theater.
Penguins	**never**	fly.	

Yukio is **always** on time.
Yukio is **never** late.
He **always** catches his train at 7:00.
Yukio is late today. He is very upset.

2. We put adverbs of frequency after the verb *be*.

Subject	Simple Present of *Be*	Adverb of Frequency	
Ted	is	always	late.
		usually	
		often	
		sometimes	
		rarely	
		never	

Function

Brenda **always** walks home from school.

Adverbs of frequency tell us how many times something happens.

		Mon.	Tue.	Wed.	Thurs.	Fri.	Sat.	Sun.
I **always** walk in the morning.		■	■	■	■	■	■	■
Julia **usually** walks in the morning.		■	■	■	■	■	■	
We **often** walk in the morning.		■	■	■	■	■		
You **sometimes** walk in the morning.		■	■	■				
Mel and Sue **rarely** walk in the morning.		■						
Satoshi **never** walks in the morning.								

3 Practice

Add the adverb of frequency to each sentence.

1. I get up at 7:00. (always) _I always get up at 7:00_ .

2. I have breakfast at 7:30. (usually) _____ .

3. I drink two cups of tea for breakfast. (often) _____ .

4. I eat eggs for breakfast. (never) _____ .

5. I watch the news on television. (sometimes) _____ .

6. I listen to the radio at home. (rarely) _____ .

7. I read the newspaper in the morning. (usually) _____ .

8. I lock my door. (always) _____ .

4 Practice

Add the adverb of frequency on the left to each sentence.

1. always   Yukio is on time.   _Yukio is always on time_ .

2. always   Yukio comes to work on time.   _____ .

3. never   Yukio is sick.   _____ .

4. usually   He works on Saturday.   _____ .

5. sometimes He feels tired.   _____ .

6. rarely   He is home early.   _____ .

7. often   He works late at the office.   _____ .

8. never   He misses a meeting.   _____ .

5 Pair Up and Talk

Work with a partner. What do you do on weekday evenings? Use *always*, *usually*, *often*, *sometimes*, *rarely*, or *never* with these phrases or your own.

A: I rarely go to the movies on weekday evenings.

B: I often work on the computer on weekday evenings.

1. eat dinner early   5. go to the movies
2. watch TV   6. do homework
3. go to bed late   7. stay at home
4. read magazines   8. see friends

Form

Every evening, Ken **sits** in front of the television, **drinks** his soda, **watches** his favorite program, and **falls** asleep.

Verb	Spelling	Examples	Pronunciation
Verb ends in voiceless *f, k, p, t* **like sleep write**	Add -s.	He like**s** soda. He sleep**s**. She often write**s** letters.	/s/
Verb ends in voiced *b, d, g, l, m, n, r, v,* or vowel **swim read run see**	Add -s.	He swim**s**. She read**s**. He run**s**. She see**s**.	/z/
Verb ends in *ch, sh, s, x, z** **watch dress finish**	Add -es.	She watch**es** TV. He dress**es**. It finish**es** at 10:00.	/iz/
Verb ends in consonant + *y* **worry cry hurry**	Drop *y* and add -ies.	He worr**ies**. The baby cr**ies** at night. She hurr**ies** to work.	/z/
Verb ends in vowel + *y* **play stay buy**	Add -s.	He play**s** football. She stay**s** at home. He buy**s** food.	/z/

*Verbs that end in *dge*, as in **judge**, add only -*s* but are pronounced with /iz/ at the end.

6 Practice
Write the third person singular of these verbs in the correct column. Then read them aloud.

ask	dance	like	play	stay	wish
begin	eat	look	put	stop	write
brush	fix	miss	say	teach	
buy	fly	open	see	try	
catch	kiss	pass	speak	walk	

/s/	/iz/	/z/
puts	_brushes_	_says_
_____	_____	_____
_____	_____	_____
_____	_____	_____
_____	_____	_____
_____	_____	_____
_____	_____	_____
_____	_____	_____
_____	_____	_____

7 Practice
A Complete the sentences with the third person singular of the verbs in parentheses. Then underline the correct pronunciation for each verb.

Dan Thomas (come) ___comes___ (s/z/iz) from Canada, but he
1

(live) _____ (s/z/iz) in New York. He (teach) _____
2   3

(s/z/iz) English. He (like) _____ (s/z/iz) to walk, so he (walk)
4

_____ (s/z/iz) to school every day. He sometimes (arrive) _____
5   6

(s/z/iz) late for class. He (enjoy) _____ (s/z/iz) his job and (love)
7

_____ (s/z/iz) his students, but he sometimes (forget) _____
8   9

(s/z/iz) their names. He usually (give) _____ (s/z/iz) a lot of homework.
10

AUDIO

DOWNLOAD

CD1, 37, 38

B Listen and check your answers. Then listen again and repeat each sentence.

C What do you think? Is Dan Thomas a good or a bad teacher? Why?

8 Practice

Complete the sentences about Wendy with the words on the left.

1.	try, always	Wendy ___*always tries*___ hard.
2.	study, usually	She _____ in the library after class.
3.	worry, often	She _____ about her homework and her tests.
4.	stay, never	She _____ out with her friends after school.
5.	enjoy, rarely	She _____ her life.
6.	cry, sometimes	She _____ .
7.	say, usually	She _____ she is happy and fine.
8.	look, often	But she _____ sad and unhappy.

9 Your Turn

Write about what you do every day. Use *always*, *usually*, *often*, *sometimes*, *rarely*, and *never*. Use these phrases or your own.

do homework   early/late to school   exercise   go to bed

1. ___*I always go to bed late*___ .

2. _____ .

3. _____ .

4. _____ .

Irregular Verbs: *Have, Do,* and *Go*

Form

Kathy's classes finish at 4:00 every day.
Then she **goes** home.
She **has** a cup of coffee and **does**
her homework.

The third person forms of *have, go,* and *do* are irregular.

I We You They	**have** a job.	He She It	**has** a job.
I We You They	**do** the work.	He She It	**does** the work.
I We You They	**go** outside.	He She It	**goes** outside.

10   Practice

Complete the sentences about Kathy and Kay with the verbs in parentheses.

1.   Kathy (go) __goes__ to work in a hospital. Kay (go) _____ to work in a big office.

2.   Both Kathy and Kay (have) _____ cars.

3.   Kathy (have) _____ a big car, but Kay (have) _____ a small car.

4.   Both Kathy and Kay (do) _____ yoga to be healthy.

5.   Kathy (do) _____ yoga in a gym, and Kay (do) _____ yoga at home.

11   Practice

Complete the sentences with the simple present form of the verbs in parentheses.

Mike (have) _____has_____ two classes in the morning. At 12:00, he (finish)
                    1

_____ his classes and (go) _____ to the cafeteria. He (eat) _____
        2   3   4

lunch with his classmates. After lunch, he (study, usually) _____ in the library.
                                                                    5

His teachers (give, often) _____ a lot of homework. Then he (take) _____
                                  6   7

the bus to his uncle's garage. He (have) _____ a job there. He (fix) _____
                                              8   9

cars and (talk) _____ to people. Mike (do) _____ a great job. His uncle
                      10   11

(pay) _____ him every week. The garage (close) _____ at 8:00. After
            12   13

work, Mike (go) _____ home. Mike's roommate Ken (be) _____ very nice.
                      14   15

He (try, always) _____ to help Mike. Ken and Mike (cook) _____ dinner,
                      16   17

and then they (eat) _____ in the kitchen. They (do, always) _____ the
                          18   19

dishes together. They (watch, usually) _____ television. They (like) _____
                                              20   21

football and other sports on TV. They (go, often) _____ to bed late.
                                                          22

Function

We use *have* and *has*:

1. For things we possess or own.
    I **have** a car.   She **has** two houses.
2. To describe people, places, animals, and things.
    It **has** two windows.   She **has** black hair.
3. For our families and people we know.
    I **have** a son.   She **has** a friend from Canada.
4. With some expressions like these:

have a cold/the flu	The children **have a cold** this week.
have a temperature	I **have a temperature**.
have a headache	Gloria **has a headache**.
have a problem	We **have a problem**.

12 Practice

A Complete the sentences with *have* or *has*.

Sam _____*has*_____ a good job. He _____ a wife, Kate. They
            1   **2**

_____ two children. Kate _____ a good job, too. She is a
        3   **4**

teacher. They _____ one car, and they _____ a small house.
                    5   **6**

The house _____ two bedrooms. It _____ a garden, too.
                7   **8**

The garden _____ trees and flowers. Sam and his family are happy.
                    9

They _____ a good life.
        10

B Listen and check your answers. Then listen again and repeat each sentence.

CD1, 39, 40

13 Practice

Complete the sentences with *is* or *has*.

1. Sam _____*is*_____ young.

2. He _____ 28 years old.

3. He _____ healthy.

4. Today, Sam _____ a problem.

5. He _____ sick.

6. He _____ a cold.

7. He _____ a headache, too.

8. Sam _____ at home today.

Form

Len **doesn't walk** in the evenings.
Len **doesn't see** his friends.
Len **doesn't go** out.
Len watches television and
eats chips.

1. In simple present negative statements, *do* and *does* are helping verbs. The base verb does not have an *-s* for the third person singular. The *-s* ending is on the helping verb (*does*).

Subject	Do Not/Does Not	Base Verb
I You We They	**do not**	work.
He She It	**does not**	

2. We usually use contractions when we speak. We often use contractions when we write.

Contractions	
do not	don't
does not	doesn't

14 Practice

Complete the negative sentences with the words on the left.

1. understand, not   I love my husband, Len, but I ___*don't understand*___ him.

2. want, not   He is always tired. He _____ to go out.

3. talk, not   He watches TV all the time. He _____ to me.

4. go, not   We _____ to the movies.

5. eat, not   He eats only chips and pizza. He _____ salads.

6. drink, not   He always drinks coffee. He _____ water.

7. like, not   He likes to watch sports on TV. He _____ to exercise.

8. have, not   We _____ many friends.

9. see, not   His mother _____ him.

10. know, not   Poor Len, I _____ what to do!

15 Practice

A   Write true sentences with these words. Make the sentences negative where necessary.

1. birds/give/milk _*Birds don't give milk*_____ .

2. fish/swim _____ .

3. a chicken/come/from an egg _____ .

4. plants/need/water to grow _____ .

5. penguins/live/in Italy _____ .

6. elephants/eat/chickens _____ .

7. rice/grow/on trees _____ .

8. the Chinese/drink/tea _____ .

B   Listen and check your answers. Then listen again and repeat each sentence.

AUDIO

DOWNLOAD

CD1, 41, 42

16 Practice

A Complete the sentences with the negative form of the verbs from the list.

be	get up	look at	sit	wait
eat	go	put on	talk	worry

It is August. The sun is hot. There ___*aren't*___ any clouds in the
                                      1

sky. Tony is in Hawaii. He _____ early. He gets up at 11:00. He
                                2

_____ his shirt and tie. He puts on his shorts. He _____
      3   **4**

to work. He goes to the beach. He _____ for the bus. He waits for
                                        5

his friends. Tony and his friends _____ in front of computers.
                                        6

They sit at a table in a café on the beach. They _____ about work.
                                                        7

They talk about fun things to do. They _____ sandwiches. They eat
                                            8

delicious food. They _____ computers. They look at the blue sea.
                          9

Tony _____ about his work. He is happy and relaxed. But Tony
        10

isn't on vacation. He is in his office. It's just a dream.

B Listen and check your answers. Then listen again and repeat each sentence.

AUDIO

DOWNLOAD

CD1, 43, 44

17 Pair Up and Talk

Tell your partner four things you do and four things you don't do on the
weekend. Use these phrases or your own.

A: I don't get up early. I get up late.

clean your room	get up early	go to the store	play sports	study English
do homework	go to school	have breakfast	see friends	watch TV

Form/Function

MEG: **Does** John wear glasses?
LINDA: Yes, he **does**.
MEG: **Does** he wear glasses all the time?
LINDA: No, he **doesn't**.

Yes/No Questions			Short Answers	
Do/Does	**Subject**	**Base Verb**	**Affirmative**	**Negative**
	I		**Yes,** you **do**.	**No,** you **don't**.
Do	you		I/we **do**.	I/we **don't**.
	we		you **do**.	you **don't**.
	they	work?	they **do**.	they **don't**.
Does	he		he **does**.	he **doesn't**.
	she		she **does**.	she **doesn't**.
	it		it **does**.	it **doesn't**.

18 Practice

A Penny wants to marry Tim. Her mother asks questions about him. Write questions with *do* or *does*. Write short answers.

1. you/love him _____*Do you love him*_____ ?
   Yes, _____*I do*_____ .

2. you/know his family _____ ?

Yes, _____ .

3. he/have a good job _____ ?

Yes, _____ .

4. he/live in a nice apartment _____ ?

Yes, _____ .

5. he/drive a nice car _____ ?

Yes, _____ .

6. he/wear nice clothes _____ ?

Yes, _____ .

7. he/smoke _____ ?

Yes, _____ .

8. he/buy you nice gifts _____ ?

Yes, _____ .

9. he/take you out _____ ?

Yes, _____ .

10. he/want to marry you _____ ?

No, _____ .

B Listen and check your answers. Then work with a partner. Listen again and repeat the questions and answers.

CD1, 45, 46

C Listen again. Why don't Penny and Tim get married? Circle the letter of the correct answer.

CD1, 47

A Tim doesn't have a car.

B Penny smokes.

C Tim doesn't want to get married.

D Penny doesn't want to get married.

19 Pair Up and Talk

A Work with a partner. You are looking for a roommate. Ask your partner six questions with *be* or *do*. Your partner gives short answers.

A: Do you listen to loud music?

B: No, I don't.

B Now practice the conversation with your partner again. Use these words or your own.

a good cook	clean	have many friends	quiet
a student	go to bed late	like parties	smoke

3G The Simple Present: *Wh-* Questions

Form/Function

SUE: **Where do** kangaroos **come** from?
KEN: Australia.
SUE: **What do** they **eat**?
KEN: Plants. (They eat plants.)
SUE: **When do** they **sleep**?
KEN: In the day. (They sleep in the daytime.)

1. We often call *where, when, what, why, who, how,* and *how many* wh- question words because most of them start with the letters *wh*. We use *wh-* question words to get information.
2. We put question words before *do* and *does*.
3. Frequency adverbs like *usually* come after the subject in a question.
    When do you **usually** get up? I **usually** get up at seven.

Wh- Word	Do/Does	Subject	Base Verb
What	do	I	do?
Where	does	he	live?
When	do	they	sleep?
Why	do	you	get up early?
Who*	does	she	call?
How many	do	they	have?
How	do	you	go?

* In formal written English, the wh- word is whom.

20 Practice

This is Paul. He plays in a group called the Purrmaster 9000. Match the questions to the answers.

A

_____c_____ 1. What instrument does he play?

_____ 2. Who does he play with?

_____ 3. Where does he live?

_____ 4. Why does he travel a lot?

_____ 5. When does he work?

_____ 6. How many guitars does he have?

B

a. Because he plays in concerts in different towns.

b. His brothers.

c. The guitar.

d. He has five.

e. In Los Angeles.

f. In the evenings.

The Simple Present **83**

21 Read

Read about Linda Barton. Then write questions with the phrases and give answers.

Linda lives in Toronto. She is married to Tom. Tom is an accountant. They have a daughter, Nancy. She is 20 years old and goes to the university. Linda is a nurse. She works in a big hospital. She starts work at 9:30 in the evening and finishes at 6:30 in the morning. She comes home and has breakfast. After breakfast, she usually watches television and goes to bed at about 9:00. She gets up at 4:00 in the afternoon, goes to the store, and prepares dinner. Her husband comes home at 7:00. They eat dinner. After dinner they talk. They also watch television together. Then Linda goes to work again, but Linda wants to change her hours of work soon.

1. Where/Linda/live?
   Where does Linda live? Linda lives in Toronto   .

2. What/Tom/do?
   _____ .

3. How many children/they/have?
   _____ .

4. What/Nancy/do?
   _____ .

5. What/Linda/do?
   _____ .

6. Where/Linda/work?
   _____ .

7. When/Linda/start and finish work?

   _____ .

8. What/she/do after breakfast?

   _____ .

9. What/they/do after dinner?

   _____ .

10. What/Linda/do then?

    _____ .

22 Your Turn
Why do you think Linda wants to change her hours? Write three reasons.

Example

She wants to change her hours because she doesn't see her daughter.

23 Practice
A   **Complete the questions with *is*, *are*, *do*, or *does*.**

1. What _____ *is* _____ the largest animal on land? It's the elephant.

2. Where _____ it live? It lives in Africa and Asia.

3. What _____ it eat? It eats plants.

4. How long _____ it live? It lives about 70 years.

5. _____ elephants intelligent? Yes, they are. Elephants are intelligent.

6. _____ elephants live alone? No, they don't. They live in groups.

7. How many kinds of elephants _____ there? There are two kinds of elephants.

8. What _____ they? They are the African elephant and the Indian elephant.

9. _____ an elephant cry? Yes, it does. An elephant cries.

10. _____ elephants laugh? Yes, they do. Elephants laugh.

The Simple Present   **85**

AUDIO
DOWNLOAD
CD1, 48, 49

24 Practice

Read the answers. Then write the questions.

Louisa   Gina

1. _Is Gina Louisa's sister_ _____ ?

   Yes, she is. (Gina is Louisa's sister.)

2. _____ ?

   Gina is 28.

3. _____ ?

   Gina works for Channel AB on television. She gives the news.

4. _____ ?

   Yes, she is famous.

5. _____ ?

   Yes, she is married to a TV producer.

6. _____ ?

   She's unhappy because she has no time for her husband and daughter.

7. _____ ?

   Yes, Louisa is happy.

8. _____ ?

   She lives at home with her parents.

25 Pair Up and Talk

A   Work with a partner. Ask your partner questions about his/her weekends. Use *what, where, when, who, how,* and *why.* Use these verbs or your own. Use adverbs of frequency in your questions and answers.

do   get up   go to bed   have lunch
eat   go   have breakfast   see

A: What do you usually do on Saturday nights?
B: I often go to a movie.

B   Now write five things that your partner does. Then write five things that you do.

Example

Tomiko often goes to the movies.

1. _____ .
2. _____ .
3. _____ .
4. _____ .
5. _____ .

Example

I usually go to bed late.

1. _____ .
2. _____ .
3. _____ .
4. _____ .
5. _____ .

26   **Read**
Read the story. Then write answers to the questions.

THE MISER AND HIS GOLD

There is a man in a village. This man loves gold. He melts down all his gold into a big brick. He then buries the gold brick in the ground behind his house. Every night, he digs it up, looks at it, and then buries it again.

One night, a thief sees him do this. The thief steals the gold brick and puts an ordinary brick in its place.

The next evening, the man comes to dig up his gold, but finds an ordinary brick in its place. He starts to cry and moan. The thief watches him from behind a tree. Then the thief comes up to the man and asks, "Why are you so upset? What is the difference if the brick is of gold or ordinary brick? You never use it!"

1.   What does this man love?

_____ .

2.   What does he do with all his gold?

_____ .

3.   Where does he bury the gold brick?

_____ .

4.   What does he do every night?

_____ .

5. Who sees him?

   _____.

6. What does the thief do?

   _____.

7. What does the man find the next evening?

   _____.

8. Does the man ever use his gold?

   _____.

Listening Puzzle

AUDIO DOWNLOAD   CD1, 50

A Listen and check the correct answer.

☐ A. *penguin*

☐ B. *seal*

☐ C. *dolphin*

B Discuss your answer with your classmates.

AUDIO DOWNLOAD CD1, 51

C Now listen again and write the sentences you hear.

A Before You Read

Answer the questions.

1. Where do camels live?
2. What is special about a camel?

B Read

CAMELS

DID YOU KNOW ... ?
A camel's nostrils close up completely to block out sand, and camels have the worst smelling breath of all animals.

Some people think that a camel stores water in its hump, but this isn't true. A camel's hump is really fat. When there is no food or water, the camel's
5 body makes the fat into food. After it uses the fat in its hump, the hump gets soft and **bounces around** from side to side. Arabian camels
10 have one hump. These camels live mainly in the Sahara Desert and the Middle East. Bactrian camels have two humps, and they live in Asia.

15   People call camels "ships of the desert." Camels often go many days or sometimes months with no water. When a camel finds water, it drinks 50 gallons (220 liters) at a time! The camel's body temperature rises from 95
20 to 104 degrees Fahrenheit (35 to 40 degrees Celsius) during the day. We rarely see this in other animals. For the desert sand, camels have a double set of eyelashes. **This** gives the camel a gentle look, but be careful!

C Notice the Grammar

Underline all forms of the simple present.

Choose the best answer.

D Look for Main Ideas

Every paragraph has a main idea or topic. It is the most important information in that paragraph. The first or second sentence in the paragraph often has the main idea.

1. What is the main idea of paragraph 2?
   - (A) why a camel is like a ship
   - (B) how a camel drinks
   - (C) how a camel lives in the desert
   - (D) why a camel is gentle

F Look for Vocabulary

6. The words **bounces around** in the reading are closest in meaning to _____ .
   - (A) moves about
   - (B) hangs
   - (C) falls
   - (D) sits

E Look for Details

2. Bactrian camels _____ .
   - (A) have one hump
   - (B) live in the Sahara
   - (C) have two humps
   - (D) live in the Middle East

G Reference the Text

7. The word **This** in the reading refers to _____ .
   - (A) the desert sand
   - (B) the double set of eyelashes
   - (C) the camel's temperature
   - (D) the camel's hump

3. A camel's hump is _____ .
   - (A) water
   - (B) food
   - (C) fat
   - (D) hot

4. A camel's hump is soft _____ .
   - (A) after it doesn't eat or drink for a long time
   - (B) all the time
   - (C) when it drinks
   - (D) when it is full of fat

5. Camels are different from most animals because _____ .
   - (A) they have long eyelashes
   - (B) they have humps
   - (C) their body temperature rises to 104 degrees Farenheit
   - (D) they live in the desert

Writing: Describe a Person

Write a paragraph about another person.

STEP 1   **Find out about a partner. Ask these questions, or use your own. Write your answers.**

1. Where do you come from?
2. Where do you live?
3. Do you have brothers and sisters?
4. Do you live alone? Who do you live with?
5. What sports do you like?
6. What language(s) do you speak?

7. What kind of music do you like?
8. What time do you get up?
9. What do you have for breakfast?
10. What do you usually have for lunch?
11. When do you go home?
12. What do you do in the evening?

STEP 2   **Rewrite your answers in paragraph form. Use your partner's name for the title. Be sure to indent the first line of your paragraph.**

We indent the first line of the paragraph. →

8

Belen Gutierrez

9

    Belen Gutierrez comes from Buenos Aires, Argentina, but now she
10 *lives in Las Vegas, Nevada, in the United States. She has …*

11

STEP 3   **Evaluate your paragraph.**

Checklist

_____ Did you indent your first line?

_____ Did you give your paragraph a title?

_____ Did you write the title with a capital letter for each word?

STEP 4   **Work with a partner to edit your paragraph. Correct spelling, punctuation, vocabulary, and grammar.**

STEP 5   **Write your final copy.**

Self-Test

1. It _____ in Hawaii.

   A. often rain   (A) (B) (C) (D)
   B. often rains
   C. rain often
   D. rains often

2. Brazilians _____ Portuguese.

   A. speak   (A) (B) (C) (D)
   B. speaks
   C. is speaking
   D. do speaks

3. The United States _____ 50 states.

   A. have   (A) (B) (C) (D)
   B. is have
   C. has
   D. does

4. Crocodiles _____ in cold countries.

   A. doesn't live   (A) (B) (C) (D)
   B. live not
   C. isn't live
   D. don't live

5. When _____ ?

   A. is summer start   (A) (B) (C) (D)
   B. does summer start
   C. start summer
   D. does start summer

6. _____ a fish _____ ?

   A. Does … sleep   (A) (B) (C) (D)
   B. Do … sleeps
   C. Don't … sleep
   D. Is … sleep

7. Where _____ ?

   A. does coffee come from   (A) (B) (C) (D)
   B. coffee come from
   C. is coffee come from
   D. coffee comes from

8. Whales give milk to _____ young.

   A. her   (A) (B) (C) (D)
   B. they
   C. their
   D. its

9. It _____ cold in Antarctica.

   A. is always   (A) (B) (C) (D)
   B. always is
   C. does always
   D. always has

10. What _____ ?

   A. is *fetch* mean   (A) (B) (C) (D)
   B. *fetch* mean
   C. does *fetch* mean
   D. does means *fetch*

1. Chinese people usually celebrates the New
          A   **B**   **C**
    Year in February.
          D

    Ⓐ Ⓑ Ⓒ Ⓓ

2. Do elephants lives in groups, or do they
    A   **B**   **C** **D**
    live alone?

    Ⓐ Ⓑ Ⓒ Ⓓ

3. The male lion is very lazy, and sleep for about 20
             A   **B** **C**
    hours a day.
    D

    Ⓐ Ⓑ Ⓒ Ⓓ

4. Babies doesn't have tears when they cry until
           A   **B**   **C**
    they are several weeks old.
          D

    Ⓐ Ⓑ Ⓒ Ⓓ

5. Giraffes don't sometimes sleep at all
       A   **B**   **C**
    for 24 hours.
        D

    Ⓐ Ⓑ Ⓒ Ⓓ

6. People in the United States use often
        A   **B**   **C**
    credit cards.
        D

    Ⓐ Ⓑ Ⓒ Ⓓ

7. July has cold in Argentina, but it's warm in
          A   **B**   **C**   **D**
    New York.

    Ⓐ Ⓑ Ⓒ Ⓓ

8. When do people have the flu, they usually
          A   **B**   **C**
    have a temperature.
        D

    Ⓐ Ⓑ Ⓒ Ⓓ

9. Gorillas rarely climb trees because of its size.
       A   **B**   **C**   **D**

    Ⓐ Ⓑ Ⓒ Ⓓ

10. How many babies does a panda has?
       A   **B** **C**   **D**

    Ⓐ Ⓑ Ⓒ Ⓓ

Unit 4

The Present Progressive

The baby **is crying**.

The Present Progressive: Affirmative Statements

Form

A: That girl **is looking** at me.
B: Which one?
A: She **is wearing** a hat. She **is lying** on the grass.

We form the present progressive (also called the present continuous) with the present form of the verb *to be* and the base verb + *-ing*.

Subject	Be	Contraction	Base Verb + -*ing*
I	am	(I'm)	
You	are	(You're)	
He She It	is	(He's) (She's) (It's)	working.
We You They	are	(We're) (You're) (They're)	

Function

The students **are studying** in the library now.
They **are reading**.
It **is snowing** right now.
The woman **is smiling**.

We use the present progressive to talk about what is happening at the moment.

1 Practice

A It's Sunday. You are looking out of the window. Complete each sentence with the present progressive form of the verb in parentheses.

1. The birds (sing) _____ *are singing* _____ .
2. Tony (work) _____ in the yard.
3. Fred and Tom (talk) _____ in the street.
4. A child (eat) _____ ice cream.
5. Children (play) _____ in the park.
6. Bob (wash) _____ his car.
7. Mike and Linda (go) _____ to the car.
8. Alex (fix) _____ his motorbike.
9. Carol (read) _____ the newspaper.
10. A man (wait) _____ for the bus.
11. An airplane (fly) _____ in the sky.
12. Two girls (watch) _____ the airplane.

B Listen and check your answers. Then listen again and repeat each sentence.

2 Practice

Look at the photos. Write the correct sentence on the lines under the pictures.

Linda is talking on the phone.   The girls are eating ice cream.
Tim is opening the door.   The baby is crying.
Peter is carrying bags and suitcases.   Paul is playing the guitar.

1.   _Paul is playing the guitar_   .

_____ .

2.   _____ .

_____ .

3.   _____ .

_____ .

4.   _____ .

_____ .

5.

6.

3 Practice

Look at these two old photos. Work with a partner. Write about the man and the woman in the photos. Use these words or your own.

Nouns

he/shirt	she/hat	she/umbrella	the woman/boots
he/shoes	she/skirt	the man/hat	the woman/coat
he/tie	she/snow	the man/suit	

Verbs

carry   hold   smile   stand   walk   wear

Example

The man is wearing a tie.

1. He _'s wearing a shirt_ .

2. She _____ .

3. The man _____ .

4. He _____ .

5. She _____ .

6. He _____ .

7. The woman _____ .

8. He _____ .

9. He _____ .

10. The man and the woman _____ .

4 Practice

Work with a partner or the class. Describe what a student in your class is wearing. Do not say the name of the student. Do not say *he* or *she*. Say *the student*. Your partner or the class guesses who it is.

Example

A: The student is wearing black shoes.

B: Is it Kang?

A: No, it isn't. The student is wearing a sweater.

5 Pair Up and Talk

A Work with a partner. Take turns. Talk about what is happening in your class right now.

A: The teacher is standing in front of the class.

B: A student is looking at his book.

B Now practice the conversation with your partner again. Use these verbs or your own.

| listen | read | stand | wear |
| look at | sit | talk to | write |

The Spelling of Verbs Ending in *-ing*

Form

The sun **is shining**.
The woman **is sitting** on a chair at the beach.
She **is typing** on her laptop.

Verb Ending	Rule	Examples	
1. Consonant + *e*	Drop the *e*, add *-ing*.	dance come	dan**cing** com**ing**
2. Consonant + vowel + consonant	Double the consonant, add *-ing*.	sit show	si**tting** show**ing**
Exception: Verbs that end in *w, x, y*	Do not double *w, x, y*.	fix say	fix**ing** say**ing**
3. Two vowels + one consonant	Do not double the consonant, add *-ing*.	eat sleep	eat**ing** sleep**ing**
4. All other verbs	Add *-ing*.	talk read	talk**ing** read**ing**

Vowels   *a, e, i, o, u*
Consonants   *b, c, d, f, g, h, j, k, l, m, n, p, q, r, s, t, v, w, x, y, z*

6 Practice

A Write the base form of each verb.

1. saving _____save_____
2. making _____
3. typing _____
4. studying _____
5. hoping _____
6. planning _____

7. adding _____
8. smiling _____
9. hurrying _____
10. driving _____
11. agreeing _____
12. giving _____

B Listen and check your answers. Then listen again and repeat each word.

AUDIO
DOWNLOAD
CD2, 4, 5

7 Practice

Use the rules for adding *-ing* with the verbs in the list. Then write them in the correct column.

cry	get	play	read	shop	stop	wash
dance	hope	put	run	show	swim	wear
fix	move	rain	save	smile	take	write

Add *-ing*	Drop *e*, add *-ing*	Double the consonant, add *-ing*
crying	dancing	getting

8 Practice

A Complete the sentences with the present progressive form of the verbs in parentheses. Use the correct spelling.

Dear Elsie,

It's Monday evening, and it (rain) _____*is raining*_____ outside. I

(sit) _____ at my desk in my room. I (watch) _____
          2   **3**

the rain from my window, and I (think) _____ of you. I really miss you!
                                              4

All the family is at home this evening. My father (read) _____
                                                                5

a book and (eat) _____ popcorn. My brother
                      6

(play) _____ video games in his room. My mother is in the kitchen.
          7

She (make) _____ a cake because it's my sister's birthday
              8

tomorrow. Right now my sister is in her room. She (do) _____
                                                            9

her homework, and she (listen to) _____ music at the same
                                        10

time. The telephone (ring) _____ , and my mother
                              11

(call) _____ me. I must go now.
          12

Write soon,

Magda

B Listen and check your answers. Then listen again and repeat each sentence.

AUDIO

DOWNLOAD

CD2, 6, 7

C Listen again. How does the speaker feel? Circle the letter of the correct answer.

AUDIO

DOWNLOAD

CD2, 8

A angry

B sad

C sleepy

D hungry

4c The Present Progressive: Negative Statements

Form/Function

The man **is not sleeping**.
He**'s not sleeping**.
OR
He **isn't sleeping**.

To form the negative of the present progressive, we use *not* after the verb *be* and the verb + *-ing*. There are two forms of contractions. Both forms of contractions are correct and have the same meaning.

are not = **'re not**   OR   **aren't**
is not = **'s not**   OR   **isn't**

Subject	Be	Not	Base Verb + -ing	Contraction
I	am			I**'m not.**
You	are			You**'re not**/You **aren't.**
He				He**'s not**/He **isn't.**
She	is	not	working.	She**'s not**/She **isn't.**
It				It**'s not**/It **isn't.**
We				We**'re not**/We **aren't.**
They	are			They**'re not**/They **aren't.**

*There is no contraction for *am not*.

9 Practice

A Look at the photo. Read the statements. Write correct negative and affirmative statements.

1. The man and the woman are standing in an office. *The man and the woman aren't standing in an office. They are standing in the street* .

2. The man is talking on the phone. _____
   _____ .

3. The man is holding a book. _____
   _____ .

4. The man is looking at cars. _____
   _____ .

5. The man is wearing a raincoat. _____
   _____ .

6. The woman is holding her handbag. _____
   _____ .

7. It is sunny. _____
   _____ .

8. The woman is working on her computer. _____
   _____ .

B Listen and check your answers. Then listen again and repeat each sentence.

The Present Progressive **105**

The Present Progressive: *Yes/No* Questions

Form

A: **Is** the woman **riding** her bicycle?
B: No, **she isn't.**
A: **Is** she **standing** next to her bicycle?
B: Yes, **she is.**

Yes/No Questions			Short Answers	
			Yes,	**No,**
Am	**I**		you **are.**	you**'re not/aren't.**
Are	**you**		I **am.**	I**'m not.**
	he		he **is.**	he**'s not/isn't.**
Is	**she**	**working** now?	she **is.**	she**'s not/isn't.**
	it		it **is.**	it**'s not/isn't.**
	we		you **are.**	you**'re not/aren't.**
Are	**you**		we **are.**	we**'re not/aren't.**
	they		they **are.**	they**'re not/aren't.**

10　Practice

A　Match the questions with the answers.

__*d*__	**1.**	Is your sister studying?
_____	**2.**	Is the sun shining?
_____	**3.**	Am I taking your seat?
_____	**4.**	Are you studying?
_____	**5.**	Is David cooking?
_____	**6.**	Are the children sleeping?

a.　No, you're not. That seat is free.

b.　Yes, they are. They're in their beds.

c.　Yes, he is. He's making rice.

d.　No, she isn't. She's watching TV.

e.　Yes, we are. We're learning grammar.

f.　No, it's not. It's cloudy.

B　Listen and check your answers. Then work with a partner. Listen again and repeat the questions and answers.

AUDIO

DOWNLOAD

CD2, 11, 12

11　Pair Up and Talk

A　Look at the photo. Practice the conversation with a partner.

A:　Is the bride wearing a white dress?

B:　Yes, she is.

B　Now practice the conversation with your partner again. Use these phrases.

the bride/wear a white dress	the bride/cry
the bride/hold flowers	the mother/cry
the mother/stand next to the groom	the groom/wear a flower on his jacket
the people/sit	the mother and the father/smile
the father/wear a suit	the mother and the father/wear hats

Form

A: **What is** the man **doing**?
B: He's talking on the phone and walking.
A: **Where is** he **walking**?
B: He's walking down the street.

Wh- Word	Be	Subject	Base Verb + -ing
Where	**is**	Tony	**working?**
What	**are**	you	**eating?**
Why	**is**	Susan	**studying?**
When	**are**	they	**coming?**
Who*	**is**	Ken	**talking to?**
How	**are**	you	**feeling?**

*In formal written English, the *wh-* word is *whom*.

12   Practice

A   Write a question for each sentence. Use the *wh-* question words in parentheses.

1. She's watching a movie. (what) _What is she watching_ ?

2. I am drinking tea. (what) _____ ?

3. Sandra is coming at six. (when) _____ ?

4. I am taking an umbrella because it's raining. (why) _____ ?

5. Peter is talking to his father. (who) _____ ?

6. Linda is feeling fine. (how) _____ ?

7. The children are playing in the park. (where) _____ ?

8. I am talking to Bill on the telephone. (who) _____ ?

B Listen and check your answers. Then work with a partner. Listen again and repeat the questions and answers.

 CD2, 13, 14

4F Nonaction or Stative Verbs

Function

I **love** Paris. I **think** Paris is beautiful.

1. There are some verbs we do not usually use in the present progressive. We call these nonaction or stative verbs. They describe a state or condition, not an action. We use the simple present with these verbs.

Nonaction Verbs			
believe	know	prefer	taste
hate	like	remember	think
have	love	see	understand
hear	need	smell	want

CORRECT:	I know the answer.	CORRECT:	Do you hear the music?
INCORRECT:	~~I am knowing~~ the answer.	INCORRECT:	~~Are you hearing~~ the music?

2. We sometimes use the verbs *think* and *have* in the present progressive.

He **thinks** it is difficult. (*Think* here means "believe.")

He **is thinking** about his family. (*Think* here means "thoughts are going through the person's mind.")

Julia **has** a car. (*Has* here means "possess.")

We **are having** a good time. ("*Have*" here means experiencing. In certain idiomatic expressions, such as *have a good/bad time* and *have a problem/difficulty*, we use *have* in the progressive form.)

---

13   Practice

A   Look at these pairs. Only one sentence is correct. Check the
      correct sentence.

1. _____ a. Mary is having a lot of work right now.

    ___✔___ b. Mary has a lot of work right now.

2. _____ a. Susan needs a new coat.

    _____ b. Susan is needing a new coat.

3. _____ a. Look! That man takes a photo of us.

    _____ b. Look! That man is taking a photo of us.

4. _____ a. Please be quiet. I study.

    _____ b. Please be quiet. I am studying.

5. _____ a. This cup of coffee is smelling good.

    _____ b. This cup of coffee smells good.

6. _____ a. I look for a new apartment.

    _____ b. I'm looking for a new apartment.

7. _____ a. The children are loving ice cream.

    _____ b. The children love ice cream.

8. _____ a. He's not understanding Japanese.

    _____ b. He doesn't understand Japanese.

B   **Listen and check your answers. Then listen again and repeat each sentence.**

CD2, 15, 16

110   Unit 4

14   Practice

A   Look at the photo and complete the sentences with the correct form of the verbs. You can use a verb more than one time. Use the simple present or present progressive.

buy   have   love   read   sit   wear

The woman in the picture _____ *has* _____ long hair. She _____
                                         1   **2**

a white blouse and a skirt. In the picture, she _____ at a table in a
                                                                3

restaurant. She _____ a book. She _____ some
                            4   **5**

flowers. She _____ flowers, so she _____
                      6   **7**

flowers from the market every week.

B   Listen and check your answers. Then listen again and repeat each sentence.

DOWNLOAD
CD2, 17, 18

C   Listen again. Why does the woman have flowers? Circle the letter of the correct answer.

DOWNLOAD
CD2, 19

A   because she likes to put them in her hair

B   because she is sitting at a restaurant

C   because she loves them

D   because she is in the flower market

The Present Progressive   **111**

Form/Function

Sally **stretches** every day.

Jon **is stretching** right now.

The Simple Present	The Present Progressive
Statements Use the simple present for actions you do all the time or again and again. I **watch** television every evening. He **studies** grammar every day.	**Statements** Use the present progressive for an action happening right now. I **am watching** television right now. He**'s studying** grammar at the moment.
Questions Use *do* and *does* plus the base verb. **Do** you watch television every day? **Does** he study grammar every day?	**Questions** Use *am*, *is*, or *are* plus the *-ing* verb form. **Are** you watching television right now? **Is** he studying grammar at the moment?
Negatives Use *do* and *does* plus *not* and the base verb. I **don't** watch television every day. He **doesn't** study grammar every day.	**Negatives** Use *am*, *is*, or *are* plus *not* and the *-ing* verb form. I**'m not** watching television right now. He **isn't** studying grammar at the moment.
Time Expressions: every day, every week, every month, every year, all the time, usually, often, sometimes, never	**Time Expressions**: (right) now, at the moment, these days

A   Complete the sentences with the words in parentheses. Use contractions when possible.

A

A: What are you doing? (study) _____*Are*_____ you _____*studying*_____ ?
                                              1   2

B: No, I (not, study) _____3_____ . I (clean) _____4_____ my car.

A: (wash) _____5_____ you _____6_____ your car every week?

B: Yes, I (like) _____7_____ a clean car.

B

A: Why (sit) _____1_____ you _____2_____ in front of the class?

     You usually (sit) _____3_____ at the back.

B: I know. I (not, have) _____4_____ my glasses with me today.

C

A: (speak) _____1_____ you _____2_____ Japanese?

B: Yes, I (speak) _____3_____ a little.

A: What (mean) _____4_____ "moshi moshi" _____5_____?

B: It (mean) _____6_____ "hello."

D

A: How often (write) _____1_____ you _____2_____ to your

     family?

B: I (not, like) _____3_____ to write letters. I (call) _____4_____

     them every week.

E

A: (go) _____1_____ you _____2_____ out now?

B: Yes, I (go) _____3_____ to the store.

     (need) _____4_____ you _____5_____ anything?

F

A: (work) _____ you _____ at the moment?
　　　　　　　　　　1　　　　　　　　　　　　2

B: Yes, I (sit) _____ at my desk right now.
　　　　　　　　3

A: (like) _____ you _____ it?
　　　　　　　　4　　　　　　　　5

B: Yes, I (love) _____ it. I (write) _____ for five
　　　　　　　　　　6　　　　　　　　　　　　　　　7

hours every day.

G

A: Why (put) _____ you _____ on your coat?
　　　　　　　　1　　　　　　　　　　　　2

B: I (go) _____ for a walk. (want) _____ you
　　　　　　3　　　　　　　　　　　　　　　4

_____ to come?
　　5

H

A: What (wait) _____ you _____ for?
　　　　　　　　1　　　　　　　　　　　2

B: I (wait) _____ for the store to open.
　　　　　　　3

A: But it (open) _____ at ten every day.
　　　　　　　　　4

B: I (know) _____ . I (want) _____ to
　　　　　　　5　　　　　　　　　　　6

be early. The sales start today.

I

A: Why (walk) _____ you _____ so fast?
　　　　　　　1　　　　　　　　　　2

You usually (not, walk) _____ fast.
　　　　　　　　　　　　3

B: I (hurry) _____ because my father (wait) _____
　　　　　　4　　　　　　　　　　　　　　　　　　5

for me.

J

A: (usually, take) _____ you _____ the bus
　　　　　　　　　1　　　　　　　　　　2

to school?

B: Yes, I (always, take) _____ the bus.
　　　　　　　　　　3

I (like) _____ it. I (not, have) _____ a problem
　　　　　4　　　　　　　　　　　5

with parking.

K

A: (remember) _____1_____ you _____2_____ Joanne?

B: Yes. (still, study) _____3_____ she _____4_____ ?

A: No. She (work) _____5_____ now. She (have) _____6_____

a very good job in a hospital.

CD2, 20, 21

B Listen and check your answers. Then work with a partner. Listen again and repeat the questions and answers.

16 Practice

A Work with a partner. Think of someone you know very well. Tell your partner three things that the person is doing now. If you are not sure, you can use *maybe* or *probably*. Then tell your partner five things that the person does regularly.

Example

Maybe he is having lunch now.

He is probably having lunch now.

He always has lunch at 1:00.

B Now write sentences about your partner's person.

Example

Her friend is having lunch now.

1. _____ .

2. _____ .

3. _____ .

4. _____ .

5. _____ .

17 Read
Read the story. Then write answers to the questions.

THE TRAVELER AND HIS DOG

A traveler is starting a journey soon. The traveler has a dog, and the dog is stretching by the door. The traveler says to his dog, "Come, what are you yawning for? Hurry up and get ready. I want you to go with me."

But the dog is just wagging its tail. Then the traveler says again, "Hurry up. What are you waiting for?" The dog wags his tail again. The dog quietly says, "I'm ready, master. It's you I'm waiting for."

1. What is the traveler doing soon?

   _____ .

2. What animal does the traveler have?

   _____ .

3. Where is the dog?

   _____ .

4. What is the dog doing?

   _____ .

5. What does the traveler think the dog is doing?

_____ .

6. What does the traveler want his dog to do?

_____ .

7. What is the dog doing when it speaks?

_____ .

8. Who is the dog waiting for?

_____ .

Listening Puzzle

  CD2, 22

A Listen and check the correct answer.

❑ A. *Mother's Day*

❑ B. *Thanksgiving*

❑ C. *Fourth of July*

B Discuss your answer with your classmates.

CD2, 23

C Now listen again and write the sentences you hear.

A Before You Read

Answer the questions.

1. What are the people doing in the photo?
2. What do you think they are celebrating?
3. What do you know about Burma?

B Read

WATER FESTIVAL

DID YOU KNOW ... ?
In Spain, *La Tomatina* festival is on the last Wednesday in August. Thousands of people throw tomatoes at each other.

Burma, also called Myanmar, is a country in Asia, and it is a country of many traditions. One tradition is the Water Festival. The Burmese ₅ celebrate the New Year in the month of April with the Water Festival or *Thingyan*. **This** means "change."

April is a very hot month ₁₀ in Burma. The shops and schools are closed, and everyone is in the streets. They are splashing and spraying water on each other. Some people are in cars. They are ₁₅ singing and spraying water on the people in the streets. People in the streets are spraying water on the people in the cars. People all over the country are celebrating the Water Festival. They are washing away the old year and the bad ₂₀ memories. They are making themselves clean and pure for the coming months. The Water Festival lasts for three days. It is great fun, but it is also a serious festival for religious people. People go to **temples**.

C Notice the Grammar

Underline all of the present progressive forms.

Choose the best answer.

Some detail questions have the words **NOT** or **EXCEPT**. Choose the answer that is **NOT** true or **NOT** in the passage. Answers that are true or in the passage are not correct.

D Look for Main Ideas

1. What is paragraph 2 mainly about?
   - A the country of Burma
   - B the many traditions of Burma
   - C why people go to temples
   - D how they celebrate the Water Festival

E Look for Details

2. The new year in Burma is _____ .
   - A always a fun time
   - B fun and serious at the same time
   - C not always in April
   - D a one-day celebration

3. People throw water on each other _____ .
   - A because it is hot
   - B because it is fun
   - C to get clean
   - D to wash away the old year

4. What does *Thingyan* mean?
   - A the Water Festival
   - B April
   - C the new year
   - D change

5. What are they NOT spraying water on?
   - A people
   - B cars
   - C streets
   - D monasteries

F Look for Vocabulary

6. The word *temples* in the reading is closest in meaning to _____ .
   - A places of worship
   - B meetings
   - C parks
   - D city buildings

G Reference the Text

7. The word *This* in the reading refers to _____ .
   - A the new year
   - B *Thingyan*
   - C water
   - D April

Writing: Describe Experiences

Write an email about a vacation.

STEP 1 Read the email and answer the questions. Then check your answers with a partner.

New	Delete	Reply	Reply All	Forward	Move

To	pamle@woohoo.net
Cc	
Subject	Here we are!

Dear Pam,

    We are here in Hawaii on the island of Oahu. We're having a great time. We're staying in a big hotel on Waikiki beach. I'm writing this email from the hotel you see in the picture. My husband, Tony, is lying on the beach. My son, Jerry, is swimming in the pool. We're enjoying the vacation very much. See you soon!

Rima, Tony, and Jerry

1. Who is writing the email?
2. Where are they staying?
3. Where are they writing the email from?

4. What are Tony and Jerry doing?
5. Are they enjoying the vacation?

STEP 2 Now write an email to a friend. Use your own information. Use the email in Step 1 to help you. Tell about the things below. Be sure to check your spelling of words that end in *-ing*.

1. where you are
2. where you are staying
3. where you are writing the email

4. what you and your family are doing
5. if you are enjoying the vacation

STEP 3 Work with a partner to edit your email. Correct spelling, punctuation, vocabulary, and grammar.

STEP 4 Write your final copy.

Self-Test

1. We _____ oxygen to live.

    A. needs   (A) (B) (C) (D)
    B. needing
    C. need
    D. are needing

2. Schools _____ in tests.

    A. believing   (A) (B) (C) (D)
    B. is believing
    C. are believing
    D. believe

3. This food _____ delicious.

    A. smelling   (A) (B) (C) (D)
    B. is smelling
    C. smells
    D. smell

4. I _____ my first day at school.

    A. remembering   (A) (B) (C) (D)
    B. remember
    C. am remembering
    D. to remember

5. It _____ right now.

    A. not rain   (A) (B) (C) (D)
    B. does not rain
    C. not raining
    D. is not raining

6. I _____ on the phone right now.

    A. talk   (A) (B) (C) (D)
    B. talking
    C. am talking
    D. be talking

7. What _____ here?

    A. you are doing (A) (B) (C) (D)
    B. you doing
    C. are you doing
    D. you do

8. We _____ English in class.

    A. are always speaking   (A) (B) (C) (D)
    B. always speak
    C. speak always
    D. are speaking always

9. Foreign students _____ some American customs.

    A. do not understand   (A) (B) (C) (D)
    B. do no understand
    C. no understand
    D. are not understanding

10. _____ the music?

    A. Are you hearing   (A) (B) (C) (D)
    B. You are hearing
    C. Do you hear
    D. You hear

1. Hippos <u>are eating</u> <u>at night</u> <u>and</u> <u>spend</u> the day
           A   **B**   **C**   **D**
   in the water.

   Ⓐ   Ⓑ   Ⓒ   Ⓓ

2. <u>Fingernails</u> <u>growing</u> more during <u>the day</u>
      A   **B**   **C**
   than <u>at night</u>.
       D

   Ⓐ   Ⓑ   Ⓒ   Ⓓ

3. Bears <u>do not</u> see well so <u>they</u> <u>smelling</u>
        A   **B** **C**
   <u>their</u> food.
    D

   Ⓐ   Ⓑ   Ⓒ   Ⓓ

4. Many people <u>are thinking</u> the heart <u>is</u> on the left,
             A   **B**
   but <u>it</u> <u>is</u> in the middle of your chest.
      C D

   Ⓐ   Ⓑ   Ⓒ   Ⓓ

5. <u>Sometimes</u> students <u>having</u> <u>problems</u> with
    A   **B**   **C**
   <u>English</u> spelling.
     D

   Ⓐ   Ⓑ   Ⓒ   Ⓓ

6. <u>Teachers</u> <u>in the United States</u> <u>are</u>
    A   **B**   **C**
   <u>not wear</u> uniforms.
    D

   Ⓐ   Ⓑ   Ⓒ   Ⓓ

7. We <u>freeze</u> here in New York right now, and
      A
   <u>people</u> <u>are lying</u> in the sun in <u>Australia</u>.
    B   **C**   **D**

   Ⓐ   Ⓑ   Ⓒ   Ⓓ

8. When <u>does</u> the semester <u>ending</u>, <u>in</u>
       A   **B** **C**
   June <u>or</u> July?
     D

   Ⓐ   Ⓑ   Ⓒ   Ⓓ

9. <u>Are</u> you <u>need</u> <u>a dictionary</u> <u>for the test</u>?
    A   **B**   **C**   **D**

   Ⓐ   Ⓑ   Ⓒ   Ⓓ

10. The students <u>are</u> not <u>take</u> a test right now; they
             A   **B**
    <u>are waiting</u> for <u>their</u> teacher.
       C   **D**

    Ⓐ   Ⓑ   Ⓒ   Ⓓ

Unit 5

Nouns and Pronouns

Whose hat is this?
It's **Jane's.**

Form/Function

TOM: What's on the pizza?
KAREN: **Tomatoes, peppers, mushrooms, cheese,** and **olives.**
TOM: No **onions**?

1. We can count some things. *Book* is a count noun. It can be singular or plural (one book, two books).
2. We cannot count other nouns. These are noncount nouns. These nouns do not have *a* or *an* in front of them, and they have no plural. Here are some noncount nouns.

Examples of Noncount Nouns	
Mass nouns	cheese, butter, meat, salt, pepper, bread, rice, sugar, money, paper, gold, tea, water, milk, oil, soup, gasoline, wood, silver
Abstract nouns	love, happiness, beauty, luck, peace
Others	advice, furniture, information, weather, help, homework, work, traffic, music

3. We use singular verbs with noncount nouns.
   Water **is** important.
   Gold **is** expensive.

1 Practice
Write *C* for count nouns and *N* for noncount nouns.

1. __N__ coffee
2. _____ letter
3. _____ city
4. _____ traffic
5. _____ cheese
6. _____ flower
7. _____ teacher
8. _____ weather
9. _____ banana
10. _____ milk
11. _____ gold
12. _____ meat
13. _____ rice
14. _____ house
15. _____ advice
16. _____ food
17. _____ bed
18. _____ sugar
19. _____ chair
20. _____ money

Count		Noncount	
1.	*apples*	4.	*milk*
2.	_____	5.	_____
3.	_____	6.	_____

5B | *A/An* and *Some*

Function

There is **an** apple. There are **some** cookies, and there's **some** milk.

1. We use *a* or *an* in front of singular count nouns. Remember, *a* and *an* mean "one."
   a table, **an** umbrella

2. We use *some* in front of noncount nouns. *Some* means "a quantity of."

   CORRECT: The cake has **some** milk in it.

   INCORRECT: The cake has ~~a milk~~ in it.

3. We also use *some* with plural count nouns.
   a book, **some** books

4. It is possible to use *milk* as a count noun, but the meaning is different.
   I want **a milk**. = I want *a serving* of milk.

3 Practice

Tony and Stella are preparing for a picnic. Here are some things they need. Complete the list with *a*, *an*, or *some*.

1. ___some___ water
2. _____ orange juice
3. _____ tablecloth
4. _____ radio
5. _____ cups
6. _____ ice chest
7. _____ fruit
8. _____ tent

9. _____ salt
10. _____ sandwiches
11. _____ napkins
12. _____ forks
13. _____ knives
14. _____ umbrella
15. _____ cookies
16. _____ volleyball

4 Practice

A What does Joe eat every morning? Complete these sentences with *a*, *an*, or *some*.

He has some coffee. He puts ___some___ milk in his coffee.
1

He also puts in _____ sugar. He has _____ bread. He
2   3

puts _____ butter on the bread. Sometimes he has _____
4   5

cheese. He likes _____ fruit in the morning. He has
6

_____ orange every morning. And he has _____
7   8

banana with _____ cookie at 10:30.
9

B Listen and check your answers. Then listen again and repeat each sentence.

CD2, 24, 25

C Listen again. How does Joe like his coffee? Circle the letter of the correct answer.

CD2, 26

A with only milk
B with only sugar

C with milk and sugar
D without milk or sugar

126 Unit 5

5c | *A/An* or *The*

Form

> There is **a** dog outside. **The** dog is big.

We use *the* with singular count, plural count, and noncount nouns.

He has a car. **The** car is black. (singular count noun)
I have two boys. **The** boys are at school. (plural count noun)
I have some information. **The** information is important. (noncount noun)

Function

1. We use *the* when the person we are speaking to knows which person or thing we are talking about.

   TONY: Where's John?

   ANNIE: He's in **the** house.

   (Both Tony and Annie know which house they are talking about.)

2. We use *a* or *an* when the person we are speaking to does not know which person or thing we are talking about. Often, we use *a* or *an* when we talk about something for the first time. We use *the* after that because the other person knows what we are talking about.

   There's **a** dog and **a** cat outside. **The** dog is chasing **the** cat.

5 Practice

A Complete the sentences with *the*, *a*, or *an*.

A

I live in _____*an*_____ apartment in the city. _____ apartment is in
           1   **2**

_____ big building. _____ building is old, but it is near
        3   **4**

transportation and stores. I usually take _____ bus or _____ tram
                                                    5   **6**

to work. _____ bus stops in front of _____ apartment building,
             7   **8**

and _____ tram is just _____ hundred yards (91 meters) from
        9   **10**

_____ building.
    11

B

DON: What do you want to do today?

KATE: I want to see _____ movie.
                           1

DON: Which movie?

KATE: There's _____ movie I want to see at _____ movie theater
                    2   **3**

near my house. I don't know _____ name of the movie. It's about
                                  4

_____ man with _____ dog. _____ dog has a special
    5   **6**   **7**

ability. It speaks like _____ person.
                            8

DON: That sounds like _____ silly movie.
                             9

C

DAVE: Do you live in _____ house or _____ apartment?
                           1   **2**

JAMES: Well, I have _____ house in the country and _____
                         3   **4**

apartment in the city. _____ house was my mother's, and I rent
                           5

_____ apartment.
    6

DAVE: Oh. I guess you have _____ car and _____ motorbike, too.
                                 7   **8**

B Listen and check your answers. Then work with a partner. Listen again and repeat each conversation. Take turns with the sentences in A.

CD2, 27, 28

5D | Generalizations

Form / Function

I love **roses**.

1. We do not use *the* when we talk about something in general.

   I smell **roses** in the air.   **Gold** is expensive.

2. We use *the* when we are specific.

   The roses in my garden are all red.   **The** gold in this jewelry is very expensive.

---

6 Practice
Complete the sentences with *the* or *X* (no article).

1. AMY: What do you like to read about?

   KEN: I love _____X_____ history. I really like to read about _____

   history of Europe.

2. BEN: Do you watch _____ football on television?

   STEVE: No, I don't like _____ football. I like _____ tennis.

3. JOE: I don't like _____ meat. I prefer _____ fish.

   PETER: _____ fish at the restaurant was very good.

4. SUI: _____ water is very important in our lives.

   LEE: _____ water in this city is bad.

5E | *Some* and *Any*

Form

> I love this place. I can get **some** peace and quiet here. There aren't **any** cars. There aren't **any** telephones. There isn't **any** noise.

1. Some We use *some* in affirmative statements with count and noncount nouns.
   I need **some** eggs (count noun) and **some** sugar (noncount noun) to make a cake.

2. **Any** We use *any* in negative statements and questions.
   Are there **any** flowers in the park?
   No, there aren't **any** flowers. There are **some** trees.
   Is there **any** noise?
   No, there isn't **any** noise.

Function

1. Some We use *some* to show a quantity when we do not know exactly how much or how many.
   I have **some** time to go on vacation.

2. **Any** In negative statements and questions, we use *any* to show a quantity when we do not
   know exactly how much or how many.
   Do you have **any** information?
   Sorry, I don't have **any** information.

7 Practice

Look at the photo. Complete the sentences with *some* or *any*.

1. Are there _____*any*_____ cars in the street? No, there aren't _____ cars.

2. Are there _____ buses in the street? No, there aren't _____ buses.

3. Are there _____ bicycles in the street? Yes, there are _____ bicycles.

4. Are there _____ churches? No, there aren't _____ churches.

5. Are there _____ plants? Yes, there are _____ plants.

8 Pair Up and Talk

A Look at the picture. Ask your partner questions with *any*. Your partner answers with *some* or *any*.

A: Is there any milk on the table?

B: Yes, there's some milk.

B Now practice the conversation with your partner again. Use these words or your own.

apples	bread	cheese	fish	milk	rice
bananas	carrots	eggs	lemons	onions	tomatoes

Form

They give you **a glass of** water and **a cup** of coffee.

After measurement words, we usually have a prepositional phrase with *of*.

a cup **of** coffee
a glass **of** water

Function

We can use measurement words with noncount nouns. We can also use them with count nouns.

I drink **a cup of** coffee every morning.
Here are some measurement words.

a bar of soap	**a can of** tomatoes	**a box of** chocolates
a bunch of bananas	**a tube of** toothpaste	**a glass of** water
a carton of milk	**a sheet of** paper	**a bottle of** wine
a piece of fruit	**a slice of** cake	**a cup of** tea
a head of lettuce	**a pack of** batteries	**a roll of** toilet paper
a jar of jam	**a loaf of** bread	**a bowl of** soup

9 Practice

A Suzy is going shopping. Here are some things she needs to buy. Add measurement words to her list.

1. ___*a bar of*___ soap
2. _____ toilet paper
3. _____ tomatoes
4. _____ milk
5. _____ bread
6. _____ cereal
7. _____ sugar

8. _____ shampoo
9. _____ batteries
10. _____ toothpaste
11. _____ mayonnaise
12. _____ oil
13. _____ cheese
14. _____ juice

B Listen and check your answers. Then listen again and repeat each phrase.

CD2, 29, 30

10 Pair Up and Talk

A Practice the conversation with a partner.

A: What food do you have at home?

B: I have a box of cereal.

B Now practice the conversation with your partner again. Use these phrases or your own.

Foods

bread	juice	milk	soda
chocolates	ketchup	rice	sugar
gum	lettuce	salt	tomatoes

Measurement Words

| a bottle of | a can of | a jar of | a pack of |
| a box of | a carton of | a loaf of | a piece of |

Quantifying Expressions

Form

David runs **a few** miles every day. He drinks **a lot of** water. He doesn't drink **any** beer or wine.

	Affirmative	Negative
Count Nouns	There are **many** eggs.	There aren't **many** eggs.
	There are **a lot of** apples.	There aren't **a lot of** apples.
	There are **some** tomatoes.	There aren't **any** tomatoes.
	There are **a few** onions.	There aren't **any** onions.
	There are **a couple of** onions.	There are **no** onions.
Noncount Nouns	There is **a lot of** juice.	There isn't **much** juice.
	There is **some** milk.	There isn't **any** milk.
	There is **a little** cheese.	There isn't **any** cheese.
		There isn't **much** cheese.

Function

1. We use *a lot of* with count and noncount nouns to talk about a large amount or a large number.
   There is **a lot of** food on the table. There are **a lot of** apples.

2. We use *a little* or *not much* with noncount nouns, and we use *a few* or *not many* with count nouns to talk about a small amount or a small number.
   There is **a little** milk in the carton.　　There are **a few** oranges left.
   There is **not much** coffee.　　There are**n't many** potatoes.

11 Practice

A Complete the sentences with *much* or *many*.

1. David doesn't eat _much_ meat.
2. He doesn't eat _____ bread.
3. He eats _____ kinds of cereal.
4. He doesn't eat _____ eggs.
5. He doesn't drink _____ milk.
6. He doesn't eat _____ cheese.
7. He doesn't eat _____ food at meals.
8. He doesn't spend _____ money on food.

B Listen and check your answers. Then listen again and repeat each sentence.

CD2, 31, 32

12 Practice

A Complete the sentences with *a few* or *a little*.

1. He drinks _a few_ glasses of juice every day.
2. When he is hungry, he eats _____ nuts.
3. He exercises for _____ hours every day.
4. He only uses _____ salt on his food.
5. He also uses _____ oil.
6. He eats _____ fish.
7. He eats _____ oranges every morning.
8. He eats _____ kinds of fruit every day.

B Listen and check your answers. Then listen again and repeat each sentence.

CD2, 33, 34

C Listen again. Read the sentences. Write *T* for *True* or *F* for *False*.

1. He likes to exercise. _____
2. He likes salty food. _____
3. He doesn't like fruit. _____
4. He wants to be healthy. _____

CD2, 35

Form/Function

JAMES: **How many** slices of bread do you eat for breakfast?

TOMMY: A lot. About six.

JAMES: **How much** milk do you drink?

TOMMY: Not much. About four glasses.

We use *how many* with plural count nouns. We use *how much* with noncount nouns.

Type of Noun	Wh- Word	Noun	
Plural Count Noun	**How many**	lemons	do you need?
		friends	do you have?
Noncount Noun	**How much**	money	do you have?
		milk	is there?

13   Pair Up and Talk

A   How much of these things do you eat? Practice the conversation with a partner.

A: How much pasta do you eat in a week?

B: Not much.

B   Now practice the conversation with your partner again. Use these words and *a lot, not much,* or *not many*.

apples	bread	eggs	fruit	meat	potatoes
bananas	chocolate	fish	ice cream	pasta	rice

5I *Whose* and Possessive Nouns

Form/Function

SAM: **Whose** dog is that?

KAREN: That's **Julia's** dog.

Whose

1. We use *whose* to ask who owns something or who something belongs to.

Whose	Noun	Verb		Answers with Possessive Nouns
Whose	dog	is	that?	It's Julia**'s** dog.
Whose	books	are	these?	They're Ken**'s** books.

Do not confuse *who's* and *whose*. *Who's* = who is. *Whose* = who owns something.

Possessive Nouns

2. We use **'s** (apostrophe *s*) or **'** (apostrophe) to talk about things that belong to people.

Nouns	Rules	Examples
Singular Nouns	Add an apostrophe + *s* ('s) to the noun.	It's John**'s** bag. It's the boy**'s** bag.
Regular Plural Nouns (end in –s)	Add an apostrophe to the noun.	They are boys**'** bags. That's the teachers**'** office.
Irregular Plural Nouns	Add an apostrophe + *s* ('s) to the noun.	They are the children**'s** toys. They sell women**'s** shoes. That's a men**'s** store.
Names and Nouns that already end in *s* (for example, Charles, the boss)	Add an apostrophe + *s* ('s) or an apostrophe (') to the name or noun.	That's Charles**'s** wife. OR Charles**'** wife. That's the boss**'s** chair. OR the boss**'** chair.

1. (bicycle/Mike)

   <u>Whose bicycle is this</u>?

   <u>It's Mike's</u>.

2. (sneakers/Ted)

   _____?

   _____.

3. (hat/Jane)

   _____?

   _____.

4. (house/Sandra)

   _____?

   _____.

5. (ball/Timmy)

   _____?

   _____.

6. (car/my parents)

   _____?

   _____.

B Listen and check your answers. Then work with a partner. Listen again and repeat the questions and answers.

15 Practice

Add ' or 's to the nouns to show possession. Write the noun in its possessive form on the line.

1. Every Saturday, we go to my mother house for dinner. _____ *mother's* _____

2. My parents house is not far, but we take the car. _____

3. I take the children in my husband car. _____

4. I have two girls and a boy. My girls names are Kate and Lila. _____

5. Kate hair is red. _____

6. The children favorite day is Saturday. ___ _____

16 Practice

Rewrite the questions.

1. What is the name of your teacher? *What's your teacher's name* ?

2. What is the name of your school? _____ ?

3. What is the name of your partner? _____ ?

4. What is the name of your best friend? _____ ?

5. What is the name of your mother/father? _____ ?

6. What is the address of your parents? _____ ?

17 Your Turn

Write the answers to the questions from Practice 16.

1. *My teacher's name is Mr. Peterson* .

2. _____ .

3. _____ .

4. _____ .

5. _____ .

6. _____ .

18   Read
Read the story. Then write answers to the questions.

THE BEST SOUND

There is a famous king. This king likes to talk. He and his friends talk about many things. His friend asks, "What is the best sound in the world?"

One man answers, "The sound of a flute."

"No," says the other man, "The sound of a tambourine is best."

The third man says, "No, the sound of a drum is best."

The king says nothing. Three days go by, and he invites his friends for dinner. When the friends enter the room, there isn't any food on the table. The king's musicians play for hours, but still there isn't any food. Five hours go by, and the friends are now very hungry.

Finally, the king calls to his waiters. The waiters bring a big pot of food. The king hits the top of the pot with a spoon and says, "The sound of dishes when you are hungry—is the best sound!"

1. What do the king and his friends talk about?

   _____ .

2. What does the king do after three days?

   _____ .

3. Is there any food on the table?

_____ .

4. What do the waiters bring?

_____ .

5. What does the king say at the end?

_____ .

Listening Puzzle

AUDIO DOWNLOAD   CD2, 38

A Listen and check the correct answer.

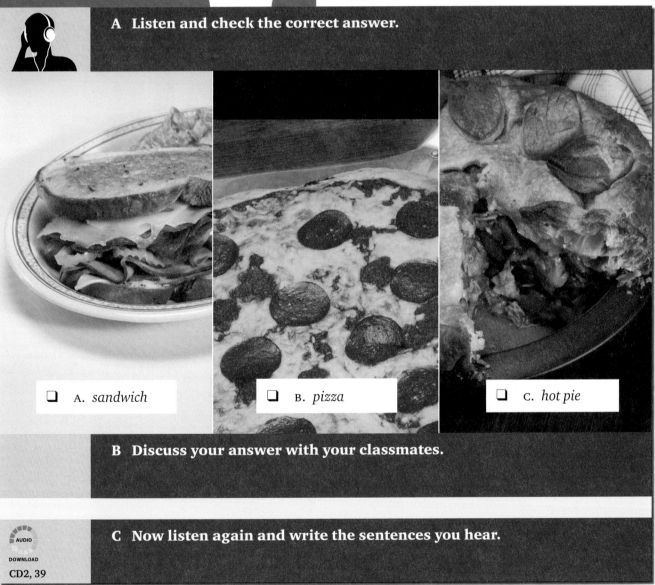

☐ A. _sandwich_   ☐ B. _pizza_   ☐ C. _hot pie_

B Discuss your answer with your classmates.

AUDIO DOWNLOAD
CD2, 39

C Now listen again and write the sentences you hear.

A Before You Read

Answer the questions.

1. Where do penguins live?
2. How many kinds of penguins are there?

B Read

PENGUINS

DID YOU KNOW ... ?

The emperor penguin is four feet (1.2m) tall and weighs over 90 pounds (40kg). It is the heaviest sea bird.

There are 18 kinds of penguins, and they all live south of the equator. The largest are the emperor penguins, which live in 5 Antarctica. They lay their eggs about 50 miles (81 kilometers) from the coast. However, there is only snow and ice **there** and nothing 10 to make a nest from.

The emperor penguins take care of their eggs in a special way. The female produces only one egg. As soon as she lays her egg, the male penguin rolls it on top of his feet. A special fold 15 of skin on the bottom of his stomach comes down over the egg to **protect** it from the cold. For two months while the females go to find food, the male penguins stand together to keep warm with their eggs on their feet. Finally, 20 when the females return, the males, which now have had no food for two months, go out to sea.

C Notice the Grammar

Underline all noncount nouns.

When you read, try to understand new words.
First, look at clues in the reading. Then write
down the new words and their meanings.

Choose the best answer.

D Look for Main Ideas

1. What is the main idea of paragraph 1?
    A how penguins make their nests
    B different kinds of penguins
    C information about emperor penguins
    D the weather in Antarctica

2. What is the main idea of paragraph 2?
    A how emperor penguins take care
       of their eggs
    B the life of the female emperor penguin
    C what emperor penguins eat
    D how the emperor penguin lays her egg

E Look for Details

3. Antarctica doesn't have any _____ .
    A ice
    B plants
    C snow
    D penguins

4. Which of the following is NOT true about
    emperor penguins?
    A They live in Antarctica.
    B They lay their eggs 50 miles from the sea.
    C They don't make nests.
    D They aren't large.

5. The male emperor penguin _____ .
    A lays the egg
    B keeps the egg on its feet
    C covers the egg with its feet
    D protects the female

6. The female emperor penguin _____ .
    A goes to find food first
    B doesn't move for two months
    C takes care of the egg for the first
       two months
    D goes to find food after the male returns

F Look for Vocabulary

7. The word *protect* in the reading is closest in
    meaning to _____ .
    A keep safe and warm
    B hide
    C change
    D keep soft

G Reference the Text

8. The word *There* refers to _____ .
    A Antarctica
    B south of the equator
    C snow
    D nest

Writing: Describe Objects

Write a descriptive paragraph.

STEP 1   Work with a partner. Ask and answer questions about what is on the table. Use *how much, how many, a/an, the, a little, a lot, a few, some, any, no*, and so forth.

Example

YOU: How many eggs are there?

YOUR PARTNER: There are two eggs.

STEP 2   Write a paragraph about what is on the table. Write one sentence in your paragraph that has three or more nouns together. Be sure to put a comma between each noun and before the word *and*.

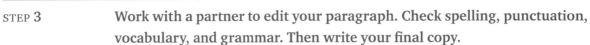

There is a lot of food on the table. There is some bread, some cheese, and some fruit on the table.

STEP 3   Work with a partner to edit your paragraph. Check spelling, punctuation, vocabulary, and grammar. Then write your final copy.

Self-Test

1. I eat _____ every day.

    A. a rice   Ⓐ Ⓑ Ⓒ Ⓓ
    B. some rices
    C. some rice
    D. any rice

2. Excuse me, I need _____ information.

    A. any   Ⓐ Ⓑ Ⓒ Ⓓ
    B. some
    C. a
    D. an

3. To make a sandwich, you need _____ bread, butter, and cheese.

    A. any   Ⓐ Ⓑ Ⓒ Ⓓ
    B. the
    C. a
    D. some

4. How _____ are there in your class?

    A. many students   Ⓐ Ⓑ Ⓒ Ⓓ
    B. many student
    C. much students
    D. students many

5. There is _____ bread on the table.

    A. a loaf   Ⓐ Ⓑ Ⓒ Ⓓ
    B. a
    C. a loaf of
    D. the loaf of

6. I have _____ umbrella for the rain.

    A. a   Ⓐ Ⓑ Ⓒ Ⓓ
    B. an
    C. the
    D. any

7. _____ that man?

    A. Whose   Ⓐ Ⓑ Ⓒ Ⓓ
    B. Who
    C. Who is
    D. Is who

8. These are _____ toys.

    A. the children's   Ⓐ Ⓑ Ⓒ Ⓓ
    B. a children's
    C. the childrens'
    D. the childs'

9. Those are _____ books.

    A. Ken   Ⓐ Ⓑ Ⓒ Ⓓ
    B. Ken's
    C. Kens'
    D. Ken his

10. _____ are big animals.

    A. Elephants   Ⓐ Ⓑ Ⓒ Ⓓ
    B. Elephant
    C. The elephants
    D. An elephant

1. <u>A</u> tube <u>toothpaste</u> sells for about <u>two dollars</u>
   <u>these days</u>.

   A B C D

2. <u>Monkeys</u> <u>don't like</u> to live in <u>cold</u> <u>weathers</u>.
   A   B   C   D

   A B C D

3. Many <u>Americans</u> like to eat <u>a bowl of</u> <u>cereal</u>
   with <u>a milk</u> for breakfast.

   A B C D

4. In Great Britain, most people <u>drink</u> <u>tea</u> with
   <u>a few</u> <u>milk</u> in it.

   A B C D

5. Many Americans are eating more <u>chickens</u>,
   <u>turkey</u>, and <u>fish</u> because too much red <u>meat</u> is
   not good for them.

   A B C D

6. Foods that <u>have</u> a lot of <u>fat</u>, <u>oil</u>, and <u>sugars</u> are
   not good for you.

   A B C D

7. <u>Life</u> was very difficult <u>two hundred years</u> ago
   when there <u>was</u> no <u>an electricity</u>.

   A B C D

8. <u>Some people</u> take <u>a little</u> <u>vitamins</u> every day;
   other people don't like to take <u>vitamins</u>.

   A B C D

9. <u>Walt Disneys'</u> <u>movies</u> and <u>his</u> cartoon
   characters are popular with <u>children</u> around
   the world.

   A B C D

10. <u>Vegetarians</u> don't eat meat, and some
    vegetarians don't eat <u>cheeses</u> or <u>eggs</u> and don't
    drink <u>milk</u>.

    A B C D

Unit 6
The Simple Past

We **flew** to Paris last April.

6A | The Simple Past: Regular Verbs

Form

Erika **worked** in a hospital last year.
She **helped** a lot of people.

To form the simple past of regular verbs, add *-ed* to the base verb. The past form is the same for all subjects.

Subject	Base Verb + *-ed*
I	
You	
He/She/It	work**ed**.
We	
They	

Function

It **rained** yesterday.
He **needed** an umbrella.

1. We use the simple past to talk about actions and situations that began and ended in the past.
2. We can use specific time expressions like *yesterday*, *last week*, and *at three o'clock* with the simple past.

1 Practice

A Complete the sentences with the simple past of the verbs in parentheses.

1. It (rain) ____rained____ yesterday.

2. Peter (wait) _____ for the bus for 30 minutes.

3. He (walk) _____ into the office at 9:10. He was late.

4. First, he (open) _____ the windows.

5. Then he (listen) _____ to his voice mail messages.

6. He (talk) _____ to customers for several hours.

7. Then he (work) _____ on his computer.

8. At 12:15, he was hungry, so he (call) _____ a restaurant.

9. He (order) _____ a sandwich and a cup of coffee.

10. He (stay) _____ in the office until 5:15 as usual.

11. Peter then (call) _____ a taxi to the airport.

12. He (board) _____ the plane in Boston, and he (arrive) _____ in
    Rio de Janeiro, Brazil at 11:45 A.M. the next day.

B What do you think? We have no news from Peter. What happened to him?
Where is he? What is he doing?

2 Practice

Complete the sentences with the simple present or the simple past of the verbs in parentheses.

1. Three years ago, Trisha (work) ___worked___ at a bakery.

2. Now, she (work) _____ in a bank.

3. Every day, customers (call) _____ her on the phone.

4. Yesterday, she (receive) _____ 75 phone calls.

5. She always (listen) _____ to the customers very carefully.

6. Usually, Trisha (answer) _____ their questions quickly, but last week, somebody (ask) _____ her a difficult question.

7. She (not, be) _____ sure of the answer.

8. On Tuesdays after work, Trisha (play) _____ baseball in the park, but last Tuesday, she (stay) _____ at work late to find the answer to that difficult question.

9. She finally (solve) _____ the problem.

10. Then last Wednesday, she (call) _____ the customer back with the answer.

3 Pair Up and Talk

A Practice the conversation with a partner.

A: What did you do last week?

B: Last week, I talked to my uncle on the phone.

B Now practice the conversation with your partner again. Use these phrases.

clean my apartment	play a sport/game	visit friends
cook dinner	stay up late	watch television
listen to music (say what kind)	talk to my relatives	work on homework

Form

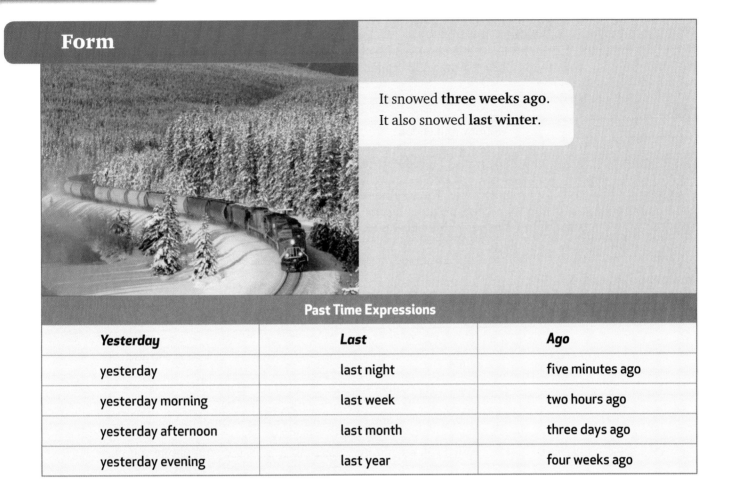

It snowed **three weeks ago**.
It also snowed **last winter**.

Past Time Expressions

Yesterday	Last	Ago
yesterday	last night	five minutes ago
yesterday morning	last week	two hours ago
yesterday afternoon	last month	three days ago
yesterday evening	last year	four weeks ago

Function

1. *Yesterday*, *last*, and *… ago* tell us when an action happened in the past. We use these words in the following ways:

Yesterday	morning, afternoon, and evening
Last	night, general periods of time (week, month, year), days of the week, and seasons (summer, winter, spring, fall)
Ago	specific lengths of time; for example, five minutes ago

2. Time expressions usually come at the beginning or at the end of a sentence. When they come at the beginning of a sentence, we use a comma after the time expression.
   Yesterday morning, I walked to school. OR I walked to school **yesterday morning**.

A Complete the conversation with *yesterday, last,* or *ago.*

PAMELA: Where were you? I called you four times _____*last*_____ week.
                                                           1

MEG: I was in New York. I was there for a conference. It started _____

      Monday and ended _____ .
               3

PAMELA: Lucky you. I love New York in the fall. I was there two years _____
                                                                         4
      in October. The weather was beautiful!

MEG: Well, this October was terrible. The rain started two weeks

      _____ and stopped _____ week for just two days. Then it
            5   **6**

      started to rain again _____
                                 7

      afternoon just as I arrived at the airport.

PAMELA: _____ afternoon? Were you in that traffic jam at the airport?
              8

MEG: Yes, I was. I was really tired _____ night when I got home.
                                          9

      I was in bed by nine and opened my eyes only an hour _____ .
                                                                10

PAMELA: Oh, I called you ten minutes _____ , but your phone was busy.
                                          11

MEG: That was my brother. He called me about 20 minutes _____ . He
                                                             12

      called me _____ evening, too, but I was asleep.
                    13

PAMELA: By the way, Mary Jane called me _____ Friday. She's
                                              14

      getting married!

MEG: Really! Who's the lucky man?

PAMELA: His name is Tony Bradson. She started to work with him three

      years _____ , and they decided to get married last year.
                15

      So they saved some money and decided the wedding date

      _____ month.
            16

MEG: Tony Bradson? Are you sure?

PAMELA: Yes, why?

B Listen and check your answers. Then work with a partner. Listen again and repeat the conversation.

CD3, 2, 3

C What do you think? Why is Meg surprised?

5 Practice

A Talk about yourself with a partner. Use the time expressions.

Example

Three months ago, I was in Rio de Janeiro.

Last night,	Last year,	Twenty minutes ago,
Last spring,	One hour ago,	Yesterday afternoon,
Last week,	Three months ago,	Yesterday morning,

B Now write about things your partner told you.

1. *Three months ago, she was in Seoul* .

2. _____ .

3. _____ .

4. _____ .

5. _____ .

6. _____ .

7. _____ .

8. _____ .

9. _____ .

Spelling of Regular Simple Past Verbs

Form

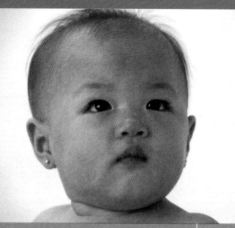

The baby **cried** and **cried**.
Then she look**ed** at me and stop**ped**.

Verb Ending	Spelling Rule	Examples	
1. Most regular verbs	Add -*ed*.	rain point	rain**ed** point**ed**
2. Verb ends in *e*	Add -*d*.	arrive smile	arrive**d** smile**d**
3. Verb ends in consonant + *y*	Change *y* to *i* and add -*ed*.	try carry	tr**ied** carr**ied**
4. Verb ends in vowel + *y*	Add -*ed*.	enjoy play	enjoy**ed** play**ed**
5. Verb ends in consonant + vowel + consonant (one-syllable verbs)	Double the consonant and add -*ed*.	stop rub	stop**ped** rub**bed**
6. Verb ends in *x, w*	Add -*ed*.	show fix	show**ed** fix**ed**
7. Verb ends in vowel + consonant and stress is on the first syllable (two-syllable verb)	Add -*ed*. Do not double the consonant.	visit answer	visit**ed** answer**ed**
8. Verb ends in vowel + consonant and stress is on the second syllable (two-syllable verb)	Double the consonant and add -*ed*.	prefer occur	prefer**red** occur**red**

6 Practice

A Write the correct spelling of the simple past form.

Base Verb	Simple Past		Base Verb	Simple Past
1. add	_added_		11. stop	_____
2. carry	_____		12. hurry	_____
3. allow	_____		13. wait	_____
4. show	_____		14. stay	_____
5. count	_____		15. cry	_____
6. erase	_____		16. drop	_____
7. fit	_____		17. study	_____
8. marry	_____		18. taste	_____
9. die	_____		19. cook	_____
10. fail	_____		20. worry	_____

B Check your answers with a dictionary. Then listen and repeat each pair of words.

CD3, 4, 5

7 Practice

Work with a partner. Read the verbs from one list. Your partner writes the simple past form. Then your partner reads the verbs from the other list and you write the simple past form. Share your answers.

List A

1. listen _listened_
2. mix _____
3. smile _____
4. kiss _____
5. pick _____
6. shop _____
7. tip _____
8. reply _____
9. admit _____

List B

1. start _____
2. study _____
3. fix _____
4. refer _____
5. hug _____
6. touch _____
7. live _____
8. clap _____
9. offer _____

8 Practice

Now write the past verb forms from Practice 7 in the correct column.

Add -*ed*	Add -*d*	Change *y* to *i* and add -*ed*	Double the consonant and add -*ed*
listened	smiled	studied	hugged

9 Your Turn

Write sentences about yourself. Use the simple past form of each verb.

1. visit *I visited my grandparents last summer* .
2. prefer _____ .
3. admit _____ .
4. answer _____ .
5. hug _____ .
6. study _____ .
7. shop _____ .
8. offer _____ .

10 Practice

A Look at the email message and complete the sentences. Use the simple past of these verbs.

arrive	climb	enjoy	prefer	shop	walk
carry	decide	enter	rain	visit	watch

New	Delete	Reply	Reply All	Forward	Move

To:	rbronson@wol.com
Cc:	
Subject:	Hi from NY

Dear Mom and Dad,

Greetings from New York! We _____*arrived*_____ last Friday. It
1

_____ all weekend, so we _____ umbrellas.
2   3

We _____ in the big stores on Fifth Avenue, but I
4

_____ the small shops in the East Village. We _____
5   6

the Statue of Liberty. We _____ at her feet and _____ up
7   8

to her head. That was great! We _____ around Central Park and
9

even _____ a parade in the streets. Last night, we
10

_____ to go to Little Italy to have dinner. The food was
11

delicious, and we _____ the lovely Italian music.
12

See you soon!

Susan

B Listen and check your answers. Then listen again and repeat each sentence.

11 Practice

A Complete the sentences with the verbs in parentheses. Use the present progressive, simple present, or simple past.

JENNIFER: Hello, Brad. It's Jennifer. How (be) _____*are*_____ you?
1

BRAD: I (be) _____ fine, Jennifer. I
2

(arrive) _____ in Hawaii yesterday morning, and right now I
3

(walk) _____ on the beach, and I (talk) _____
4 5

to you.

JENNIFER: It (sound) _____ wonderful! (think) _____
6 7

you _____ about me?
8

BRAD: Of course, I (think) _____ about all the work you have
9

in the office.

JENNIFER: Yes, I (have) _____ so much work. By the
10

way, Tommy Jones (call) _____ you at the office yesterday.
11

He (ask) _____ about you and (want) _____
12 13

to speak to you. I said you (be) _____ out of town.
14

BRAD: Good.

JENNIFER: By the way, where (stay) _____ you _____?
15 16

BRAD: I (stay) _____ at the Sands Hotel on Waikiki
17

Beach. I (have) _____ a beautiful room.
18

JENNIFER: (have) _____ it _____ a view?
19 20

BRAD: Yes, it (have) _____ a beautiful view of the ocean.
<u>21</u>

JENNIFER: How (be) _____ the meeting yesterday?
<u>22</u>

BRAD: The meeting (be) _____ fine. After the
<u>23</u>

meeting, we all (walk) _____ to a restaurant on the
<u>24</u>

beach. The waiter (offer) _____ us a
<u>25</u>

table under the stars and (allow) _____ us to
<u>26</u>

choose the music. And we (dance) _____ all
<u>27</u>

night. I really (enjoy) _____ it.
<u>28</u>

JENNIFER: Oh, really? You (dance) _____ ! Who with?
<u>29</u>

B Listen and check your answers. Then work with a partner. Listen again and repeat the conversation.

CD3, 8, 9

C Listen again. Why did Brad go to Hawaii? Circle the letter of the correct answer.

CD3, 10

A   to see Tommy Jones
B   to walk on the beach
C   to attend a meeting
D   to dance under the stars

D What do you think? What does Brad say next? Write the next two lines of the conversation from Part A.

BRAD: _____

_____ .

JENNIFER: _____

_____ .

Form

Elizabeth graduat**ed** last summer.
I want**ed** to take her picture, so she smil**ed** and I photograph**ed** her with some of her friends.

Verb Ending	Pronunciation	Examples
1. Verb ends in voiceless *p, k, f, s, sh, ch*	/t/	helped washed cooked
2. Verb ends in voiced *b, g, v, z, zh, th, j, m, n, ng, l, r,* or a vowel sound	/d/	played lived rained
3. Verb ends in *d* or *t*	/id/	waited wanted needed

12 Practice

A Complete the sentences with the simple past of the verbs. Then read the sentences aloud and check the line for the pronunciation of each verb.

	/t/	/d/	/id/
Luis (open) _____opened_____ his eyes. **1**	____	✔	____
The hands on the clock (point) _____ **2**	____	____	____
to 9:20. He (yawn) _____ and **3**	____	____	____
(stay) _____ in bed until 10:30. **4**	____	____	____
Then he (shower) _____ and **5**	____	____	____
(shave) _____ . **6**	____	____	____

	/t/	/d/	/id/

He (dress) _____ at 12:00 and ___ ___ ___
7

(finish) _____ at around 1:00. ___ ___ ___
8

Then he (walk) _____ to the café on the ___ ___ ___
9

corner and (order) _____ breakfast. ___ ___ ___
10

He (enjoy) _____ it as usual. ___ ___ ___
11

It (start) _____ to rain, so ___ ___ ___
12

he (call) _____ his friend and ___ ___ ___
13

(invite) _____ him to his apartment ___ ___ ___
14

to watch videos.

His friend (arrive) _____ at 6:00 P.M., ___ ___ ___
15

and they (watch) _____ videos and they ___ ___ ___
16

(laugh) _____ a lot. ___ ___ ___
17

At 10:00 P.M., the rain (stop) _____ ___ ___ ___
18

and his friend (want) _____ to go ___ ___ ___
19

back home. It was then 11:00 P.M., and Luis

(return) _____ to his favorite place—his bed! ___ ___ ___
20

B   **Listen and check your answers. Then listen again and repeat each sentence.**

AUDIO
DOWNLOAD   CD3, 11, 12

13   Practice

A   **Complete the sentences with the simple past of these verbs. Then underline the final -ed sound: /t/, /d/, or /id/.**

answer	dry	need	play	talk	wash
cook	fold	pick	shop	turn on	watch

At 8:30 A.M. yesterday, Ann ___*played*___ (t/*d*/id) tennis
1

with a friend. At 10:00, she _____ (t/d/id) her
2

clothes. Then she _____ (t/d/id) her clothes in
3

the dryer and _____ (t/d/id) them.
4

The Simple Past   **161**

At 12:00, she _____ (t/d/id) lunch. After lunch, she

_____ (t/d/id) her computer and _____ (t/d/id)
                    6   7

her email. Then she _____ (t/d/id) on the telephone with her friends.
                            8

She _____ (t/d/id) to buy a birthday gift for a friend. So
        9

she _____ (t/d/id) in the stores and _____
        10   11

(t/d/id) out a gift. By 9:00 P.M., she was at home and tired, so she _____
                                                                            12

(t/d/id) television.

B   Listen and check your answers. Then listen again and repeat each sentence.

CD3, 13, 14

14   Pair Up and Talk

A   Practice the conversation with a partner.

A: What did you do yesterday?

B: I enjoyed a nice dinner.

B   Now practice the conversation with your partner again. Use the past forms
          of these words. Say a few things that you did.

call	finish	look at	play	visit	wash
enjoy	listen to	need	talk	walk	watch

The Simple Past: Irregular Verbs

Form

She **went** to Africa last year.
She **saw** a chimpanzee there.

Many verbs do not use the -*ed* form. The past form of these verbs is irregular.

Subject	Past Form of Verb (*Go*)	
I		
You		
He/She/It	**went**	to Africa last year.
We		
They		

These are some common irregular verbs.

Base Form	Past Form	Base Form	Past Form	Base Form	Past Form	Base Form	Past Form
be	was/were	feel	felt	meet	met	spend	spent
become	became	find	found	put	put	stand	stood
begin	began	fly	flew	run	ran	take	took
buy	bought	get	got	say	said	teach	taught
come	came	give	gave	see	saw	tell	told
do	did	have	had	sit	sat	think	thought
drink	drank	hear	heard	sleep	slept	throw	threw
eat	ate	make	made	speak	spoke	write	wrote

15 Practice

A Complete the sentences with the simple past of the irregular verbs in parentheses.

A Trip to Paris

Last April, Pete and Paula (fly) _____*flew*_____ to Paris from New York. They
                                         1

(find) _____ a small hotel in the center of town. The hotel (not, be) _____
            2   **3**

expensive, and it (be) _____ clean. Every morning, they (eat) _____
                               4   **5**

French bread and (drink) _____ strong French coffee. They (take) _____
                                   6   **7**

the Metro all the time. They (hear) _____ people sing in the subway.
                                            8

One day, they (make) _____ friends with a French person. They
                              9

(be) _____ lucky because he (speak) _____ English. He (tell) _____
        10   **11**   **12**

them all the interesting places to visit. He also (teach) _____ them two French words,
                                                                   13

bonjour and *merci*. They (take) _____ a trip on the river Seine, and they
                                          14

(see) _____ a lot of interesting places. One day, they (go) _____ shopping.
         15   **16**

They (buy) _____ French perfume for gifts. Then they (sit) _____ outside
                17   **18**

in a café and (have) _____ an expensive lunch. They (spend) _____ a lot of
                           19   **20**

money that day. Pete and Paula (think) _____ Paris was a very romantic city.
                                                21

AUDIO
DOWNLOAD
CD3, 15, 16

B   Listen and check your answers. Then listen again and repeat each sentence.

AUDIO
DOWNLOAD
CD3, 17

C   Listen again. What did Pete and Paula do every day in Paris? Circle the letter of the correct answer.

A   They cleaned their hotel room.

B   They ate French bread and drank strong coffee.

C   They made friends with French people.

D   They shopped for gifts.

16   Practice

A   Complete the life story of Jane Goodall. Write the correct form of the verb in parentheses. Use the simple present, the present progressive, or the simple past.

Jane Goodall was born in London, England, in 1934. As a child, she

(love) _____*loved*_____ stories about Africa. She (finish) _____

        1   **2**

school and (work) _____ for a film company. One day, a friend

          3

(invite) _____ her to Kenya, in Africa. She (save) _____

     4   **5**

money for the trip, and she (go) _____ there. Jane (be) _____

                6   **7**

23 years old.

In Kenya, she (meet) _____ Louis Leakey. He (be) _____ a

        8   **9**

famous anthropologist (a person who studies humans and where they come from).

Jane Goodall (become) _____ his assistant. She
                               10

(travel) _____ with Louis Leakey and his wife in Africa.
            11

    In 1960, she (begin) _____ to study chimpanzees.
                              12

She (live) _____ alone in the forest in Africa. Every morning,
              13

she (go) _____ to the same place in the forest.
             14

The chimpanzees (see) _____ her, but they (stand) _____
                          15   **16**

far away. After about six months, the chimpanzees (come) _____ near her.
                                                              17

Jane Goodall (begin) _____ to know each chimpanzee. She
                          18

(give) _____ each chimpanzee a name.
          19

    After years of work, she (discover) _____ many things about the
                                            20

chimpanzees. For example, chimpanzees (eat) _____ meat.
                                                21

    Today, sadly, there are fewer chimpanzees. People (kill) _____ the
                                                                 22

chimpanzees or (cut) _____ down the forests where they live. Jane
                          23

(study) _____ chimpanzees for over 40 years. Now she
            24

(travel) _____ around the world and (talk) _____ about
            25   **26**

how to save chimpanzees.

B   Listen and check your answers. Then listen again and repeat each sentence.

CD3, 18, 19

17   Practice
Complete the sentences about the story. Use the simple present or the
simple past of these verbs.

| become | begin | come | go | hear | live | talk | travel |

1. Today, Jane Goodall ____*travels*____ all over the world.

2. In her lectures, she usually _____ about how to save chimpanzees.

3. I _____ her speak in New York last year.

4. Ms. Goodall and a friend first _____ to Kenya over 40 years ago.

5. In 1960, she _____ to study chimpanzees in Africa.

6. She _____ in the forests of Africa to study the chimpanzees.

7. After about six months, the chimpanzees _____ near her.

8. Jane Goodall _____ an expert on chimpanzees.

6F The Simple Past: Negative

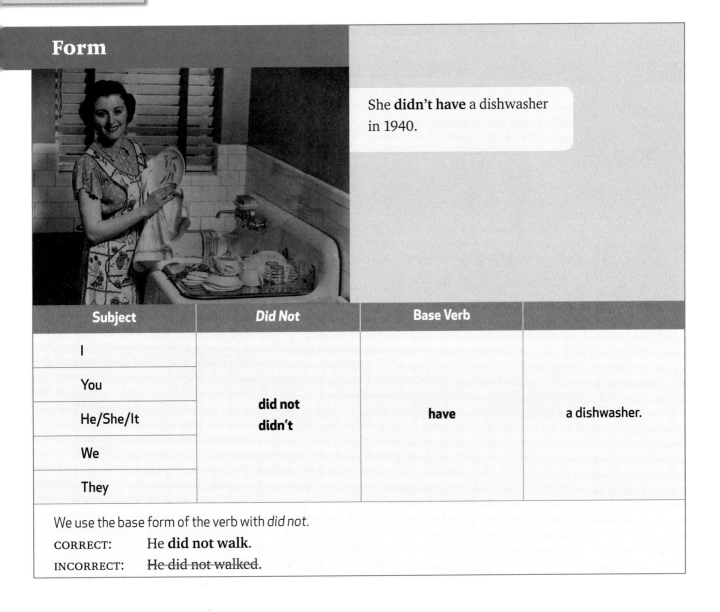

Form

She **didn't have** a dishwasher in 1940.

Subject	*Did Not*	Base Verb	
I			
You			
He/She/It	**did not** **didn't**	**have**	a dishwasher.
We			
They			

We use the base form of the verb with *did not*.

CORRECT: He **did not walk**.

INCORRECT: ~~He did not walked~~.

18 Practice

A Look at the photo of people in 1948. Write affirmative and negative simple past statements about what people did and didn't do in 1948.

1. Children/wear/jeans _Children didn't wear jeans_ .

2. People/watch/a lot of television _____ .

3. Many mothers/stay/at home _____ .

4. Many mothers/work/outside the home _____ .

5. People/eat/fast food _____ .

6. Homes/have/computers _____ .

7. Children/play/video games _____ .

8. People/use/microwaves _____ .

9. People/drink/a lot of soda _____ .

10. Mothers/read/books to their children _____ .

B What do you think? Work with a partner. Say two things people did and two things people didn't do in the 1940s. Was life good or bad then? Why?

19 Practice

Monica is nice to Paul, but he isn't nice to her. Give the past form of the verb in parentheses. Then complete the sentences with the negative form.

1. Monica (say) _____said_____ hello to Paul today, but he _didn't say hello to her_.
2. Monica (ask) _____ Paul "How are you?," but _____.
3. Monica (call) _____ Paul yesterday, but _____.
4. Monica (write) _____ Paul a postcard, but _____.
5. Monica (give) _____ Paul a gift, but _____.
6. Monica (go) _____ to see Paul, but _____.
7. Monica (smile) _____ at Paul, but _____.
8. Monica (wait) _____ for Paul last week, but _____.
9. Monica (kiss) _____ Paul last week, but _____.
10. Monica (invite) _____ Paul to have lunch, but _____.

20 Practice

Work in groups or teams. Write and discuss six statements. Make some statements true and some statements false. Then ask a person from the other team: "Is this true or false?" For a false statement, Student B makes the statement negative.

A: Edison invented the telephone. Is this true or false?
B: False. Edison didn't invent the telephone.
A: It snowed last January in this city. Is this true or false?
B: True.

21 Your Turn

Write a paragraph about your life (or another person's life). Use affirmative and negative simple past statements. Use these regular or irregular verbs or your own.

arrive	come	give	have	pass my exams	see	stay	visit
be	finish	go	live	play	start	study	work

Example

I was born in Cairo. My family lived in an apartment in the city.

The Simple Past: *Yes/No* Questions

Form

DORIS: **Did** you **lock** the door?

ALBERT: **Yes,** I **did.**

Questions				Short Answers	
Did	Subject	Base Verb		Affirmative	Negative
Did	I			**Yes,** you **did.**	**No,** you **didn't.**
	you			I/we **did.**	I/we **didn't.**
	he			he **did.**	he **didn't.**
	she	work	yesterday?	she **did.**	she **didn't.**
	it			it **did.**	it **didn't.**
	we			you **did.**	you **didn't.**
	they			they **did.**	they **didn't.**

22   Practice

A   **Complete the conversation. Use the simple past of the words in parentheses.**

BILLY: (enjoy) _____*Did*_____ you _____*enjoy*_____
                              1   **2**

your vacation, Dolores?

DOLORES: No, I _____ .
                              3

BILLY: Why not?

DOLORES: Well, I (not, like) _____4_____ the food.

BILLY: (like) _____5_____ you _____6_____ the city?

DOLORES: No, I _____7_____ .

BILLY: What about the weather? (like) _____8_____ you

_____9_____ it?

DOLORES: No, I _____10_____ . It (rain) _____11_____ every day.

BILLY: (be) _____12_____ the hotel good?

DOLORES: No, it _____13_____ . Every time I (call) _____14_____ the

reception desk, nobody (answer) _____15_____ .

BILLY: (visit) _____16_____ you _____17_____ any museums?

DOLORES: No, I _____18_____ . They (be) _____19_____ all closed. It

(be) _____20_____ a holiday.

BILLY: That's terrible. (go) _____21_____ you _____22_____

shopping at least?

DOLORES: Yes, I _____23_____ , but I (not, buy) _____24_____

anything. It (be) _____25_____ very expensive.

BILLY: Well, (have) _____26_____ you _____27_____

a good flight?

DOLORES: No, I _____28_____ . The flight (be) _____29_____ five

hours late and the service (be) _____30_____ terrible.

BILLY: So, it (not, be) _____31_____ a good vacation, I guess.

DOLORES: No, it (be) _____32_____ NOT!

B Listen and check your answers. Then work with a partner. Listen again and repeat the conversation.

AUDIO

DOWNLOAD

CD3, 20, 21

23 Pair Up and Talk

A Practice the conversation with a partner.

A: Did you write a letter yesterday?

B: I didn't write a letter yesterday. I made a phone call.

B Now practice the conversation with your partner again. Use these phrases. Say what activities you did or didn't do yesterday.

cook a meal	make a phone call	speak English	walk for 20 minutes
go to the library	play a sport	take a shower	watch television
listen to music	read a paper	visit a museum	write a letter

24 Pair Up and Talk

A Practice the conversation with a partner.

A: Did you stay in a hotel?

B: No, I didn't. I stayed in a guesthouse.

B Now think of three questions to ask your partner about his/her last vacation or trip. Use these phrases or your own. Your partner gives a short answer and then a long answer to explain.

eat in a nice restaurant	go to the beach	meet interesting people
go shopping	have a good time	spend a lot of money
go sightseeing	have good weather	visit museums

25 Practice

Work in groups. One person in the group thinks of a famous person from the past. The others in the group ask 20 *yes/no* questions to guess who the person is.

Example

Was this person a man?	Yes./No.
Did he/she live in the U.S.A.?	Yes./No.

6H | The Simple Past: *Wh-* Questions

Form

BRAD: **Where did** you **go** on Sunday?
DAN: I went to the beach.
BRAD: **What did** you **do**?
DAN: I went surfing, of course.

Wh- Word	*Did*	Subject	Base Verb
What		I	**talk** about?
When		you	**go** to the beach?
What time		he	**get** there?
Where	**did**	she	**stay**?
Who*		you	**call**?
How		we	**find** the place?
Why		they	**stay** at the beach all day?

Wh- Word as Subject	Past Verb Form
What	**happened**?
Who	**called**?

* In formal written English, the *wh-* word is *whom*.

26 Practice

This is a photo of Steve's grandmother. Janine is asking Steve questions about his grandmother. Match the questions to the answers.

A

_h_ **1.** How many children did she have?

_____ **2.** When did she die?

_____ **3.** How did she meet your grandfather?

_____ **4.** Why did she want to go to Hollywood?

_____ **5.** Where did she go in 1938?

_____ **6.** Where did she grow up?

_____ **7.** Who did she go to Hollywood with?

_____ **8.** What did your grandfather do?

_____ **9.** What happened to her parents?

B

a. They stayed in New York.

b. Because she wanted to be an actress.

c. He was an actor.

d. They were on the same train to California.

e. In 1998.

f. She went alone.

g. In Chicago.

h. Six.

i. To Hollywood.

27 Practice

A Look at the pictures and write questions for the answers. Use the underlined words to help you choose the correct question word.

1. _Who did you see_ ?
   I saw <u>Karen</u>.

2. _____ ?
   I saw her <u>yesterday morning</u>.

3. _____ ?
   I saw her <u>in a café</u>.

4. _____ ?
   She looked <u>happy</u>.

5. _____ ?
   She found <u>an apartment</u>.

6. _____ ?
   She looked <u>in the newspaper</u>.

Items 1–6

7. _____ ?
   <u>Dave</u> had a bad day yesterday.

8. _____ ?
   He came home <u>at 10 P.M.</u>

9. _____ ?
   He felt <u>tired</u>.

10. _____ ?
   <u>Because he had a lot of work</u> to do.

Items 7–10

11. _____ ?

I saw <u>Tina</u> yesterday.

12. _____ ?

She was <u>in the street</u>.

13. _____ ?

I saw her <u>in the afternoon</u>.

14. _____ ?

She looked <u>happy</u>.

15. _____ ?

She said <u>hello</u>.

Items 11–15

B Listen and check your answers. Then work with a partner. Listen again and repeat the questions and answers.

AUDIO
DOWNLOAD
CD3, 22, 23

28 Pair Up and Talk
A Practice the conversation with a partner.

A: Where did you go to school?

B: I went to school near my house.

A: Did you walk to your school?

B: Yes, I did.

B Now ask your partner more questions about when he or she was a child. Use these phrases or your own.

go on vacation   make a phone call   speak English

listen to music   play a sport   watch television

29   Read
Read the story. Then write answers to the questions.

THE FARMER AND HIS SONS

Once there was an old farmer. The farmer was dying. Before he died, he wanted to teach his three sons how to be good farmers. He called his sons to him and said, "Boys, before I die, I want you to know that there is a lot of money and gold buried in the vineyard. Promise me that you will look for it when I am dead." The sons promised to look for the money.

After their father died, they started to look for the money. Every day, they worked in the hot sun. They thought about the money all the time and worked hard to find it. They worked and worked but found nothing. They were very upset. But then the grapes started to grow on the vines. The grapes were the biggest and the best grapes in the neighborhood. The brothers sold the grapes and had a lot of money. Now they understood their father's words and lived happily until the end of their lives.

1. How many sons did the farmer have?

    _____ .

2. Who did the farmer call?

    _____ .

3. What did the sons promise?

    _____ .

4. When did they start to look for the money?

    _____ .

5. What did they find?

_____.

6. How did they feel?

_____.

7. What started to grow on the vines?

_____.

8. What did they do with the grapes?

_____.

9. What did they have in the end?

_____.

10. What happened at the end of the story?

_____.

30   Practice

Work with a partner. Ask each other *wh-* questions about yesterday. Then tell the class about your partner's day.

Example

A: What time did you get up?

B: At 8:00.

A: What did you have for breakfast?

B: Toast and tea.

A: Where did you go after class?

B: To the café.

The Simple Past: Time Clauses with *Before* and *After*

Form/Function

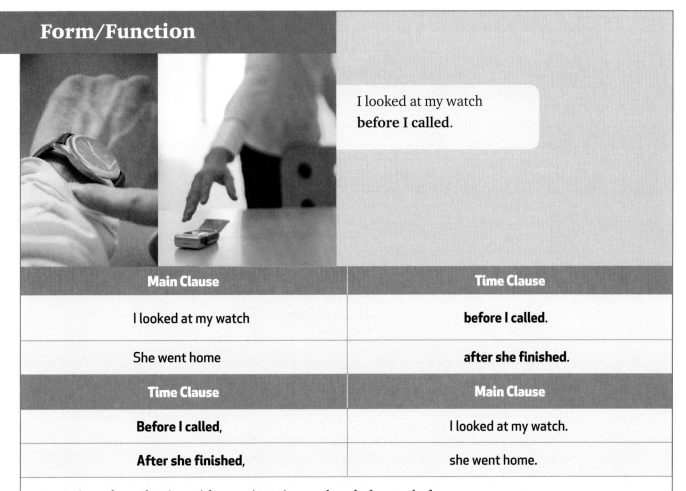

> I looked at my watch **before I called.**

Main Clause	Time Clause
I looked at my watch	**before I called.**
She went home	**after she finished.**

Time Clause	Main Clause
Before I called,	I looked at my watch.
After she finished,	she went home.

1. A time clause begins with a conjunction such as *before* and *after*.
2. A time clause has a subject and a verb, but it is not a complete sentence.
3. A time clause needs a main clause to make a complete sentence.
4. A time clause can come before or after a main clause. The meaning is the same. If the time clause comes first, it has a comma after it.

Underline the time clauses in the sentences. Circle the main clauses. Then rewrite each sentence and change the order of the clauses.

1. After she got up, (she brushed her teeth.)

   She brushed her teeth after she got up .

2. She took a shower before she had breakfast.

   _____ .

3. She got dressed after she had breakfast.

   _____ .

4. Before she locked the door, she turned off the lights.

   _____ .

5. After she arrived at the office, she answered the phone.

   _____ .

6. She finished her day's work before she left the office.

   _____ .

7. She cooked dinner after she got home.

   _____ .

8. After she ate dinner, she washed the dishes.

   _____ .

9. She watched television before she went to bed.

   _____ .

10. Before she went to sleep, she read a book.

    _____ .

Combine the two sentences about the photos. Write one sentence with *after* and another with *before*. Then work with a partner to check the punctuation.

1. They got married. They had a baby.

   After they got married, they had a baby .

   Before they had a baby, they got married .

2. He learned to walk. He rode a bicycle.

   _____ .

   _____ .

3. He graduated from college. He worked for a company.

   _____ .

   _____ .

4. He became the president of the company. He … (Use your own idea.)

_____ .

_____ .

33   Pair Up and Talk

A   Practice the conversation with a partner.

A: What did you do before you came to class today?

B: I had breakfast before I came to class today.

A: What did you do before you had breakfast today?

B   Now write nine things you did before and after you came to class today. Use these phrases or your own. Be sure to use *before* and *after* in your sentences. Then ask and answer questions with a partner about what you did before and after you came to class.

Example

I did my homework before I came to class today.

do my homework	listen to the news	take a shower
email a friend	lock my door	take the bus/train
have breakfast	put my books in my bag	talk to my classmates

A Listen and check the correct answer.

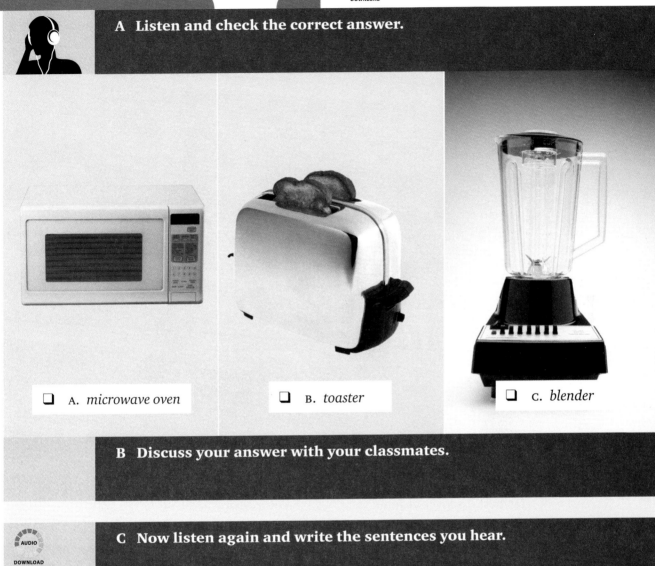

☐ A. *microwave oven*

☐ B. *toaster*

☐ c. *blender*

B Discuss your answer with your classmates.

AUDIO

DOWNLOAD

CD3, 25

C Now listen again and write the sentences you hear.

Reading Challenge

A Before You Read

Answer the questions.

1. Where did they find these figures?
2. Why did a Chinese emperor make these figures?

B Read

THE TERRACOTTA ARMY

DID YOU KNOW ... ?
There is a replica of the Terracotta Army in Texas. It is called Forbidden City and has 6,000 terracotta soldiers.

In 1974 in China, some farmers discovered some figures under the ground. **They** were made of terracotta. Later, researchers found more figures. In all, they found over 8,000 figures. **They** were figures of soldiers and horses and were life-size. Each one is different from the other. Their hairstyles are different, too. **They** were all part of the **tomb** of Qin Shi Huangdi, (Ch'in shir hwang-dee), the first emperor of China. Today, we call them the Terracotta Army.

Shi Huangdi was the first Qin emperor. The name China comes from the name Qin. He started to rule at the age of 13. This was over 2,225 years ago. Shi Huangdi made many changes in China. He started to build the Great Wall. He also started to build his tomb. It took over 700,000 people and 36 years to complete it. The emperor wanted to show that even in death, he was powerful in the next world.

C Notice the Grammar

Underline all forms of the simple past regular and irregular verbs.

Choose the best answer.

D Look for Main Ideas

1. What is the main idea of paragraph 1?
   - A the tomb of the emperor of China
   - B what Chinese farmers discovered
   - C the soldiers and horses of the emperor
   - D the army of the first emperor

2. What is the main idea of paragraph 2?
   - A who the first emperor was and what he did
   - B how he made the tomb
   - C how he made the Great Wall
   - D how China got its name

E Look for Details

3. Shi Huangdi _____ .
   - A died young
   - B started to build the Great Wall
   - C had an army of 700,000 men
   - D put real soldiers in his tomb

4. The tomb of the first emperor had _____ .
   - A real horses in it
   - B soldiers with all the same hairstyle
   - C soldiers and horses made of terracotta
   - D 2,225 terracotta soldiers and horses

5. Which of the following is NOT true about Shi Huangdi?
   - A He started to build the Great Wall.
   - B He finished his tomb by age 36.
   - C He made many changes in China.
   - D He began to rule when he was 13.

Look for a connection between the pronoun <u>they</u> and a noun that comes before it. If you see the connection, you can understand better.

6. To complete the tomb, it took _____ .
   - A 700,000 people
   - B 2,225 people
   - C 8,000 soldiers and horses
   - D 2,225 years

F Look for Vocabulary

7. The word **tomb** in the reading is closest in meaning to _____ .
   - A a special place made for an important dead person
   - B a palace
   - C a place to hide people
   - D a gift people give for the next world

G Reference the Text

8. The word **they** refers to _____ .
   - A the Great Wall
   - B the changes
   - C the figures
   - D the next world

Writing: Narrate Events

Write a narrative paragraph.

STEP 1   Work with a partner. Find out about your partner's last vacation. Ask these questions. Write the answers to the questions.

1. Where did you go?
2. When did you go?
3. Who/with?
4. How/get there?
5. Where/stay?
6. How long/stay?

7. How/hotel?
8. How/food?
9. How/weather?
10. What/buy?
11. Did you have a good time?
12. Did you have any problems?

STEP 2   Rewrite your answers in paragraph form. Be sure to use correct past forms.

STEP 3   Write a title in three or four words, for example, "My Friend's Last Vacation." Center the title above your paragraph.

My Friend's Last Vacation

On her last vacation, my friend went to ...

STEP 4   Evaluate your paragraph.

Checklist

_____ Did you indent the first line?

_____ Did you give your paragraph a title?

_____ Did you put the title in the center, above your paragraph?

_____ Did you capitalize the title correctly?

STEP 5   Work with a partner to edit your paragraph. Check for correct spelling, punctuation, vocabulary, and grammar.

STEP 6   Write your final copy.

Self-Test

A Choose the best answer, A, B, C, or D, to complete the sentence. Darken the oval with the same letter.

1. Who _____ on the phone?

   A. you talk   Ⓐ Ⓑ Ⓒ Ⓓ
   B. talked you
   C. did you talk to
   D. did talk you

2. When I asked Richard a question, he _____ me.

   A. didn't answered   Ⓐ Ⓑ Ⓒ Ⓓ
   B. didn't answer
   C. not answered
   D. no answered

3. When _____ home yesterday?

   A. you come   Ⓐ Ⓑ Ⓒ Ⓓ
   B. come you
   C. did you come
   D. you came

4. Before I _____ to class yesterday, I studied for the test.

   A. came   Ⓐ Ⓑ Ⓒ Ⓓ
   B. did come
   C. cames
   D. come

5. What _____ ?

   A. he did said   Ⓐ Ⓑ Ⓒ Ⓓ
   B. did he said
   C. he said
   D. did he say

6. We went to a movie _____ .

   A. yesterday night   Ⓐ Ⓑ Ⓒ Ⓓ
   B. last yesterday
   C. last night
   D. night yesterday

7. Why _____ famous?

   A. did Lindberg become   Ⓐ Ⓑ Ⓒ Ⓓ
   B. Lindberg he became
   C. did Lindberg became
   D. Lindberg became

8. Mozart _____ music when he was a child.

   A. write   Ⓐ Ⓑ Ⓒ Ⓓ
   B. wrote
   C. did write
   D. writed

9. Thomas Edison _____ the airplane.

   A. didn't invent   Ⓐ Ⓑ Ⓒ Ⓓ
   B. not invented
   C. not invent
   D. didn't invented

10. Where _____ yesterday afternoon?

    A. you went   Ⓐ Ⓑ Ⓒ Ⓓ
    B. did you go
    C. did you went
    D. you did go

1. Plato <u>was</u> a Greek philosopher who <u>lived</u> and
       A   **B**
   <u>died</u> more than 2,000 years <u>before</u>.
    C   **D**

   Ⓐ   Ⓑ   Ⓒ   Ⓓ

2. <u>In</u> 1897, Boston <u>puts</u> streetcars underground
   A   **B**
   and <u>completed</u> the first American subway.
    C   **D**

   Ⓐ   Ⓑ   Ⓒ   Ⓓ

3. Webster's American Spelling Book, which he

   <u>wroted</u> in 1783, <u>sold</u> over 100 million copies
      A   **B**
   and <u>became</u> <u>a</u> best-selling book.
        C **D**

   Ⓐ   Ⓑ   Ⓒ   Ⓓ

4. Coffee <u>came from</u> Ethiopia and <u>was</u> popular
           A   **B**
   before <u>it</u> <u>comes</u> to Europe.
        C **D**

   Ⓐ   Ⓑ   Ⓒ   Ⓓ

5. <u>How long</u> <u>ago</u> <u>did</u> the Egyptians <u>built</u>
      A   **B** **C**   **D**
   the pyramids?

   Ⓐ   Ⓑ   Ⓒ   Ⓓ

6. Helen Keller <u>was born</u> in 1889 and <u>becomes</u> deaf
           A   **B**
   and blind at the age of 20 <u>months</u> after she <u>had</u> a
                    C   **D**
   fever.

   Ⓐ   Ⓑ   Ⓒ   Ⓓ

7. Peter the Great <u>tried</u> to modernize Russia and <u>its</u>
                A   **B**
   old <u>customs</u>, and he also <u>moves</u> the capital from
      C   **D**
   Moscow to St. Petersburg.

   Ⓐ   Ⓑ   Ⓒ   Ⓓ

8. <u>When</u> Marco Polo and his father <u>returned</u> to
    A   **B**
   Italy from China in the 1200s, <u>they</u> <u>bring</u> with
                    C **D**
   them ways to make noodles.

   Ⓐ   Ⓑ   Ⓒ   Ⓓ

9. <u>How long</u> <u>it take</u> to travel across
      A   **B**
   the <u>Atlantic Ocean</u> by ship 200 years <u>ago</u>?
         C   **D**

   Ⓐ   Ⓑ   Ⓒ   Ⓓ

10. The Wright brothers <u>invented</u> the airplane, <u>but</u>
                   A   **B**
    <u>they</u> <u>not invent</u> the telephone.
     C   **D**

    Ⓐ   Ⓑ   Ⓒ   Ⓓ

Unit 7

The Past Progressive

At 10:00 yesterday morning, the women **were working**.

7A | The Past Progressive

Form

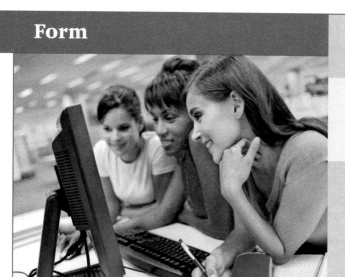

A: **What were** the women **doing** at 10:00 yesterday morning?

B: They **were working**, of course!

Affirmative and Negative Statements

Subject	Past of *Be* (+*Not*)	Base Verb + -*ing*
I	was was not wasn't	
You	were were not weren't	
He/She/It	was was not wasn't	working.
We They	were were not weren't	

Yes/No Questions

Was	I	
Were	you	
Was	he/she/it	working?
Were	we/you/they	

Short Answers

Yes,	No,
you **were**.	you **weren't**.
I **was**.	I **wasn't**.
he **was**. she **was**. it **was**.	he **wasn't**. she **wasn't**. it **wasn't**.
you **were**. we **were**. they **were**.	you **weren't**. we **weren't**. they **weren't**.

Wh- Questions			
Wh- Word	Past of Be	Subject	Verb + -ing
What	was	I	saying?
Where	were	you	going?
When	was	he/she/it	working?
Why	were	you	running?
Who*	were	they	watching?

*In formal written English, the wh- word is whom.

Function

Tony **was sleeping** at 10:00 yesterday.

We use the past progressive for an action that was already happening at a particular time in the past.

Tony **was sleeping** at 10:00 yesterday. (He started to sleep before 10:00. He **was** still **sleeping** at 10:00 yesterday.)

1 Practice

Work with a partner. What was happening in the neighborhood on Sunday at 11:00 in the morning? Look at the photos. Ask and answer questions. Use the words and phrases.

1. Dad/wash/his car

   What was Dad doing ?

   He was washing his car .

2. Karen/play/the violin

   _____ ?

   _____ .

3. Bob/get/dressed

   _____ ?

   _____ .

4. Nancy/talk/on the phone

   _____ ?

   _____ .

5. Mike/drive/his car

   _____ ?

   _____ .

6. the cat/watch/the birds

   _____ ?

   _____ .

7. Tim/work/on his computer

_____ ?

_____ .

8. Eric and Sherry/jog

_____ ?

_____ .

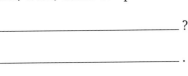

9. Laurie/swim

_____ ?

_____ .

10. Ben/shop/at the market

_____ ?

_____ .

11. Julio/garden

_____ ?

_____ .

12. Cheryl and Benny/make cookies

_____ ?

_____ .

2 Pair Up and Talk
A Practice the conversation with a partner.

A: What were you doing at seven o'clock yesterday evening?

B: I was eating dinner.

B Now practice the conversation with your partner again. Use these phrases or your own.

an hour ago

at 12:00 noon on Sunday

at midnight last night

at seven this morning

at this time yesterday

five minutes ago

three days ago

yesterday evening

3 Practice

A Answer the questions with a negative past progressive verb. Then add a statement. Use the phrases in parentheses.

1. Was Sue doing her homework when I called?

   No, *she wasn't doing her homework* .

   (clean the apartment) *She was cleaning the apartment* .

2. Were Dave and Bob talking about the basketball game?

   No, _____ .

   (talk about the soccer game) _____ .

3. Were you trying to reach me?

   No, _____ .

   (try to reach your brother) _____ .

4. Was I speaking too loudly?

   No, _____ .

   (speak too softly) _____ .

5. Were you reading the *New York Times*?

   No, _____ .

   (read the *Los Angeles Times*) _____ .

6. Was Mr. Black explaining the present progressive?

   No, _____ .

   (explain the past progressive) _____ .

B Listen and check your answers. Then work with a partner. Listen again and repeat the questions and answers.

AUDIO

DOWNLOAD

CD3, 26, 27

Form

> **While he was driving**, a man crossed the street.

1. *While* can begin a time clause.
2. The verb in a *while* clause is often in the past progressive.

While	
Main Clause	**Time Clause**
A man crossed the street	**while he was driving.**
Time Clause	**Main Clause**
While he was driving,	a man crossed the street.

3. *When* can begin a time clause.
4. The verb in a *when* clause is often in the simple past.

When	
Main Clause	**Time Clause**
Jenny was working at the office	**when Tony called.**
Time clause	**Main Clause**
When Tony called,	Jenny was working at the office.

5. A time clause can go at the beginning or at the end of a sentence. If it is at the beginning, we use a comma after it.
6. A time clause alone is not a complete sentence. We must use it with a main clause to form a complete sentence.

COMPLETE SENTENCE: When Tony called, Jenny was working at the office.

INCOMPLETE SENTENCE: ~~When Tony called.~~

4 Practice

Tony and Linda had a bad day yesterday. Find out what happened.
Match the sentence parts.

	A		B
_f_	**1.**	Tony was sleeping when	**a.** the water heater broke.
____	**2.**	Linda was walking to the store when	**b.** it had a problem.
____	**3.**	Linda was waiting for the bus when	**c.** she burned her finger.
____	**4.**	Linda was standing in the rain when	**d.** the bus finally came.
____	**5.**	Tony was driving to work when	**e.** she tripped and fell.
____	**6.**	Tony was taking a shower when	**f.** the telephone rang and woke him up.
____	**7.**	Tony was working on his computer when	**g.** he had an accident.
____	**8.**	Linda was cooking when	**h.** it started to rain and she got wet.

5 Practice

A Complete the sentences with the simple past or past progressive of the verbs in parentheses.

We (talk) _____were talking_____ about the questions on the test when
$\quad\quad\quad\quad\quad\quad\quad$ **1**

the teacher (walk) _____ into the classroom. While she
$\quad\quad\quad\quad\quad\quad\quad$ **2**

(give) _____ out the tests, we (sit) _____ in silence.
$\quad\quad$ **3** $\quad\quad\quad\quad\quad\quad\quad\quad\quad\quad\quad\quad$ **4**

We started the test at 9:15. While we (take) _____ the test, the teacher
$\quad\quad\quad\quad\quad\quad\quad\quad\quad\quad\quad\quad$ **5**

(watch) _____ us. While Leo (take) _____
$\quad\quad\quad$ **6** $\quad\quad\quad\quad\quad\quad\quad\quad\quad\quad$ **7**

the test, he (talk) _____ to himself. He (talk) _____
$\quad\quad\quad\quad\quad\quad$ **8** $\quad\quad\quad\quad\quad\quad\quad\quad\quad\quad$ **9**

to himself when the teacher (tell) _____ him, "Be quiet, Leo."
$\quad\quad\quad\quad\quad\quad\quad\quad\quad$ **10**

His face became red.

I (finish) _____ my last answer when the teacher
                11
(say) _____ ,"STOP." I (smile) _____ when I
         12   13
(leave) _____ the classroom. While I (walk) _____ home,
           14   15
I (say) _____ to myself, "I did a great job on that test."
          16

B Listen and check your answers. Then listen again and repeat each sentence.

CD3, 28, 29

C Listen again. Which activity started first? For each pair below, put *1* next to the activity that started first and *2* next to the activity that started second.

CD3, 30

A _____ We talked about the test questions.

_____ The teacher entered the classroom.

B _____ The teacher said, "Be quiet, Leo."

_____ Leo talked to himself.

C _____ I left the classroom.

_____ I smiled.

D _____ The teacher said "STOP."

_____ I completed the test.

E _____ I left school.

_____ I told myself I did a great job.

Function

The students **were studying** English grammar.

Verb Form	Function	Examples
Past Progressive	Use the past progressive for an action that was already happening at a particular time in the past.	The students **were studying** English grammar at 10:15 yesterday morning. (They were studying before 10:15 and at 10:15.)
	We use the past progressive for an action that was happening when another action interrupted it.	She **was working** when Jim **called**. While Bob **was sleeping** last night, the telephone **rang**.
Simple Past	We use the simple past for an action that began and ended at a particular time in the past.	I **called** my mother last Sunday. She **arrived** at 9:30 yesterday. They **went** to Mexico in June last year.
	We use the simple past to show that one action immediately followed another action.	When I **opened** the door, I **saw** my sister. (First, I opened the door. Then I saw my sister.)

6 Practice

A Use the simple past or past progressive of the verbs in parentheses.

A

One day, I (study) _____*was studying*_____ in the library when I
                              1

(see) _____ her. She (come) _____ towards me and
              2   3

(sit) _____ down in the chair next to me. Then she
           4

(put) _____ on her glasses and (start) _____ to read
           5   **6**

a book. While she (read) _____ , I (look) _____ at
                              7   **8**

her quickly for a moment. Suddenly our eyes (meet) _____ .
                                                          9

I (smile) _____ , and then she (smile) _____ .
             10   **11**

B

I had a bad dream last night. In my dream it was Sunday morning. It was

ten o'clock, and I (read) _____ a book in the yard in front of the house.
                               1

Suddenly the sky (become) _____ dark. It (start) _____
                                2   **3**

to rain, so I (go) _____ inside the house. I (close) _____
                        4   **5**

the windows and (turn) _____ on the television to listen to the news
                             6

and weather. I (watch) _____ the news when the storm (begin)
                             7

_____ . I remember that the wind (blow) _____ and the
       8   **9**

windows (shake) _____ when I (hear) _____ a
                       10   **11**

terrible noise like a big bang. Then I (wake) _____ up on the floor.
                                                     12

C

It (get) _____ dark when I (get) _____ off the train.
              1   **2**

There was no one in the street. While I (walk) _____ down the street,
                                                      3

I (hear) _____ footsteps behind me. When I (begin) _____
              4   **5**

to walk fast, the footsteps (get) _____ fast. When I (begin)
                                        6

_____ to run, the footsteps (get) _____ faster. Finally,
       7   **8**

I (get) _____ to my house. I (shake) _____ when I (put)
              9   **10**

_____ the key in the door. Just then I (hear) _____ a man's
       11   **12**

voice behind me. "Is this your purse? You left it on the train."

B Listen and check your answers. Then listen again and repeat each sentence.

AUDIO

DOWNLOAD

CD3, 31, 32

7 Practice

Look at the information about Mike and Lillian. Then complete the sentences about them. Use the past progressive or the simple past.

Mike

1994–2000	lived in Boston
2000–2001	took computer course
2001–2002	lived and worked in Japan
2002–2005	worked for Microdisc
2002	met Lillian
2004	married Lillian

Lillian

1996	arrived in New York
1996–2004	lived in New York
1996–1999	studied at the university
1998–2000	worked for a computer company
2002	met Mike
2004	married Mike

1. In 1994, Mike _____*was living*_____ in Boston.

2. When Lillian _____ in New York in 1996, Mike _____ in Boston.

3. In 2000, Lillian _____ in New York.

4. From 1996 to 1999, Lillian _____ at a university in New York.

5. In 2001, Mike _____ in Japan, and he _____ there, too.

6. In 2002, Lillian _____ Mike.

7. Lillian _____ in New York when she _____ Mike.

8. In 1999, Lillian _____ for a computer company.

9. Mike _____ for Microdisc when he met Lillian.

10. Lillian married Mike while he _____ for Microdisc.

8 Practice

Look at the following results of different actions. What do you think the person was doing in each situation? Work with a partner and write an answer. Then compare your answers in groups.

1. He burned his finger.

   Maybe he was cooking when he burned his finger .

2. She started to cry.

   _____ .

3. He fell down.

   _____ .

4. It fell and broke to pieces.

   _____ .

5. He fell asleep.

   _____ .

6. We heard a strange noise.

   _____ .

7. I saw a man's head in the window.

   _____ .

8. The lights went out.

   _____ .

9. She laughed loudly.

   _____ .

9 Your Turn

Describe a bad day that you had to the class. Use *while* and *when*. What unexpected thing happened while you were doing something else?

Example

I had a very bad day last week. While I was watching television at home …

10   Read
Read the story. Then write answers to the questions.

THE SACK

A man was walking sadly along the road to town when Mula came up to him.

"What's wrong?" he asked.

The man held up his old bag and cried, "All I have in this whole world is in this miserable old bag."

"Too bad," said Mula, and with that he took the bag from the man's hands and ran down the road with it.

The man now had nothing. He was now very, very sad. He was crying and walking down the road at the same time. Meanwhile, Mula ran ahead, turned around the corner, and put the man's bag in the middle of the road. When the man saw his bag in the road in front of him, he was so happy, he shouted "My bag! I'm so happy I found you!"

Mula was watching the man from the bushes and said to himself, "Well, that's one way to make a person happy!"

1. What was the man doing when Mula came up to him?

    _____ .

2. Why was the man sad?

    _____ .

3. What did Mula do?

    _____ .

4. Why was the man crying?

    _____ .

5. Where did Mula put the man's bag?

_____ .

6. How did the man feel when he saw his bag?

_____ .

7. What was Mula doing when the man found the bag?

_____ .

Listening Puzzle

CD3, 33

A Listen and check the correct answer.

❑ A. *toast*   ❑ B. *cornflakes*   ❑ C. *yogurt*

B Discuss your answer with your classmates.

CD3, 34

C Now listen again and write the sentences you hear.

A Before You Read
Answer the questions.

1. What are some advantages of travel by ship?
2. What are some disadvantages of travel by ship?
3. What kind of people travel long voyages by ship?

B Read

THE *TITANIC*

DID YOU KNOW ... ?
The *Titanic* was designed to hold 32 lifeboats, but there were only 20 on board. The management thought too many boats destroyed the beauty of the ship.

On Wednesday, April 10, 1912, the *Titanic* **set out** on its first voyage from England to the United States. The ship was unique.
5 **It** was very large and luxurious. Everyone thought it was unsinkable. There were 2,200 people aboard. Many of them were rich
10 and famous.

It was Sunday, April 14th. There was ice in the water, but the captain told the crew to move full speed ahead.

15 At about 11:40 P.M. the crew saw something. They radioed the captain and said there was an iceberg straight ahead. The captain tried to turn the ship, but it was too late.

When the ship hit the iceberg, many of the
20 passengers were sleeping. While the ship was sinking, people reacted in different ways. Some people were crying; some were dancing. Other people were praying, and others were saying good-bye to ones they loved.

25 Some of the passengers, mostly women and children, escaped on lifeboats. There weren't enough lifeboats for everyone. Fifteen hundred people died.

C Notice the Grammar
Underline all forms of the past progressive.

Choose the best answer.

D Look for Main Ideas

1. What is the main idea of paragraph 2?
   - (A) why the *Titanic* was unique
   - (B) the people on board the *Titanic*
   - (C) what happened on April 14th
   - (D) why the ship was sailing at full speed

2. What is the main idea of paragraph 3?
   - (A) what happened when the *Titanic* hit the iceberg
   - (B) why people were crying
   - (C) why people were sleeping
   - (D) why people were going to the United States

E Look for Details

3. Which of the following is NOT true about the *Titanic*?
   - (A) It was a very luxurious ship.
   - (B) It was very big.
   - (C) It was going to the United States.
   - (D) It had the richest people in the world on board.

4. Who saw the iceberg first?
   - (A) the captain
   - (B) the crew
   - (C) the people
   - (D) no one

5. Who escaped on lifeboats?
   - (A) almost everyone
   - (B) women and children
   - (C) the crew
   - (D) fifteen hundred people

6. When the captain saw the iceberg, he _____ .
   - (A) didn't do anything
   - (B) went full speed ahead
   - (C) tried to turn
   - (D) radioed the crew

F Look for Vocabulary

7. The word *set out* in the reading is closest in meaning to _____ .
   - (A) drove
   - (B) left
   - (C) found
   - (D) originated

G Reference the Text

8. The word *It* in the reading refers to _____ .
   - (A) the *Titanic*
   - (B) the size
   - (C) the voyage
   - (D) the people

Writing: Narrate Events

Write a descriptive paragraph.

STEP 1   Write four important things that happened in your life and give the dates.

Example

1986–2003	lived in Mexico City, Mexico
2004	started college

STEP 2   Work with a partner. Ask and answer questions. Find out what your partner was doing at the time important things happened in your life. Write the answers to these questions. Then rewrite your partner's answers. Use *when* and *while*.

Example

A: What were you doing while I was living in Mexico from 1980 to 1999?

B: I was living in Seoul, Korea.

STEP 3   Write a title. Be sure to use a comma when the time clause comes first.

> *Two Lives*
>
> While I was living in Mexico City, Kim was living in Seoul.

STEP 4   Evaluate your paragraph.

Checklist

_____ Did you indent the first line?

_____ Did you use verbs correctly?

_____ Did you capitalize the title correctly?

STEP 5   Work with a partner to edit your paragraph. Correct spelling, punctuation, vocabulary, and grammar.

STEP 6   Write your final copy.

Self-Test

1. It _____ here every winter.

   A. snows   (A) (B) (C) (D)
   B. was snowed
   C. is snowing
   D. snow

2. _____ now?

   A. It is raining   (A) (B) (C) (D)
   B. Is it raining
   C. Does it rain
   D. Is raining

3. At 11:00 yesterday morning, we _____ in this classroom.

   A. sat   (A) (B) (C) (D)
   B. sitting
   C. were sat
   D. were sitting

4. When she heard the news, she _____ to cry.

   A. was beginning   (A) (B) (C) (D)
   B. begin
   C. began
   D. begins

5. I saw Karen in a store yesterday, but she _____ me.

   A. does not see   (A) (B) (C) (D)
   B. did not see
   C. was not seeing
   D. not saw

6. I woke up when the alarm clock _____ .

   A. rings   (A) (B) (C) (D)
   B. did ring
   C. was ringing
   D. rang

7. While I _____ to school, I met my friend.

   A. was walking   (A) (B) (C) (D)
   B. walked
   C. walk
   D. am walking

8. I _____ my room when I found my keys.

   A. am cleaning   (A) (B) (C) (D)
   B. cleaned
   C. clean
   D. was cleaning

9. _____ when you arrived?

   A. Were they sleeping   (A) (B) (C) (D)
   B. They slept
   C. Did they sleep
   D. They were sleeping

10. I'm sorry. I _____ time to call you yesterday.

   A. didn't have   (A) (B) (C) (D)
   B. wasn't having
   C. don't have
   D. wasn't have

1. We <u>walking</u> <u>in the park</u> <u>when</u> the rain <u>started</u>.
        A   **B**   **C**   **D**

    (A) (B) (C) (D)

2. <u>Buildings</u> <u>began</u> to shake <u>when</u> people
        A   **B**   **C**
    <u>were sleeping</u>.
       D

    (A) (B) (C) (D)

3. The Titanic <u>traveled</u> fast <u>when</u> <u>it</u> <u>hit</u> a huge
                A   **B** **C D**
    iceberg in the sea.

    (A) (B) (C) (D)

4. <u>While</u> Mozart <u>was born</u>, <u>his father</u> <u>worked</u> as a
      A   **B**   **C**   **D**
    violinist at the court of Salzburg in Austria.

    (A) (B) (C) (D)

5. The explorer, Marco Polo, <u>was</u> in <u>a</u> prison
                       A   **B**
    <u>when</u> he <u>is writing</u> about his travels in the East.
     C   **D**

    (A) (B) (C) (D)

6. <u>When</u> Thomas Edison <u>was</u> <u>a child</u>, he
     A   **B**   **C**
    <u>wasn't liking</u> to go to school.
       D

    (A) (B) (C) (D)

7. <u>Last night</u>, my brother <u>was watching</u> television
      A   **B**
    and <u>eat</u> <u>chocolates</u> at the same time.
       C   **D**

    (A) (B) (C) (D)

8. <u>When</u> <u>was</u> the semester <u>begin</u>, on the 14th <u>or</u>
     A   **B**   **C**   **D**
    15th of September?

    (A) (B) (C) (D)

9. <u>When</u> I <u>was seeing</u> the <u>president's wife</u>, she
     A   **B**   **C**
    <u>was wearing</u> a red dress.
       D

    (A) (B) (C) (D)

10. <u>While</u> they <u>were traveling</u> across Europe by car,
      A   **B**
    they <u>were having</u> <u>an accident</u>.
       C   **D**

    (A) (B) (C) (D)

Unit 8

The Future

If the temperature **falls** below zero Celsius (32 degrees Fahrenheit), water **turns** to ice.

Form

Jamie is hungry.
She**'s going to eat** the cookie.
She**'s not going to save** it.

Affirmative and Negative Statements

Subject + *Be*	*(Not) Going To*	Base Verb
I **am**		
You **are**		
He/She/It **is**	(not) going to	eat.
We **are**		
They **are**		

Yes/No Questions · Short Answers

Be + Subject	*Going To*	Base Verb	Affirmative	Negative
Am I			Yes, you **are**.	No, you **aren't**.
Are you			I **am**.	I'm **not**.
Is he/she/it	going to	eat?	he/she/it **is**.	he/she/it **isn't**.
Are we			you **are**.	you **aren't**.
Are you			we **are**.	we **aren't**.
Are they			they **are**.	they **aren't**.

Wh- Questions				
Wh- Word	Be	Subject	Going To	Base Verb
What				
Where				
When	are	you	going to	eat?
Why				
How				
Who*	are	you	going to	see?

* In formal written English, the *wh-* word is *whom.*

Note: We often pronounce *going to* as "gonna" when we speak.

Function

Look at those clouds!
It**'s going to rain** soon.

1. We use *be* + *going to* + base verb to make predictions about the future (what we know or think is going to happen very soon).
   It's **going to rain** soon.
2. We use *be* + *going to* + base verb to talk about plans for the future.
   We**'re going to buy** a house next year.

1 Practice

Look at the photos. Then complete the sentences with the correct form of *be going to* and one of these phrases.

buy some fruit   order a meal   take a photo

drink a cup of coffee   paint the wall   write a check

1. Jim has a camera.

     Jim is going to take a photo .

2. Brad has a paintbrush.

     _____ .

3. Sue is in the supermarket.

     _____ .

4. Tony is in a café.

     _____ .

5. Mel has a checkbook and a pen.

     _____ .

6. Ted is in a restaurant.

     _____ .

2 Practice

A Yuko is talking to Meg about her trip to London next week. Complete the conversation with forms of *be going to.*

YUKO: Guess what! I (go) __*am going to go*__ to London next week!
                                     1

MEG: Lucky you! You (not, work) _____ ! How long
                                              2

(stay) _____ you _____ ?
              3   **4**

YUKO: I (stay) _____ for five days.
                        5

MEG: What (do) _____ you _____ ?
                      6   **7**

YUKO: On Monday, I (see) _____ St. Paul's and then I
                                    8

(walk) _____ in the parks. On Tuesday, I (visit)
              9

_____ the Houses of Parliament. On Wednesday,
        10

I (go) _____ to some museums. On Thursday, I (shop)
              11

_____ on Oxford Street. I (buy) _____
        12   **13**

some English tea.

MEG: (eat) _____ you _____ fish and chips?
                  14   **15**

English people eat fish and chips, you know.

YUKO: That's one thing I (not, do) _____ . I don't like fish.
                                              16

I (eat) _____ hamburgers as usual.
              17

B Listen and check your answers. Then work with a partner. Listen again and repeat the conversation.

AUDIO
DOWNLOAD
CD4, 2, 3

C Listen again. Write the number of the activity on the line next to the correct day.

AUDIO
DOWNLOAD
CD4, 4

____ Monday   1. going to museums

____ Tuesday   2. walking in the parks

____ Wednesday   3. buying English tea

____ Thursday   4. visiting the Houses of Parliament

The Future **213**

3 Practice

A Your friend is going to have a party. Write eight questions about it. Use the phrases to make your questions. Write your own answers.

1. When/you/have the party?

   QUESTION: *When are you going to have the party* ?

   ANSWER: *Saturday* .

2. What kind of food/you/have?

   QUESTION: _____ ?

   ANSWER: _____ .

3. What food/you/make?

   QUESTION: _____ ?

   ANSWER: _____ .

4. What/you/wear?

   QUESTION: _____ ?

   ANSWER: _____ .

5. How many people/you/invite?

   QUESTION: _____ ?

   ANSWER: _____ .

6. Where/you/have the party?

   QUESTION: _____ ?

   ANSWER: _____ .

7. What time/the party/start?

   QUESTION: _____ ?

   ANSWER: _____ .

8. What kind of music/you/have?

   QUESTION: _____ ?

   ANSWER: _____ .

B Listen and check your answers. Then work with a partner. Listen again and repeat the questions. Your partner will answer.

AUDIO

DOWNLOAD

CD4, 5, 6

Form

Jane is happy. She got a letter from Paul. He's going to come back **next Friday**! That's **in eight days**!

Next		Tomorrow	In		Other Expressions
next	week month weekend summer Friday	tomorrow	in	ten minutes three hours four days five weeks six months two years	**soon** **tonight** **the day after tomorrow** **a week from today/now**

Function

We use future time expressions at the beginning or end of the sentence. We use a comma (,) after the time expression when it is at the beginning of the sentence.

In eight days, Paul is going to come home.
Paul is going to come home **in eight days**.

4 Your Turn

Write about your life. Use time expressions and *be going to*.

1. Next summer, _*I'm going to visit my aunt in California*_ .

2. In a couple of months, _____ .

3. In two days, _____ .

4. A week from now, _____ .

5. Next Monday, _____ .

6. Tomorrow evening, _____ .

7. Tonight, _____ .

8. Later today, _____ .

5 Pair Up and Talk

A Practice the conversation with a partner.

A: What are you going to do tomorrow morning?

B: I'm going to sleep late. OR I'm not going to write letters.

B Now practice the conversation with your partner again. Use these words and phrases or your own. Make affirmative or negative statements. Use future time expressions.

clean your room	do the laundry	phone your friends	visit a relative
cook a meal	go shopping	play a sport	watch television
do homework	meet a friend	see a movie	work on a computer

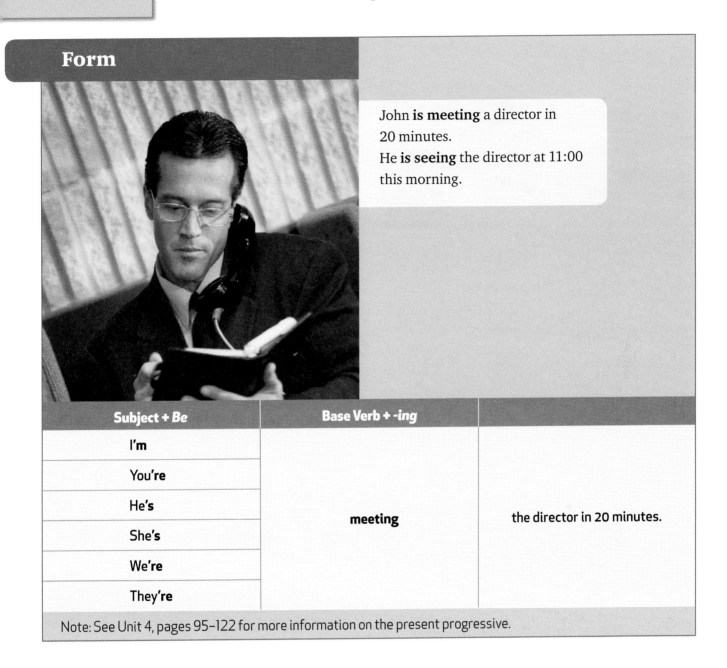

Form

John **is meeting** a director in 20 minutes.
He **is seeing** the director at 11:00 this morning.

Subject + *Be*	Base Verb + *-ing*	
I'm		
You're		
He's		
She's	meeting	the director in 20 minutes.
We're		
They're		

Note: See Unit 4, pages 95–122 for more information on the present progressive.

Function

Steve **is leaving** for New York in two hours.
He's at the airport now.

1. We can use the present progressive to talk about future plans. We often use a time expression with the present progressive. We use the present progressive especially with verbs of movement and transportation such as *come, go, fly, travel,* and *leave.*

2. We can also use *be going to* for future plans.
   Steve **is going to leave** for New York in two hours.
   OR
   Steve **is leaving** for New York in two hours.

3. We cannot use the present progressive for future predictions.
   CORRECT: Look at those dark clouds! It's going to rain soon.
   INCORRECT: Look at those dark clouds! It's raining soon.

6 Practice

A Jan is going to New York on a business trip. Look at her schedule. Write about what she is doing on Monday. Use the present progressive of the verbs in parentheses.

Monday

8:45	Arrive in New York and take a taxi to the hotel
9:30	Leave the hotel
10:00	Meet Tim and Donna at the office
10:00–12:00	Work with Tim and Donna
12:00–2:00	Have lunch with Tim, Donna, and the boss
2:30	See Tod Cordel
4:00	Return to the office and work with Donna
6:00	Go back to the hotel
7:00	Wait for Alex in the hotel lobby and go to dinner
10:00	Return to the hotel and prepare for meeting on Tuesday at 9:00

1. (arrive) _At 8:45 she is arriving in New York_ .
2. (take) _____ .
3. (leave) _____ .
4. (meet) _____ .
5. (work) _____ .
6. (have) _____ .
7. (see) _____ .
8. (return) _____ .
9. (go back) _____ .
10. (wait for) _____ .
11. (go) _____ .
12. (prepare) _____ .

B Work with a partner. Write questions and give answers.

1. What time/arrive/in New York? _What time is she arriving in New York_ ?
   She is arriving in New York at 8:45 .

2. Who/meet/at 10:00? _____ ?
   _____ .

3. What/do/between 12:00 and 2:00? _____ ?
   _____ .

4. Where/wait/for Alex? _____ ?
   _____ .

5. What/do/at 4:00? _____ ?
   _____ .

6. When/go back/to the hotel? _____ ?
   _____ .

7. Who/have lunch/with? _____ ?
   _____ .

8. Where/prepare for/Tuesday's meeting? _____ ?
   _____ .

Form

One day, people **will go** to the moon for vacations.

Affirmative and Negative Statements			Wh- Questions			
Subject	**Will (Not)**	**Base Verb**	**Wh- Word**	**Will**	**Subject**	**Base Verb**
I			What		I	**do**?
You			Where		you	**stay**?
He/She/It	**will**		When		he/she/it	**know**?
We	**'ll**	**go**.	Why	**will**	we	**wait**?
	will not		How			**know**?
	won't		How long		they	**drive**?
They			Who*			**see**?

*In formal written English, the wh- word is *whom*.

Yes/No Questions			Short Answers	
Will	**Subject**	**Main Verb**	**Affirmative**	**Negative**
	I		Yes, you **will**.	No, you **won't**.
	you		I/we **will**.	I/we **won't**.
	he		he **will**.	he **won't**.
Will	she	**go**?	she **will**.	she **won't**.
	it		it **will**.	it **won't**.
	we		you **will**.	you **won't**.
	they		they **will**.	they **won't**.

Note: Do not use contractions in affirmative short answers.

CORRECT: Yes, they will.

INCORRECT: Yes, ~~they'll~~.

Function

Scientists **will find** a cure for cancer one day.

1. We use *will* to make predictions about the future (what we think will happen).

Those shoes are very comfortable. **I'll buy** them.

2. We use *will* for the future when we decide to do something at the moment of speaking.
3. We do not use *will* for the future when plans were made before this moment.

    ANGIE: What are your plans for tomorrow?

    DICK: We**'re going to drive** to Disneyland.

    OR   We**'re driving** to Disneyland.

    NOT   We~~'ll drive~~ to Disneyland.

7 Practice

A Make predictions for the year 2050. Say what you think will happen. Use *will* or *won't*.

1. People _____*will*_____ drive electric cars.

2. Everybody _____ have a computer at home.

3. People _____ carry money.

4. People _____ take vacations on the moon.

5. All people _____ speak the same language.

6. People around the world _____ use the same currency (money).

7. People _____ find life on other planets.

8. People _____ get serious diseases like cancer.

9. Trains _____ travel very fast.

10. People _____ live to be 130 years old.

11. Men and women _____ continue to marry.

12. Children _____ go to school five days a week.

B Discuss your answers with your partner or the class. Then write eight sentences about what you think will happen. Use *will* or *won't*.

1. _____ .

2. _____ .

3. _____ .

4. _____ .

5. _____ .

6. _____ .

7. _____ .

8. _____ .

8 Practice

A Complete the conversations with the present progressive, *will*, or *be going to.*

A

JULIA: I (go) _____am going_____ to the supermarket right now. Do you
                        1
      want anything?

LEYLA: Yes. Can you get some orange juice?

JULIA: Sure. It's on my list, so I (get) _____ it.
                                         2

LEYLA: I also wanted to pick up my photos today, but I don't have time to do it.

JULIA: Don't worry. I (pick) _____ them up for you.
                                    3

      I (be) _____ back soon. (be) _____
              4   5

      you _____ here?
             6

LEYLA: I (go) _____ to work now.
                7

JULIA: OK. I (see) _____ you later. Remember Tony and Suzy
                  8

      (come) _____ by tonight.
                 9

B

STEVE: Hi, Dave. (go) _____ you _____ to the picnic
                1   2

      on Saturday?

DAVE: I don't think I can. I (help) _____ Joanne move from
                        3

      her apartment.

STEVE: Oh, no! I forgot she (move) _____ this weekend.
                            4

DAVE: Well, (come) _____ you _____ to help?
                  5   6

STEVE: Sure. What time (go) _____ you _____
                        7   8

      to Joanne's apartment?

DAVE: I don't know right now. I (call) _____ you tomorrow night,
                        9

      and I (tell) _____ you.
               10

STEVE: OK. Someone is knocking on the door right now. I (see) _____
                                  11

      who it is. I (call) _____ you right back. Bye.
                      12

DAVE: OK. Bye.

B Listen and check your answers. Then work with a partner. Listen again and repeat each conversation.

AUDIO
DOWNLOAD
CD4, 7, 8

8E | *May and Might*

Form

Oh, no! I'm late!
I **may** miss my flight.

Affirmative Statements			Negative Statements		
Subject	***May/Might***	**Base Verb**	**Subject**	***May/Might Not***	**Base Verb**
I			I		
You			You		
He			He		
She	**may** **might**	**go.**	She	**may not** **might not**	**go.**
It			It		
We			We		
They			They		

Contractions for *may* or *might* are very rare.
We don't usually use *might* in *yes/no* questions.

224   Unit 8

e-Workbook 8E

Function

1. We use *may* or *might* to talk about something that is possible now or in the future.

   I **may/might** go to Mexico next year.

   You **may/might** have a problem with your computer.

   May and *might* have the same meaning. They both express a possibility.

2. We can also use *may* (but not *might*) to give, refuse, or ask for permission.

   You **may** use a dictionary during the test.

   You **may** not go early.

   May I use your phone?

3. We use *will*, *be going to*, or the present progressive when we are certain about something. We use *may/might* when we are not certain.

   I **may** be late. (It's possible.)

   I'**ll** be late. (It's certain.)

   I'**m going to** be late. (It's certain.)

9 Practice

A   A friend is traveling around the world. Use *will* if you are certain. Use *may* or *might* if you are not certain.

1.   FRIEND: I'm going to Boston this winter.

     YOU: Take warm clothes. It _____*will*_____ be cold. It's always cold there in winter.

2.   FRIEND: I'm going to Los Angeles in the summer.

     YOU: Take your shorts and light clothes. It _____ be hot. It's always hot there in the summer.

3.   FRIEND: I want to walk around New York at night.

     YOU: Be careful. It _____ be dangerous. People sometimes get hurt.

4.   FRIEND: In June, I'm going to Bangkok, in Thailand.

     YOU: Take an umbrella. It _____ be rainy. It always rains there in June.

5.   FRIEND: I'm going to stay in Tokyo for a month.

     YOU: Take a lot of money. It _____ be expensive. Tokyo is always expensive.

6.   FRIEND: I'm flying from New York to Sydney, Australia.

        YOU: It's a long trip. Take a book with you. You _____ get bored.

7.   FRIEND: I want to go to Rio de Janeiro for the Carnival.

        YOU: Make a hotel reservation. It _____ be crowded. It's always crowded then.

8.   FRIEND: I'm going to Africa to see wild animals.

        YOU: Take some medicine with you. You _____ get sick. People sometimes get sick when they travel there.

B   Listen and check your answers. Then work with a partner. Listen again and repeat each conversation.

CD4, 9, 10

10   Practice
Underline the correct verb.

1. I'**m going**/**might go** to New York next week. I have my ticket already.

2. I **may stay**/**'m staying** at the Ambassador Hotel. I have a reservation for next week.

3. I'**ll go**/**may go** to New Jersey or perhaps to Boston from New York.

4. I **won't spend**/**may not spend** much time out of New York because my work will keep me too busy.

5. I'**ll finish**/**might finish** my work in New York before Friday of next week. My return flight is on that day.

6. I'**ll see**/**might see** a show on Broadway. I'm not sure.

7. It's my birthday on Wednesday. I **may celebrate**/**will celebrate** it in New York!

8. I'**ll go**/**may go** to an expensive restaurant. I'm not sure.

Future Time Clauses with *Before*, *After*, and *When*

Form/Function

She**'ll wear** her new suit when she **goes** to the interview.

1. A future time clause can begin with *before*, *after*, or *when*.
2. When a time clause refers to the future, the verb is in the simple present.

Time Clause				Main Clause		
Simple Present				**Future**		
Before	I	**go**	to bed,	I	**will do**	my homework.
When	she	**goes**	to the interview,	she	**will wear**	her new suit.
After	we	**finish**	the test,	we	**will go**	home.

CORRECT: Before I go to bed, I will do my homework.

INCORRECT: Before I ~~will go~~ to bed, I will do my homework.

3. We can put the time clause before or after the main clause. The meaning is the same.
4. When the time clause comes first, we put a comma (,) after the time clause.

Note: See Unit 6, pages 179–182 for more information on time clauses.

11   **Practice**

Laura has an interview tomorrow. Underline the time clauses in the
sentences about her.

1. She'll have breakfast <u>before she goes to the interview</u>.

2. Before she leaves home, she'll take some important letters with her.

3. She'll try to relax before she goes to the interview.

4. When the interviewer asks questions, she'll answer all of them.

5. She'll meet her friend after the interview.

6. When they meet, they'll talk about the interview.

7. She'll be worried before she gets the news about her job.

8. When she gets the job, she'll celebrate.

12   **Practice**

A   Jim and Paula Newley are planning a trip to Istanbul, Turkey. Complete the
sentences with the correct form of the verbs in parentheses.

1. We (change) _____'ll change_____ some money before we leave.

2. We (make) _____ a list of all the interesting places before we leave.

3. When we (get) _____ there, we'll stay at the Hilton® hotel.

4. After we see the city, we (visit) _____ museums.

5. When we stay in Istanbul, we (not, go) _____ to other cities.

6. We won't have time to see everything before we (leave) _____ .

7. We'll go to the bazaar after we (visit) _____ the museums.

8. When we go to the bazaar, we (buy) _____ a rug.

9. When we walk around the bazaar, we (take) _____ photos.

10. When we (stay) _____ in Istanbul, we won't need a car.

11. We'll take a taxi when we (want) _____ to go somewhere.

12. Before we leave Istanbul, we (get) _____ lots of souvenirs.

B Listen and check your answers. Then work with a partner. Listen again and repeat each sentence.

AUDIO
DOWNLOAD
CD4, 11, 12

13 Pair Up and Talk

A Practice the conversation with a partner.

A: What are you doing before you take the test?

B: I'm going to study for another hour before I take the test.

B Now practice the conversation with your partner again. Use these phrases or your own.

after you eat dinner   before you eat dinner   when you have dinner

after you leave class   before you go to the party   when your friend comes to visit

14 Your Turn

Where do you want to go this year? What will you do when you get there? Write six sentences. Use future time clauses with *before*, *after*, and *when*.

1. _____ .
2. _____ .
3. _____ .
4. _____ .
5. _____ .
6. _____ .

8G | Future Conditional Sentences

Form

> **If** the weather **is** nice tomorrow, we**'ll go** fishing.

1. A conditional sentence has a main clause and a dependent clause that starts with *if*. We call this kind of dependent clause an *if* clause.
2. In future conditional sentences, we use the simple present in an *if* clause to express future time. We use a future form in the main clause.

	If Clause			Main Clause	
	Present			**Future**	
If	I	**have** time,	I	**will see**	you.
If	you	**don't hurry**,	you	**will be**	late.
If	she	**gets** the job,	she	**is going to buy**	a car.
If	it	**is** sunny,	we	**will go**	fishing.
If	we	**leave** now,	we	**will arrive**	in time.
If	they	**don't run**,	they	**will miss**	the bus.

3. An *if* clause can come before or after the main clause. The meaning is the same.

   If the weather **is** nice tomorrow, we**'ll** go fishing.

   We**'ll** go fishing **if** the weather **is** nice tomorrow.

   CORRECT: **If** I **have** time tomorrow, I **will visit** you.

   INCORRECT: If I ~~will have~~ time tomorrow, I will visit you.
4. When the *if* clause comes first, we put a comma (,) after it.

Function

We use future conditional sentences to say that one situation in the future depends on another situation.

If I **have time** tomorrow, I **will visit** you. (I may or may not have time, so I may or may not visit you.)

If she **sees** Tony, she**'ll invite** him to the party. (She may or may not see Tony, so she may or may not invite him.)

15 Practice

A Jim is going to be away from home. His mother is worried about him. Match the sentence parts. Then write sentences.

	A		B
___c___ 1.	go out without a coat	**a.**	be hungry
_____ 2.	lie in the sun	**b.**	not pass your exam
_____ 3.	don't eat breakfast	**c.**	catch a cold
_____ 4.	eat too many french fries	**d.**	be lonely
_____ 5.	don't study hard	**e.**	be tired the next day
_____ 6.	don't call home	**f.**	get sunburned
_____ 7.	go to bed late	**g.**	miss class
_____ 8.	get sick	**h.**	get fat

1. *If you go out without a coat, you'll catch a cold* _____ .

2. _____ .

3. _____ .

4. _____ .

5. _____ .

6. _____ .

7. _____ .

8. _____ .

B   **Listen and check your answers. Then listen again and repeat each sentence.**

CD4, 13, 14

16   Practice

Complete the sentences with the correct future form of the verbs in parentheses. Sometimes three answers are possible.

1. What are we doing this Saturday? Well, if the weather is nice, we (go) _will go/are going to go/are going_ to the park.

2. If it (rain) _____ , we'll stay at home.

3. If we stay at home, we (watch) _____ television.

4. I (order) _____ a pizza if we eat at home.

5. If the pizza is expensive, Tony (make) _____ pasta.

6. If we go to the park, we (play) _____ baseball.

7. If we (get) _____ tired, we (sit) _____ on the grass.

8. If we (go) _____ to the park, we (have) _____ a picnic.

9. I (go) _____ to the store to get some things if we (have) _____ a picnic.

10. We (have) _____ a good time if we (go) _____ to the park. We always do.

8H | The Simple Present with Time Clauses and *If* Clauses

Form

When you **get** thirsty, you **drink** water.

We sometimes use the simple present in the dependent clause (the *if* clause or the time clause) and also in the main clause.

Time Clause/If Clause	Main Clause
Before the teacher **walks** into the classroom,	the students **make** a lot of noise.
After I **get** up,	I usually **have** a cup of tea.
When you **get** thirsty,	you **drink** water.
If you **water** plants,	they **grow**.

Function

If the temperature **falls** below zero Celsius (32 degrees Fahrenheit), water **turns** to ice.

We use the simple present in both the dependent clause and the main clause when:

1. The action is habitual. (It happens all the time.)
2. We are expressing something that is always true.

   If the temperature **falls** below zero, water **turns** to ice. (Always true.)

   When I **go** to Mexico, I usually **stay** with my grandmother. (Habitual action.)

   BUT

   When I **go** to Mexico next summer, I **will stay** with my grandmother. (Specific action in future.)

17 Practice

Match the sentence parts. Then write sentences.

A

			B	
_c_	1.	don't water plants	a.	it goes bad
_____	2.	put food in the refrigerator	b.	you get gray
_____	3.	put water in the freezer	c.	they die
_____	4.	walk in the rain	d.	it stays fresh
_____	5.	mix black and white	e.	it turns into ice
_____	6.	don't put milk in the refrigerator	f.	you get wet

1. _If you don't water plants, they die_____ .
2. _____ .
3. _____ .
4. _____ .
5. _____ .
6. _____ .

18 Practice

Complete the sentences with main clauses about you.

1. If I have a headache, _____ _I take an aspirin_____ .
2. If I eat too much, _____ .
3. If I don't sleep, _____ .
4. If I miss my class, _____ .
5. If I get very angry, _____ .
6. When I am sad, _____ .
7. When I am happy, _____ .
8. When I have a test, _____ .

19 Practice

A   Complete each sentence with the correct form of the verb in parentheses.

1. Julia works in an office from 9:00 to 5:00. When she has some extra work, she (stay) _____ *stays* _____ until 6:00.

2. If she has a lot of work tomorrow, she (stay) _____ until 8:00.

3. If she's at the office, she usually (see) _____ Terry at lunchtime.

4. If the weather is nice, they usually (go) _____ out for lunch.

5. Julia usually gets tired when she (work) _____ on the computer all day.

6. Tomorrow, she (go) _____ to meetings before she works on the computer.

7. When she (come) _____ home tomorrow, it (be) _____ about 8:30.

8. If she (be) _____ tired tomorrow, she (not, make) _____ dinner.

9. She (buy) _____ a sandwich before she (come) _____ home from work tomorrow.

10. Tomorrow, Julia (not, turn) _____ on her computer after she (have) _____ dinner.

11. After she (have) _____ dinner tomorrow, she (go) _____ to bed.

12. If she (work) _____ like this all year, Julia (ask) _____ for more money from her boss.

B   Listen and check your answers. Then listen again and repeat each sentence.

CD4, 15, 16

C   Listen again. What will Julia do for dinner tomorrow if she's tired? Circle the letter of the correct answer.

CD4, 17

A   go out with Terry

B   have a salad or a bowl of soup

C   have a sandwich at her desk

D   buy a sandwich before she comes home

THE FOX AND THE SPIDERS

A fox is walking in the forest. He is very hungry. He sees a spider on a tree. He wants to eat the spider so he picks it up.

"What are you going to do?" asks the spider.

"I'm going to eat you, of course," says the fox.

"Wait. I hear some people. They are talking about you. I will go and see what they're saying."

"OK, but come back soon," says the fox.

The spider doesn't come back. The fox walks on and finds another spider. He is going to eat it.

"Wait," says the second spider, "Why do you think I'm on this tree?"

"I don't know."

"I hold on to this tree, close my eyes, and I see everything in the world. Trees are magic. That is why spiders are always on trees."

"Really?" asks the fox.

"Yes. Just close your eyes and hold on to this tree. You'll see everything, too."

The fox closes his eyes and the spider runs away. The fox never sees anything.

1. What is the fox doing?

    _____ .

2. What is the fox going to do with the spider?

    _____ .

3. What does the spider hear?

_____ .

4. What is the spider going to do?

_____ .

5. What is the fox going to do with the second spider?

_____ .

6. What does the second spider say will happen if the fox closes his eyes?

_____ .

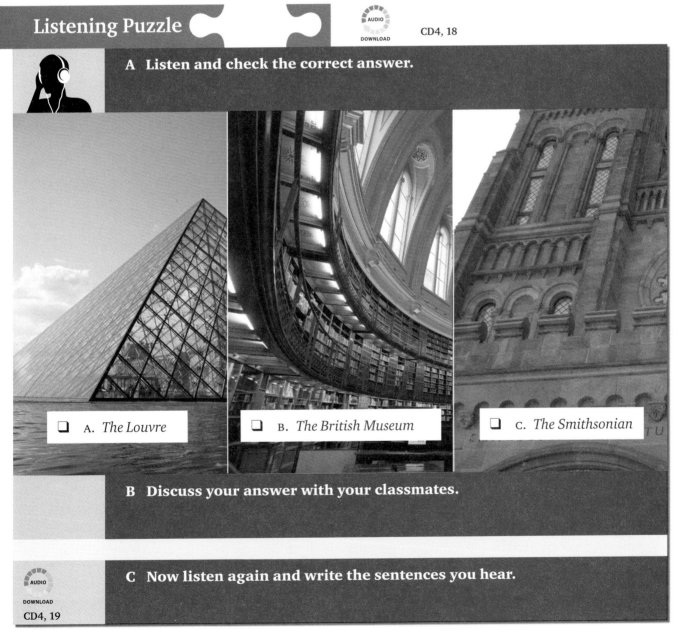

Listening Puzzle

AUDIO DOWNLOAD   CD4, 18

A Listen and check the correct answer.

❑ A. *The Louvre*   ❑ B. *The British Museum*   ❑ C. *The Smithsonian*

B Discuss your answer with your classmates.

AUDIO DOWNLOAD
CD4, 19

C Now listen again and write the sentences you hear.

A Before You Read

Answer the questions.

1. What will happen if the Earth gets warmer?
2. What will happen if the sea level rises?

B Read

GLOBAL WARMING

Many scientists are finding that in recent years our planet is growing warmer. Scientists call this global warming. In the last 100 years,
5 the average temperature around the world has risen by one degree Fahrenheit [1] (.56 degree Celsius). Some scientists believe that humans are causing global warming.
10 Other scientists believe that nature is the cause.

What will happen if global warming continues? Some things are already happening. It is so warm at the South Pole that the glaciers
15 are melting. As the ice melts, it falls into the sea and the sea level goes higher. When the sea level rises, some animals will move to new locations. In the future, some animals and plants may become **extinct**. There may be more storms,
20 floods,[2] and heat waves.[3] When sea levels rise, people will move away from the coast. Towns by the sea like New Orleans might even disappear. As the earth grows warmer, there may be no rain for long periods, and rivers will dry up.
25 Some areas may become too dry for farming, and more land will become desert.

We may or may not believe the scientists. It is still reasonable for us to do whatever we can to stop **this** process.

DID YOU KNOW … ?
Scientists think global warming will bring more diseases such as malaria.

[1] *Fahrenheit = a scale of temperature in which water freezes at 32° F*

[2] *flood = a large amount of water covers an area which is usually dry*

[3] *heat wave = a period of time during which the weather is much hotter than usual*

C Notice the Grammar

Underline all forms of the future.

Choose the best answer.

D Look for Main Ideas

1. What is the main idea of paragraph 1?
    - (A) We do not know why the world is growing warmer.
    - (B) Humans are the cause of global warming.
    - (C) Scientists are the cause of global warming.
    - (D) Nature is the cause of global warming.

2. What is paragraph 2 mainly about?
    - (A) why animals will move
    - (B) why cities will disappear
    - (C) the effects global warming will have
    - (D) why rivers will dry up

E Look for Details

3. Which of the following is NOT true about global warming?
    - (A) It causes sea levels to rise.
    - (B) It may cause animals to move.
    - (C) It may cause heat waves and floods.
    - (D) It may make more farmland.

4. With the ice melting, some animals _____ .
    - (A) may have a better life
    - (B) change the color of their fur
    - (C) may move
    - (D) may increase in numbers

5. Global warming may cause _____ .
    - (A) more land for farming
    - (B) some cities to disappear
    - (C) some animals to get big
    - (D) more waves in the sea

F Make Inferences

6. We can infer from the passage that global warming is _____ .
    - (A) nothing to worry about
    - (B) something that scientists can all agree on
    - (C) something to worry about
    - (D) nothing we can change

G Look for Vocabulary

7. The word **extinct** in the reading is closest in meaning to _____ .
    - (A) get bigger
    - (B) get smaller
    - (C) change
    - (D) no longer exist

H Reference the Text

8. The word **this** in the reading refers to _____ .
    - (A) our planet
    - (B) some scientists
    - (C) global warming
    - (D) recent years

Writing: Describe Future Plans

Write a paragraph about future plans.

STEP 1   Work with a partner. A friend is coming to your town/city for three days. It is his/her first visit. Make a list of four good places to go.

    1. _____   3. _____

    2. _____   4. _____

STEP 2   Plan your three days. Where are you going to go first, second, third, and last? Your friend is arriving at 4:00 at the airport near your town. Ask your partner questions like these. Write the answers to the questions.

    1. Where are you going to take your friend after he/she arrives at the airport?

    2. What are you going to do that evening? Why?

    3. What are you going to do on Sunday? How will you get there?

    4. What are you going to do if the weather is bad?

    5. What special food will you give your friend to eat? What will you do if he/she doesn't like it?

    6. Your friend is going back at 6:00 on Monday. Where will you go on Monday?

STEP 3   Rewrite your partner's answers in paragraph form. Be sure to use a comma when the time clause or *if* clause comes first.

STEP 4   Write a title in three to five words, for example, "Mila's Friend Visits Chicago."

STEP 5   Work with a partner to edit your paragraph. Correct spelling, punctuation, vocabulary, and grammar.

STEP 6   Write your final copy.

Self-Test

1. When I go to London, I _____ Buckingham Palace.

   A. am to visiting   Ⓐ Ⓑ Ⓒ Ⓓ
   B. going visit
   C. am going to visit
   D. will visiting

2. What _____ on the weekend?

   A. are you going to do   Ⓐ Ⓑ Ⓒ Ⓓ
   B. are you going
   C. you are going to do
   D. you doing

3. Paul and Jane _____ married next year.

   A. going to   Ⓐ Ⓑ Ⓒ Ⓓ
   B. are going to be
   C. will to be
   D. being

4. A: Would you like to come to our place this Thursday?
   B: OK, I _____ at 7:00.

   A. am going to come   Ⓐ Ⓑ Ⓒ Ⓓ
   B. 'll come
   C. am coming
   D. will coming

5. Oh, no! Look at that car! It _____ !

   A. crashing   Ⓐ Ⓑ Ⓒ Ⓓ
   B. will crash
   C. is going to crash
   D. crashes

6. In 20 years, more people _____ electric cars.

   A. are driving   Ⓐ Ⓑ Ⓒ Ⓓ
   B. will drive
   C. going drive
   D. is going to drive

7. I will be worried before I _____ to the interview.

   A. will go   Ⓐ Ⓑ Ⓒ Ⓓ
   B. go
   C. am going
   D. may go

8. If you study hard tonight, you _____ your math test tomorrow.

   A. pass   Ⓐ Ⓑ Ⓒ Ⓓ
   B. are passing
   C. will pass
   D. passing

9. If you mix blue and yellow, you _____ green.

   A. are getting   Ⓐ Ⓑ Ⓒ Ⓓ
   B. will be get
   C. get
   D. might to get

10. After I get up, I usually _____ a shower.

    A. am taking   Ⓐ Ⓑ Ⓒ Ⓓ
    B. am going to take
    C. will take
    D. take

1. How will be jobs different in the future?
   A   B   C   D

   (A) (B) (C) (D)

2. In the United States, you leave a tip when you
                              A   B
   having dinner in a restaurant.
   C   D

   (A) (B) (C) (D)

3. If you will heat water to 212 degrees Fahrenheit
          A   B
   (100 degrees Celsius), it boils.
                          C D

   (A) (B) (C) (D)

4. In 20 years, people will to visit other planets.
   A   B   C D

   (A) (B) (C) (D)

5. The next TOEFL™ test is going to be last June.
                        A   B   C D

   (A) (B) (C) (D)

6. In the future, men and women will be continue to
                  A   B   C   D
   marry.

   (A) (B) (C) (D)

7. If sharks do not move all the time, they
             A   B   C
   will be die.
   D

   (A) (B) (C) (D)

8. If plants won't get water, they die.
             A   B   C   D

   (A) (B) (C) (D)

9. You need a passport when you will travel to
       A   B   C
   other countries.
   D

   (A) (B) (C) (D)

10. Before people will get on a plane, their bags
                   A   B
    go through an X-ray machine for security.
    C   D

   (A) (B) (C) (D)

Unit 9

Quantity and Degree Words

It's **very** cold today.

9A	*All Of*, *Almost All Of*, *Most Of*, *Some Of*, and *None Of*	
	(Almost all of them are here.)	
9B	*Every*	
	(Every woman is a winner.)	
9C	*Very* and *Too*	
	(It's very cold today. It's too cold to go out.)	
9D	*Too Many* and *Too Much*	
	(There are too many cars and too much noise.)	
9E	*Too* + Adjective + Infinitive;	
	Too + Adjective + *For* + Noun/Pronoun + Infinitive	
	(He's too young to drive. It is too big for her to wear.)	
9F	Adjective + *Enough*	
	(He's old enough to vote.)	
9G	*Enough* + Noun	
	(I don't have enough money.)	
◆	Listening Puzzle: Mountains	
◆	Reading Challenge: The Sahara Desert	
◆	Writing: Describe a Place	
◆	Self-Test	

All Of, Almost All Of, Most Of, Some Of, and *None Of*

Form/Function

All of the people in the photo are men.
Almost all of them are wearing dark jackets.
Most of them are sitting.
Some of them are standing.
None of them are women.

1. We use *all of, almost all of, most of, some of,* and *none of* to show quantity.

All of							
Almost all of							
Most of							
Some of							
None of							

2. We can use *the* plus a plural count noun or a noncount noun after these expressions. We can also use a pronoun.

   All of **the computers** are old. (plural noun)

   All of **the information** is correct. (noncount noun)

   All of **it** is correct. (pronoun)

3. With these quantity words, the verb can be singular or plural. The noun tells you which one to use.

   All of the **books are** dictionaries.   (*Books* is plural, so the verb is plural.)

   All of the **cake is** chocolate.   (*Cake* is singular, so the verb is singular.)

   Some of the **water is** in the glass.   (*Water* is singular, so the verb is singular.)

   Some of the **girls are** young.   (*Girls* is plural, so the verb is plural.)

4. We can use a plural or singular verb after *none of*. Both are correct.

   None of the books **is** black.

   None of the books **are** black.

   In formal English, we use a singular verb after *none of*. In everyday English, we can use either a singular or plural verb.

1 Practice

Look at the photo. Complete the sentences with *all of the, almost all of the, most of the, some of the,* and *none of the.*

1. _____*All of the people*_____ are men.

2. _____ are wearing hats.

3. _____ are wearing a shirt and tie.

4. _____ are wearing dark pants.

5. _____ have beards.

6. _____ are standing.

7. _____ are wearing jackets.

8. _____ are wearing glasses.

2 Practice

Look at another photo. Complete the sentences with the quantity expressions from Practice 1.

1. _____*Some of the people*_____ are wearing hats.

2. _____ are women.

3. _____ are wearing white.

4. _____ are holding something.

5. _____ are looking at the camera.

6. _____ are wearing dresses.

7. _____ are young girls.

8. _____ are children.

3 Practice

A   Read the sentences about Mario's Restaurant. Underline the correct verb.

1. All of the food (<u>is</u>/are) delicious.

2. All of the dishes (come/comes) with a salad.

3. Most of the desserts (is/are) Italian.

4. None of the dishes (is/are) expensive.

5. Almost all of the dishes (have/has) pasta with them.

6. Some of the servers (is/are) Italian.

7. All of the music (is/are) Italian.

8. Almost all of the furniture (is/are) Italian.

9. All of the fish (is/are) very fresh.

10. Some of the pizzas (is/are) wonderful.

B   Listen and check your answers. Then listen again and repeat each sentence.

AUDIO

DOWNLOAD

CD4, 20, 21

9B | *Every*

Form/Function

Every woman is running.

1. We use *every* plus a singular count noun with a singular verb. *Every* means "all."
   Every runner **has** a number.

2. *Every* plus a singular noun means the same thing as *all of the* with a plural noun.
   Every runner was fast. = **All of the** runners were fast.

3. We do not use *every* with plural nouns, noncount nouns, or pronouns. We use *all of (the)* with them.

   CORRECT: All of the students passed the test.   INCORRECT: ~~Every~~ students passed the test.

   CORRECT: All of the furniture is new.   INCORRECT: ~~Every~~ furniture is new.

   CORRECT: All of them worked very hard.   INCORRECT: ~~Every~~ them worked very hard.

4 Practice
A Rewrite each sentence with *every*. Make any other necessary changes.

1. All of the classrooms have a number.

   Every classroom has a number .

2. All of the people in this school are from my country.

   _____ .

3. All of the teachers speak excellent English.

_____.

4. All of the teachers give a lot of homework.

_____.

5. All of the students in this class are learning English.

_____.

6. All of the students have a grammar book.

_____.

7. All of the units in the book have a test.

_____.

8. All of the tests have 20 questions.

_____.

9. All of the questions have four answers.

_____.

10. All of the questions are interesting.

_____.

B Listen and check your answers. Then listen again and repeat each sentence.

DOWNLOAD

CD4, 22, 23

5 Your Turn

Think of a game you play at home or outside as a sports activity. Describe the game to the class. The class guesses the game.

Example

Every team has 11 players. The two teams wear different colors.

Every player has a number. Only the goalkeeper can touch the ball with his hands.

What is the game?

Form/Function

It's **very** cold today. It's **too** cold for a long walk.

1. We use *very* and *too* before adjectives.
   Very adds emphasis. It makes the word that comes after it stronger.
   It is cold. It is **very** cold.
2. *Too* shows there is a problem.
   Rosa is young. She is **too** young to drive. (She cannot drive.)
   It is **very** cold today.
   It's **too** cold to have a picnic. (We cannot have a picnic.)
   He is **very** busy.
   He is **too** busy to go. (He cannot go.)

6 Practice
Match the sentences.

_____h_____ 1.   Tony drives very fast.   **a.**   I want to go there again.

_____ 2.   He drinks too much coffee.   **b.**   We can't go for a picnic in this weather.

_____ 3.   It's too cold.   **c.**   I can't go to work.

_____ 4.   This exam will be very hard.   **d.**   I can't lift it.

_____ 5.   The book is very interesting.   **e.**   I will study a lot and pass it.

_____ 6.   The island was very beautiful.   **f.**   He can't sleep at night.

_____ 7.   This suitcase is too heavy.   **g.**   I want to finish reading it this week.

_____ 8.   I have a very bad cold.   **h.**   I don't worry because he's a good driver.

7 Pair Up and Talk

A Look at this picture. Practice the conversation with a partner.

A: What's the problem?

B: The weight is too heavy to lift.

B Look at each picture. Now practice the conversation with your partner again. Use these words.

big   hot   sleepy

8 Practice

A Complete each conversation with *too* or *very* and one of these words.

difficult	fresh	small	tired
expensive	intelligent	sweet	young

1. JULIA: That jacket is beautiful, and it's _____*very expensive*_____ .

   PAM: Are you going to buy it?

   JULIA: Yes, I am.

2. BERTA: Do you like our new teacher?

   MARIO: Yes, I do. She's an excellent teacher, and she's _____ .

3. SUE: I didn't like that cake.

   PAM: What was wrong?

   SUE: It was _____ .

4. LOUIS: Does your sister drive?

   MARIA: No, she doesn't. She's only 13. She's _____ .

5. JO: Do you want to play tennis with us this afternoon?

   KAREN: I'm _____ , but I think I will. Thanks.

6. MEL: Can you read this tiny writing?

   JIM: Sorry, I can't read it without my glasses. It's _____ .

7. CHRIS: Can you help me with this statistics problem?

   JAN: Sorry, I can't. It's _____ .

8. LISA: Did you like the new fish restaurant yesterday?

   MIKE: Yes, I did. The fish was _____ .

B Listen and check your answers. Then work with a partner. Listen again and repeat each conversation.

DOWNLOAD

CD4, 24, 25

Form/Function

There are **too many** cars and **too much** noise.

1. We often use *too* with *much* and *many* to talk about quantities.
2. We use *too many* before plural count nouns. We use *too much* before noncount nouns.
   We have **too many** exercises to do.
   The teacher gave us **too much** homework.

9 Practice

A Some people don't like big cities. Complete each sentence with *too much* or *too many*.

1. There is _____ *too much* _____ crime.

2. There are _____ cars.

3. There is _____ traffic.

4. There are _____ people.

5. There is _____ pollution.

6. There is _____ noise.

7. There are _____ buildings.

B Listen and check your answers. Then listen again and repeat each sentence.

CD4, 26, 27

10 Practice

A Mr. Lang had a party yesterday. Complete each sentence with *too much* or *too many*.

1. Mr. Lang spent _____*too much*_____ money.

2. There were _____ guests and _____ food.

3. There were _____ flowers everywhere.

4. There were _____ drinks.

5. There were _____ sandwiches.

6. There was _____ fruit.

7. There was _____ meat.

8. There was _____ fish.

9. There were _____ cakes.

10. There were _____ waiters.

B Listen and check your answers. Then listen again and repeat each sentence.

DOWNLOAD

CD4, 28, 29

11 Pair Up and Talk

A Practice the conversation with a partner.

A: What's wrong with our school?

B: We get too much homework.

B Now practice the conversation with your partner again. Use these words or your own. Use *too much* and *too many*.

classes	homework	noise	students
grammar	mistakes	rules	tests

Quantity and Degree Words   253

Too + Adjective + Infinitive; *Too* + Adjective + *For* + Noun/Pronoun + Infinitive

Form

He's **too small to wear** the clothes.
The clothes are **too big for him to wear**.

Subject	Verb	Too	Adjective	Infinitive
I	am		tired	to study.
John	is	too	sick	to work.
The weather	is		cold	to play tennis.

Subject	Verb	Too	Adjective	For + noun	Infinitive
The coat	is		expensive	for Jane	to buy.
The clothes	are	too	big	for him	to wear.
It	is		heavy	for her	to carry.

1. We can use *too* + adjective with an infinitive after it.
   It is **too cold to have** a picnic. (*too* + adjective + infinitive)
2. We can also use *too* + adjective + *for* + noun/pronoun + infinitive.
   The clothes are **too big for him to wear**. (*too* + adjective + *for* + pronoun + infinitive)

12 Practice

A Make one sentence from the two sentences. Use *too* and the infinitive.

1. I am tired. I can't drive.

   I am too tired to drive   .

2. This room is small. It isn't comfortable.

   _____ .

3. This computer is old. It doesn't work well.

   _____ .

4. Peter is sleepy. He can't study.

   _____ .

5. Janet is busy. She can't go.

   _____ .

6. The children are excited. They can't sleep.

   _____ .

B Listen and check your answers. Then listen again and repeat each sentence.

AUDIO
DOWNLOAD
CD4, 30, 31

13 Practice

Sandy went to stay with her uncle Ned, but she didn't like it. Write sentences with the same meaning. Use *too* + adjective + *for* + noun/pronoun + infinitive.

1. The room was cold. She couldn't sit in it.

   The room was too cold for her to sit in   .

2. The room was dark. She couldn't read.

   _____ .

3. The bed was hard. She couldn't sleep in it.

   _____ .

4. The tea was strong. She couldn't drink it.

   _____ .

5. The weather was stormy. She couldn't go out.

   _____ .

6. The bathroom was cold. She couldn't take a shower.

   _____ .

9F Adjective + *Enough*

Form/Function

The little girl is not **old enough** to talk.

Subject	Verb	(Not)	Adjective	Enough	
I	am		old		to drive.
He	is	(not)	tall	enough	to play basketball.
They	are		rich		to buy the house.

1. We put *enough* after an adjective.
   I am **old enough**. (adjective + *enough*)
2. *Enough* means sufficient. It has a positive meaning. It means something is possible.
   He is **old enough** to drive.
3. *Not* + adjective + *enough* means not sufficient. It has a negative meaning. It means something is not possible.
   He is **not tall enough** to reach the shelf.

A   Mrs. Parkway complains about everything. She goes to a restaurant and complains. Use the words in parentheses to write one sentence with *too* and one sentence with *enough*.

1.   The chair is (uncomfortable). It is not (comfortable).

   The chair is too uncomfortable. It is not comfortable enough .

2.   The water is (hot). It is not (cold).

   _____ .

3.   The soup is (warm). It is not (cool).

   _____ .

4.   The server is (slow). He is not (fast).

   _____ .

5.   The bread is (old). It is not (fresh).

   _____ .

6.   The portion is (small). It is not (large).

   _____ .

7.   The coffee is (weak). It is not (strong).

   _____ .

8.   The table is (small). It is not (big).

   _____ .

9.   The meat is (tough). It is not (tender).

   _____ .

10. The meal is (expensive). It is not (cheap).

   _____ .

B   **Listen and check your answers. Then listen again and repeat each sentence.**

AUDIO

DOWNLOAD

CD4, 32, 33

Quantity and Degree Words   **257**

9G *Enough* + Noun

Form

We don't have **enough chairs**.
We have **enough coffee**, but we don't have **enough cups**.

We can use *enough* + noun. *Enough* comes before a noun.

There's **enough light** here for me to work, but I don't have **enough space**. I can't put a desk in here.
Do you have **enough money** for a car?
I have **enough money**, but I don't have **enough time** this week to look for a car.

15   Practice
Ted had a party yesterday, but people were not happy. Complete the sentences with *enough* and a word from the list.

chairs	food	money	room
drinks	glasses	people	time

Ted had a week to plan the party, but his apartment is very small.

He had _____*enough time*_____ , but he didn't have _____*enough room*_____ . Many
                        1   **2**

of his friends came. There were _____ at the party. People
                                                      3

were standing because they had no place to sit down. There weren't

_____ . There were 20 people and ten large bottles of soda.
               4

There were _____ . There were only two glasses for 20 people.
                               5

There weren't _____ . Ted did not spend much money. He didn't have
                            6

_____ to spend. People were hungry. There wasn't _____ .
         7   **8**

16 Practice

A Complete Janet's questions about her party. Use *enough* and one of these words.

CDs   chairs   food   people   soda   time

1. Did I invite ____enough people____ ?
2. Do I have _____ for people to eat?
3. Do I have _____ to get ready?
4. Is there _____ to drink?
5. Are there _____ to listen to?
6. Are there _____ to sit on?

B Listen and check your answers. Then listen again and repeat each sentence.

CD4, 34, 35

17 Pair Up and Talk

A Practice the conversation with a partner.

A: Do you have enough time to go to a movie?

B: No, I don't have enough time to go to a movie.

B Now practice the conversation with your partner again. Use these phrases or your own.

bread/to make six sandwiches   money/to buy a CD
eggs/to make an omelet   paper/to take notes in class
gas/to drive to New York   time/to go to a movie

VISITS OF KINGS

One morning, His Majesty the King visited a small teahouse. He was very hungry. He asked for an omelet. The owner served the omelet on a simple table in his teahouse. He apologized over and over. He said his food was too simple and his furniture was not good enough for a king.

"It's fine," the king said. "How much is the omelet?"

"For you, your majesty, the omelet will be 1,000 pieces of gold."

"Whoa!" exclaimed the king. "Omelets are very expensive around here. Is it because there aren't enough eggs?"

"It's not because there aren't enough eggs, your majesty," said the owner. "It's because there aren't enough visits of kings!"

1. Why did the king ask for an omelet?

    _____ .

2. Why did the owner apologize for his food?

    _____ .

3. Why did the owner apologize for his furniture?

    _____ .

4. What did the king think about the price of the omelet?

    _____ .

5. Why did the king think the price of the omelet was high?

    _____ .

6. According to the owner, why was the omelet very expensive?

    _____ .

Listening Puzzle

CD4, 36

A Listen and check the correct answer.

☐ A. *Mt. Kilimanjaro*   ☐ B. *Mt. Everest*   ☐ C. *Mt. Fuji*

B Discuss your answer with your classmates.

C Now listen again and write the sentences you hear.

CD4, 37

A Before You Read

Answer the questions.

1. Where is the Sahara Desert?
2. What things live in the Sahara Desert?

B Read

THE SAHARA DESERT

DID YOU KNOW … ?
Sahara is the Arabic word for "desert."

The Sahara Desert is the hottest and largest desert in the world. It is in North Africa and covers an area the size of the United States. At night, the ⁵ temperature often goes below freezing, but during the day it goes up to 135 degrees Fahrenheit (57 degrees Celsius).

¹⁰ When people think of the Sahara, they think of an oasis. An oasis is desert land that receives enough water for plants to grow. Oases can be big or small. Small oases have enough water for a few palm trees to grow. Large oases have ¹⁵ enough water for a city.

Almost all of the people who live in the Sahara live in the oases. Some people called nomads travel from oasis to oasis.

Many animals live in the Sahara ²⁰ Desert. There are many small creatures like grasshoppers, scorpions, and spiders. These animals are nocturnal, or active at night, when it is cool. Larger animals such as certain kinds of sheep, deer, and foxes live in the Sahara, ²⁵ too. During the day they try to find some shade. **This** is difficult to find because there are no trees. Sometimes different animals get together and share the same **shade** or burrow¹ in the ground.

¹·*burrow = a hole in the ground made by an animal*

C Notice the Grammar

Underline all quantity words.

This is also a word that often refers to a noun. Remember to look for a connection between *this* and a noun.

Choose the best answer.

D Look for Main Ideas

1. What is paragraph 2 mainly about?
   - (A) the temperature of the Sahara Desert
   - (B) the oases in the Sahara
   - (C) why nomads travel from place to place
   - (D) the special plants of the desert

2. What is the main idea of paragraph 4?
   - (A) the small animals that live in the Sahara Desert
   - (B) where to find shade in the desert
   - (C) the animals that live in the Sahara Desert
   - (D) how small and large animals live together in the Sahara

E Look for Details

3. The Sahara Desert is _____ .
   - (A) very hot during the day and night
   - (B) an oasis
   - (C) freezing in the winter
   - (D) the size of the United States

4. The Sahara Desert is a place where _____ .
   - (A) animals come out at night
   - (B) people live in small oases only
   - (C) there are no big animals
   - (D) there are no plants

5. Which of the following is NOT true of oases?
   - (A) They can be big.
   - (B) They have plants.
   - (C) People don't live in them.
   - (D) They have water.

F Make Inferences

6. What can we infer from the reading?
   - (A) People and animals can live in the Sahara.
   - (B) Oases aren't real.
   - (C) The Sahara is a dangerous place.
   - (D) People lived in the Sahara for thousands of years.

G Look for Vocabulary

7. The word *shade* in the reading is closest in meaning to _____ .
   - (A) a place to rest
   - (B) a place where there is water
   - (C) a place where there is no sun
   - (D) a place where there is wind

H Reference the Text

8. The word *This* in the reading refers to _____ .
   - (A) some shade
   - (B) trees
   - (C) the day
   - (D) larger animals

Writing: Describe a Place

Write about your city or town.

STEP 1 Work with a partner. Talk about your city or town. Talk about crime, traffic, buildings, and people who work in the city. Make sentences with these words and phrases.

all of	every	not enough	too	too much
enough	most of	some of	too many	very

Example

My city is very beautiful. Most of the offices are downtown.
Almost all of the people take the bus or subway to the city because …

STEP 2 Write your sentences.

STEP 3 Rewrite your sentences in paragraph form. Be sure to use correct spelling for quantity and degree words.

STEP 4 Write a title in three to five words, for example, "My City and Its Problems."

STEP 5 Evaluate your work.

Checklist

_____ Did you indent the first line?

_____ Did you give your paragraph a title?

_____ Did you use capital letters correctly?

_____ Did you use verb forms correctly?

STEP 6 Work with a partner to edit your paragraph. Correct spelling, punctuation, vocabulary, and grammar.

STEP 7 Write your final copy.

Self-Test

1. I love Paris. It's a _____ city.

    A. very beautiful   (A) (B) (C) (D)
    B. too beautiful enough
    C. too beautiful
    D. enough beautiful

2. We don't _____ to finish the test.

    A. have enough time   (A) (B) (C) (D)
    B. time have enough
    C. time enough have
    D. enough have time

3. She isn't _____ to drive.

    A. enough old   (A) (B) (C) (D)
    B. old enough
    C. enough age
    D. old is enough

4. I have _____ tonight.

    A. too many homeworks   (A) (B) (C) (D)
    B. too many homework
    C. too much homework
    D. very much homeworks

5. The movie was _____ . I want to see it again.

    A. too very funny   (A) (B) (C) (D)
    B. enough funny
    C. very funny enough
    D. very funny

6. This homework is _____ . I can't do it.

    A. difficult enough   (A) (B) (C) (D)
    B. too difficult
    C. difficult very
    D. enough difficult

7. Tom doesn't study _____ to pass his exams.

    A. hard enough   (A) (B) (C) (D)
    B. hard very
    C. enough hard
    D. very too hard

8. He doesn't _____ to make a pizza.

    A. have enough flour   (A) (B) (C) (D)
    B. enough flour have
    C. have very flour
    D. have too flour

9. I can't drink this tea. It _____ .

    A. isn't enough cool   (A) (B) (C) (D)
    B. is enough cool
    C. isn't cool enough
    D. isn't cool very

10. Give yourself _____ , and you can do it.

    A. time very   (A) (B) (C) (D)
    B. enough time
    C. too time
    D. very time

1. <u>An</u> elephant <u>eats</u> about five tons of <u>food</u>
     A   B   C
   every <u>days</u>.
          D

   Ⓐ Ⓑ Ⓒ Ⓓ

2. <u>Almost</u> of the <u>seas</u> in the world have <u>fish</u>
      A   B   C
   in <u>them</u>.
       D

   Ⓐ Ⓑ Ⓒ Ⓓ

3. All of the <u>players</u> <u>has</u> numbers and names on
             A   B
   their <u>shirts</u>.
     C   D

   Ⓐ Ⓑ Ⓒ Ⓓ

4. <u>Every</u> <u>state</u> in the United States <u>have</u> <u>its</u> own
     A   B   C D
   state flag.

   Ⓐ Ⓑ Ⓒ Ⓓ

5. <u>Almost all</u> of the <u>restaurants</u> in the city <u>accepts</u>
       A   B   C
   <u>credit cards</u>.
      D

   Ⓐ Ⓑ Ⓒ Ⓓ

6. Most <u>of the</u> <u>country</u> in <u>Europe</u> now <u>use</u> the
         A   B   C   D
   euro currency.

   Ⓐ Ⓑ Ⓒ Ⓓ

7. <u>Every</u> flower <u>have</u> <u>its</u> own <u>smell</u>.
     A   B C   D

   Ⓐ Ⓑ Ⓒ Ⓓ

8. <u>Every</u> <u>students</u> <u>in</u> this class <u>is learning</u> English.
     A   B   C   D

   Ⓐ Ⓑ Ⓒ Ⓓ

9. <u>Most people</u> <u>are</u> not <u>enough tall</u> to be
     A   B   C
   basketball <u>players</u>.
            D

   Ⓐ Ⓑ Ⓒ Ⓓ

10. <u>A boy of 14</u> is not <u>enough old</u> to <u>drive</u> <u>a car</u>.
       A   B   C   D

    Ⓐ Ⓑ Ⓒ Ⓓ

Unit 10
Objects and Pronouns

This is her toy. It's **hers**.

10A | Object Pronouns

Form/Function

This is a picture of my brother and **me**.
I like **him** very much.

Many sentences in English have a subject, a verb, and an object.

Noun Subject	Verb	Noun Object	Pronoun Subject	Verb	Pronoun Object
John	likes	**rice**.	He	likes	**it**.
Mika and Rosie	love	**their children**.	They	love	**them**.

1. The subject can be a noun: a person, a place, or a thing (*Mike, a restaurant, a movie*).
2. The subject can also be a pronoun (*he, they*).
3. The object can be a noun (*rice, their children*) or a pronoun (*it, them*).
4. We often use a pronoun in place of a noun.
   Here are the subject and object pronouns:

Subject Pronouns	Object Pronouns
I	me
you	you
he	him
she	her
it	it
we	us
they	them

A Replace the underlined words with a subject or object pronoun.

1. <u>My friend and I</u> study English at the same school.

   We study English at the same school .

2. <u>John Blackie</u> is our teacher.

   _____ .

3. He teaches <u>the other students and me</u> English grammar.

   _____ .

4. He uses <u>this book</u> to teach grammar.

   _____ .

5. The students like <u>John Blackie</u>.

   _____ .

6. <u>The students</u> ask John Blackie questions.

   _____ .

7. He answers <u>the questions</u>.

   _____ .

8. Linda is a student in our class. <u>Linda</u> always asks questions.

   _____ .

9. We don't like to listen to <u>Linda</u>, but Mr. Blackie is very patient.

   _____ .

10. <u>Mr. Blackie</u> always answers her questions.

    _____ .

B Listen and check your answers. Then listen again and repeat each sentence.

AUDIO

DOWNLOAD

CD5, 2, 3

2 Practice

A Complete the sentences with subject or object pronouns.

A

At the moment, I am studying English. _____*It*_____ is a difficult language.
                                            1

Most of my friends are in the school with _____ . Our teachers are good,
                                               2

but _____ give _____ a lot of homework. _____ are having a
      3   **4**   **5**

test next week, and I want to pass _____ . Then my parents will not
                                      6

worry about _____ so much.
                7

B

JOHN: Do you know that woman?

PETE: Yes, I work with _____ .
                            1

JOHN: Is she nice?

PETE: Yes, _____ is very nice. We work in the same office.
               2

        Come with _____ to the office, and I will introduce you to
                     3

        _____ . Her husband is my boss. _____ is a great boss.
            4   **5**

        Do you want me to introduce you to _____ , too?
                                               6

JOHN: No. That's OK.

C

NICK: My father bought me a new computer, but I don't know how to use

        _____ . Can you help _____ ?
            1   **2**

DAVE: Sure, I'll show _____ how it works. When do you want _____
                           3   **4**

        to teach you?

NICK: Can you come tomorrow?

DAVE: OK. I'll see _____ at ten tomorrow. You need to learn some
                        5

        basic steps. You can learn _____ in a few hours.
                                       6

B Listen and check your answers. Then work with a partner. Listen again and repeat each conversation. Take turns with the sentences in A.

CD5, 4, 5

3 Pair Up and Talk

A Practice the conversation with a partner.

A: Do you like Brad Pitt?

B: Yes, I like him because he is very cute.

B Practice the conversation with your partner again. Use these words and phrases or your own.

cheese	jogging	snow	tight shoes
classical music	Madonna	*Star Wars*	Tom Cruise
Jackie Chan	mountains	The Rolling Stones	watching TV

C Write a paragraph about the person or thing that you talked about in Part B. Write about why you like this person or thing. Use personal pronouns.

My favorite opera singer is ...

_____

_____

_____

_____

_____

_____

_____

Form/Function

Tony gave **Karen** some flowers.

1. Some sentences have two objects after a verb: a direct object and an indirect object.
   a. A direct object answers the question *what* or *whom** (or *who*).
   b. An indirect object answers the question to *whom* or *what*.

Subject	Verb	Direct Object	*To* + Indirect Object
I	sent	a gift	to **my mother.**

2. We can put the indirect object before the direct object. Then we do not use a preposition (*to*).

Subject	Verb	Indirect Object	Direct Object
I	sent	**my mother**	a gift.

3. When the direct object is a pronoun, we put the pronoun before the indirect object. Some verbs that follow this pattern are: *email, give, hand, lend, mail, pass, send, show, tell*, and *write*.

Subject	Verb	Pronoun Direct Object	Indirect Object
I	sent	**it**	to my mother.

* In speech and informal writing, we usually use *who* for objects. In formal writing, we use *whom*.

4 Practice

Underline the direct object and circle the indirect object.

1. The teacher handed <u>the paper</u> to (me).
2. He sends newspapers to my parents.
3. She showed the photos to us.
4. My grandfather told stories to us.
5. I write letters to my brother.
6. John passed the book to Maria.
7. We lent ten dollars to Kim.
8. My father gave a watch to me.
9. His parents gave an old computer to him.
10. Her brother gave the message to her.

5 Practice

A Look at Practice 4. Rewrite the sentences. Change the position of the indirect object. Do not use *to*.

1. *The teacher handed me the paper* .
2. _____ .
3. _____ .
4. _____ .
5. _____ .
6. _____ .
7. _____ .
8. _____ .
9. _____ .
10. _____ .

B Listen and check your answers. Then listen again and repeat each sentence.

AUDIO

DOWNLOAD

CD5, 6, 7

6 Practice

A Underline the direct objects. Then change the direct objects to pronouns. Rewrite the sentences.

1. JIM: I gave my mother <u>the house</u>.

   TOM: Who did you give it to?

   JIM: *I gave it to my mother* .

2. TOM: I sold Mr. Black my car.

   JIM: Who did you sell it to?

   TOM: _____ .

3. JIM: I offered my neighbor the television.

   TOM: Who did you offer it to?

   JIM: _____ .

4. TOM: I sent my friends an email.

   JIM: Who did you send it to?

   TOM: _____ .

5. JIM: I told my boss the news.

   TOM: Who did you tell it to?

   JIM: _____ .

6. TOM: I showed my friends the photos.

   JIM: Who did you show them to?

   TOM: _____ .

7. JIM: I gave my roommate a birthday gift.

   TOM: Who did you give it to?

   JIM: _____ .

8. TOM: I handed my sister a theater ticket.

   JIM: Who did you hand it to?

   TOM: _____ .

B Listen and check your answers. Then work with a partner. One partner is Tom, and the other is Jim. Listen again and repeat each conversation.

AUDIO

DOWNLOAD

CD5, 8, 9

Form/Function

Ed opened the door **for us**.

1. We use *for* with the indirect object with some verbs. With these verbs, the direct object comes first. Then *for* + the indirect object follow.

Subject	Verb	Direct Object	Indirect Object
My father	fixed	my bicycle	**for me**.

2. With these verbs use *for* + indirect object:

answer   cash   fix   open   prepare   pronounce

CORRECT: My teacher answered the questions **for me**.

INCORRECT: My teacher answered ~~me the questions~~.

7 Practice

A Complete the sentences with *to* or *for*.

1. A teacher answers questions _____*for*_____ the students.

2. A server shows the menu _____ you in a restaurant.

3. A teacher pronounces words _____ the students.

4. A comedian tells jokes _____ you.

5. A teller in a bank cashes checks _____ its customers.

6. A customer hands money _____ a salesperson.

7. A mechanic fixes cars _____ customers.

8. A teacher gives tests _____ the students.

B Listen and check your answers. Then listen again and repeat each sentence.

AUDIO

DOWNLOAD

CD5, 10, 11

8 Pair Up and Talk

A What do you do for friends and family on special holidays like Mother's Day, Father's Day, or the New Year? Practice the conversation with a partner.

A: What do you do for friends or family for the New Year?

B: We hand envelopes with money to our children.

B Now practice the conversation with your partner again. Use these words or your own.

cook	give	open	send	tell
email	hand	prepare	show	write

9 Practice

A Work with a partner. It's a classmate's birthday. Tell your partner four things you will do. Use these verbs. Use *to* or *for*.

get   give   send   write

Example

We will give a photo of the class to him.

B Now write five sentences about what you will do for your classmate's birthday. Use the verbs from Part A and add one of your own.

1. _____ .
2. _____ .
3. _____ .
4. _____ .
5. _____ .

Form/Function

She bought gifts **for me**.

1. We can use two patterns with the verbs *buy*, *get*, and *make*.

Verb	With *For*	Without *For*
buy	She bought gifts **for** you.	She bought you gifts.
get	I got a tie **for** my father.	I got my father a tie.
make	Jim made breakfast **for** his son.	Jim made his son breakfast.

2. We can use only one pattern with the verbs *explain*, *introduce,* and *repeat*.

Verb	With *To* or *For*
explain	I explained the problem **to the teacher**.
introduce	He introduced me **to the teacher**.
repeat	The teacher repeated the rules **for us**.

CORRECT: She explained the answer **to me**.
INCORRECT: She explained me the answer.

10   **Practice**
Jenny is looking at gifts. Complete the sentences with the words in
parentheses. Write each sentence two ways.

1. She bought (a tie/her father) *She bought a tie for her father*   .
    She bought her father a tie   .

2. She got (a blouse/her mother) _____.
    _____ .

3. She made (a sweater/her brother) _____ .
    _____ .

4. She bought (a toy/her niece) _____ .
    _____ .

5. She got (books/her sister) _____ .
    _____ .

6. She made (a cake/her neighbors) _____ .
    _____ .

7. She bought (a wallet/Brian) _____ .
    _____ .

8. She got (a plant/her boss) _____ .
    _____ .

1. The teacher explained (us/the answer)
    The teacher explained the answer to us   .

2. The teacher introduced (us/indirect objects)
    _____ .

3. The teacher repeated (us/the questions)
    _____ .

4. The teacher explained (me/the meaning of the word)

    _____ .

5. The student repeated (her/the sentence)

    _____ .

6. The teacher introduced (us/the new student)

    _____ .

7. The student explained (the teacher/her problem)

    _____ .

8. The teacher introduced (the class/the speaker)

AUDIO
DOWNLOAD
CD5, 12, 13

12 Practice
Write sentences with the words in parentheses. Use *to* or *for* when necessary. Sometimes two patterns are possible.

1. Tim bought (a gift/his wife)

    Tim bought a gift for his wife _____ .

2. He fixed (the car/her)

    _____ .

3. He made (dinner/her)

    _____ .

4. He got (flowers/her)

    _____ .

5. He opened (the door/her)

    _____ .

6. He showed (a letter/her)

    _____ .

7. His wife told (her ideas/him)

    _____ .

8. She gave (advice/him)

    _____ .

Form/Function

LORI: Is this pen **yours**?
KEN: No, it's not **mine**.
I think it's Susan's.

Possessive Pronouns	Possessive Adjectives
mine	my
yours	your
hers	her
his	his
its	its
ours	our
yours	your
theirs	their

1. We put a possessive adjective before a noun. We use a possessive pronoun alone.
   This is **my** pen. This pen is **mine**.
   That is **their** television. It's **theirs**.
2. We use possessive adjectives and possessive pronouns to show that something belongs to somebody.
   Excuse me, is this **your** umbrella? OR Excuse me, is this **yours**?
3. Do not confuse *its* and *it's*. *Its* is a possessive adjective or possessive pronoun.
   The bus needs **its** tire fixed.
   It's is a contraction of *it is*.
   It's time to go.

13 Practice

Match the objects with the people. Write sentences with the possessive forms. Follow the example.

1. _These are the teacher's books_ .
   These are his books .
   These are his .

2. _____ .
   _____ .
   _____ .

3. _____ .

_____ .

_____ .

4. _____ .

_____ .

_____ .

5. _____ .

_____ .

_____ .

14 Practice
Look at Practice 13 and answer the questions.

1. Are the books the teacher's?

   Yes, they're his .

2. Is the thermometer the taxi driver's?

   _____ .

3. Are the suitcases the travelers'?

   _____ .

4. Is the taxi the teacher's?

   _____ .

5. Are the toys the nurse's?

   _____ .

6. Are the toys the children's?

   _____ .

15 Practice
A   Underline the correct form.

1. KAREN: Don't forget (<u>your</u>/yours) umbrella!

   JAMIE: That's not my umbrella. (My/Mine) is black.

2. JIM: Do the Petersons live there?

   DAVE: Yes, they do.

   JIM: Is that (their/theirs) house?

   DAVE: No, it isn't. (Theirs/Their) is around the corner.

3. BOBBY: That's (my/mine) teddy bear!

   JENNY: No, it isn't! It's (mine/my) teddy bear.

   MOTHER: Stop it children! Jenny, give Bobby his teddy bear.

   JENNY: It isn't his. It's (mine/my).

4.   LARRY: My brother rents his apartment, and I rent (my/mine) apartment.

     SHERRY: (My/Mine) roommate and I rent (our/ours), too. (Our/Ours) apartment is small, but it's big enough for us.

5.   TONY: Where is (their/theirs) car parked?

     PETE: (Their/ Theirs) is on the street.

     TONY: Is Maria's car on the street, too?

     PETE: No, (her/hers) is in the driveway.

6.   BEN: Shall we take (your/yours) car or (my/mine) car?

     JERRY: Let's take (my/mine). It's faster than (your/yours).

     BEN: Yes, but (mine/my) car is more comfortable.

7.   SUZY: Is that (your/yours) bag over there?

     LAURA: No, it isn't (my/mine). I thought it was (your/yours).

8.   BEN: (Our/Ours) classroom is very neat and organized.

     JERRY: That's true. The teacher has (her/hers) table and chair, and we have (our/ours).

B   Listen and check your answers. Then work with a partner. Listen again and repeat each conversation.

DOWNLOAD

CD5, 14, 15

16   Practice

Complete the sentences with *it's* and *its*.

1.   _____It's_____ cold outside so take a coat.

2.   My sofa was old, so I changed _____ cover.

3.   _____ not far. You can walk.

4.   The store is near here, but I can't remember _____ name.

5.   _____ a beautiful apartment. How much is the rent?

6.   How much is the jacket? I don't see _____ price.

7.   A: Who is it?

     B: _____ me.

8.   The new town has _____ bank and shopping area in the center.

17 Your Turn

Work with a partner. Compare your hair, eyes, shoes, hands, and other things about you.

Example

My hair is long. Yours is short.

18 Pair Up and Talk

A   Practice the conversation with a partner.

A: What are you going to do tonight?

B: I'm going to give my neighbors that TV. It's theirs.

B   Now practice the conversation with your partner again. Use these phrases or your own. Make sentences with objects and possessive pronouns.

bring these books/sister	give that toy/son	send this jacket/uncle
bring your CD/you	return the car/parents	take these groceries/wife

Form

JAMES: I don't see **anything** here for dessert.

SERVER: There's **something** on special today.

	Some-	**Any-**	**No-**
Things	something	anything	nothing
People	someone somebody	anyone anybody	no one nobody

Function

1. We use *some-* (*something, someone, somebody*), and *no-* (*nothing, no one, nobody*) in affirmative statements.
   Someone is at the door.
2. We use *any-* (*anything, anyone, anybody*) in negative statements.
   I can't see **anyone**.
3. We use *some-* or *any-* in questions.
   Can you see **something**? OR Can you see **anything**?

19 Practice

Complete the sentences with *something, someone, somebody, anything, anyone, anybody, nothing, no one,* and *nobody.*

1. LIN: There's ___*someone*___ at the door.

   JIM: There's _____ here. There must be _____ wrong with your ears!

2. JOHN: Let's have _____ to eat. How about a sandwich?

PETE: No, thanks. I'm not hungry. I don't want _____ to eat.

3. KEN: I went to the store to buy _____ for Jamie's birthday,

but there was _____ !

JEN: I didn't buy _____ for Jamie either.

4. KIM: Is there _____ in the mail for me?

NANCY: Sorry, there's _____ for you, but there's

_____ for me.

5. SYLVIA: I think there's _____ in my eye.

BEN: Your eye is red, but I can't see _____ in it.

6. TOM: _____ is wrong. Jim is never late.

JON: Does _____ know _____ ?

7. DON: Did you lose _____ ?

KEVIN: No, I didn't lose _____ . I just can't see

_____ without my glasses.

8. MIKE: Do you know _____ about Japanese history?

BOB: _____ , sorry. Maybe Tony knows _____ . Ask him.

9. KIM: I'm thirsty. Is there _____ in the fridge?

LENA: No, there's _____ . How about _____ hot, like tea?

10. ERIK: Do you hear _____ ?

LOUIS: No, I don't hear _____ .

ERIK: Do you see _____ ?

LOUIS: No, I don't see _____ .

THE PURSE OF GOLD

A beggar found a leather purse in the market. He opened it and found 100 pieces of gold. Then he heard a merchant shout, "A reward! A reward for the person who finds my leather purse!"

The beggar was an honest man, so he went to the merchant and gave the purse to him. He said, "Here's your purse. May I have the reward now?"

"Reward?" said the merchant while he was counting his gold. "The purse I dropped had 200 pieces of gold in it. You stole more than the reward! Give me my money, or I'll call the police."

"I'm an honest man," continued the beggar.

"We will go to court, and a judge will decide."

They went to court, and the judge listened to both sides of the story. He said, "I believe you both. Justice is possible! Merchant, you said that the purse you lost had 200 pieces of gold. Well, that's a lot of money. But the purse this beggar found had only 100 pieces of gold. Therefore, this purse isn't yours."

And, with that, the judge gave the purse and all the gold to the beggar.

1. What did the beggar find?

   _____.

2. What did he do after he found it?

   _____.

3. What did the beggar ask from the merchant?

   _____.

4. Who did the judge believe?

   _____.

5. Who did the judge give the purse and all the gold to?

   _____.

Listening Puzzle

 AUDIO DOWNLOAD   CD5, 16

A Listen and check the correct answer.

☐ A. *Albert Einstein*   ☐ B. *Thomas Edison*   ☐ C. *Henry Ford*

B Discuss your answer with your classmates.

AUDIO DOWNLOAD CD5, 17   **C Now listen again and write the sentences you hear.**

Reading Challenge

A Before You Read

Answer the questions.

1. What are some inventions that have changed our lives?
2. What did you do before you had a cell phone?

B Read

ALEXANDER GRAHAM BELL

As a boy, Alexander Graham Bell was interested in sound because of his family. His mother was deaf,[1] and his father taught deaf people to speak. When Alexander was 23, the Bells moved from Scotland to the United States. While they were living in Boston, Alexander started a school for the deaf.

Later, he became a professor at Boston University. While he was teaching, he met Mabel Hubbard, one of his deaf students. Bell married her five years later.

[1]deaf = hearing impaired

One day Bell got an idea for an invention. He wanted to use electricity to send the human voice from one place to another. He started to work on this idea with his assistant Thomas Watson. They rented rooms in a house. Bell was on one floor and Watson on another. They tried to send words to each other. One day, Watson suddenly heard the words: "Mr. Watson, come here. I want you." It was March 19, 1876, and these became the memorable words of the world's first telephone call.

Today, we have telephones because of Bell. Then in April 1973, Dr. Martin Cooper made the first call on a cell phone, and today there are millions of cell phones.

> **DID YOU KNOW ... ?**
> Bell was one of the people who started the *National Geographic* magazine because he believed the best way to learn was through pictures.

C Notice the Grammar

Underline all direct and indirect objects.

Choose the best answer.

D Look for Main Ideas

1. What is paragraph 1 mainly about?
    - (A) how Bell met his wife
    - (B) Bell's life before his invention
    - (C) why the Bells moved to the United States
    - (D) Bell's life as a professor

2. What is the main idea of paragraph 3?
    - (A) how Bell invented the telephone
    - (B) why Bell invented the telephone
    - (C) where Bell lived at the time of his invention
    - (D) the words of the first telephone call

E Look for Details

3. Bell's _____ .
    - (A) father was deaf
    - (B) mother taught the deaf to speak
    - (C) wife was a teacher
    - (D) mother and wife were deaf

4. In which paragraph does the author talk about Bell's marriage?
    - (A) paragraph 1
    - (B) paragraph 2
    - (C) paragraph 3
    - (D) paragraph 4

5. Which of the following is NOT true about Bell?
    - (A) He became a professor in Boston.
    - (B) He met his wife in Boston.
    - (C) Bell himself was deaf.
    - (D) His father taught the deaf.

F Make Inferences

6. What can we infer about Bell?
    - (A) He wanted to invent something only to make money.
    - (B) He wanted to become famous all his life.
    - (C) He got the idea for this invention from his wife.
    - (D) He really cared about the deaf.

G Look for Vocabulary

7. The word *memorable* in the reading is closest in meaning to _____ .
    - (A) something easy to remember
    - (B) something you remember because it is special
    - (C) something that has no meaning
    - (D) something hard to remember

H Reference the Text

8. The word *these* in the reading refers to _____ .
    - (A) Watson and Bell
    - (B) the memorable words
    - (C) "Watson come here. I want you."
    - (D) March 19, 1876

Writing: Write an Expository Paragraph

Write a paragraph about gifts.

STEP 1   Work with a partner. Ask questions like these about a person your partner sends cards and gifts to. Write the answers to the questions.

1. Who is a person you always send a card or give a gift to?

2. On what occasion (birthday, Valentine's Day, New Year's Day, other holiday) do you send a card?

3. What kind of card do you usually send this person (funny card, card with flowers, other card)? What do you say in the card?

4. What kind of gifts do you get for this person? How much money or time do you spend on a gift? Do you like to buy gifts for this person, or is it difficult to buy a gift? Why?

5. Does this person also send you a card and buy you gifts?

6. Do you like your cards and gifts? Do you keep them?

STEP 2   Rewrite your partner's answers in paragraph form. Be sure to use possessive pronouns correctly.

STEP 3   Write a title in three to five words, for example, "My Friend's Cards and Gifts."

STEP 4   Evaluate your paragraph.

Checklist

_____ Did you indent the first line?
_____ Did you give your paragraph a title?
_____ Did you use capital letters correctly?
_____ Did you use verb forms correctly?

STEP 5   Work with your partner to edit your paragraph. Correct spelling, punctuation, vocabulary, and grammar.

STEP 6   Write your final copy.

Self-Test

A Choose the best answer, A, B, C, or D, to complete the sentence. Darken the oval with the same letter.

1. Mr. Cotton sold _____ .

   A. Tim it   Ⓐ Ⓑ Ⓒ Ⓓ
   B. to Tim it
   C. for Tim it
   D. it to Tim

2. Ken introduced _____ .

   A. me his friend   Ⓐ Ⓑ Ⓒ Ⓓ
   B. me to his friend
   C. his friend me
   D. for me his friend

3. The teacher explained _____ .

   A. me the question   Ⓐ Ⓑ Ⓒ Ⓓ
   B. for me the question
   C. the question to me
   D. the question me

4. We sent _____ .

   A. to Jim a letter   Ⓐ Ⓑ Ⓒ Ⓓ
   B. for Jim a letter
   C. a letter Jim
   D. a letter to Jim

5. I didn't _____ yesterday. I just watched television.

   A. do anything   Ⓐ Ⓑ Ⓒ Ⓓ
   B. do nothing
   C. do something
   D. anything do

6. John gave _____ .

   A. the check me   Ⓐ Ⓑ Ⓒ Ⓓ
   B. for me the check
   C. to me the check
   D. me the check

7. Will you please _____ ?

   A. lend to me it   Ⓐ Ⓑ Ⓒ Ⓓ
   B. lend for me it
   C. lend me it
   D. lend it to me

8. The students handed _____ .

   A. their papers to the teacher   Ⓐ Ⓑ Ⓒ Ⓓ
   B. their papers the teacher
   C. to the teacher their papers
   D. for the teacher their papers

9. My friend fixed _____ .

   A. for me my car   Ⓐ Ⓑ Ⓒ Ⓓ
   B. my car to me
   C. my car for me
   D. to me my car

10. We prepared _____ .

    A. dinner to our friends   Ⓐ Ⓑ Ⓒ Ⓓ
    B. dinner for our friends
    C. to our friends dinner
    D. dinner for ours friends

1. Most people send <u>birthday cards</u> <u>for</u> <u>their</u>
                     A   **B**   **C**

   <u>friends and relatives</u>.
         D

   Ⓐ   Ⓑ   Ⓒ   Ⓓ

2. The Chinese <u>have</u> <u>theirs</u> New Year <u>in</u> January
              A   **B**   **C**

   <u>or</u> February.
   D

   Ⓐ   Ⓑ   Ⓒ   Ⓓ

3. In Antarctica, there <u>isn't</u> <u>something</u> <u>for</u> the
                     A   **B**   **C**

   penguins to make <u>their</u> nests with.
                  D

   Ⓐ   Ⓑ   Ⓒ   Ⓓ

4. <u>Doctors</u> tell <u>ours</u> <u>what</u> to do when we <u>get sick</u>.
     A   **B**   **C**   **D**

   Ⓐ   Ⓑ   Ⓒ   Ⓓ

5. <u>Do</u> you <u>know</u> <u>anyone</u> about Mexican <u>customs</u>?
    A   **B**   **C**   **D**

   Ⓐ   Ⓑ   Ⓒ   Ⓓ

6. Plants make <u>theirs</u> <u>food</u> from simple things like
                A   **B**

   <u>air</u> and <u>water</u>.
   C   **D**

   Ⓐ   Ⓑ   Ⓒ   Ⓓ

7. <u>A baby chimpanzee</u> will travel some of the time
     A

   on <u>it</u> mother's back until <u>it</u> is about five <u>years</u> old.
      B   **C**   **D**

   Ⓐ   Ⓑ   Ⓒ   Ⓓ

8. The brain <u>needs</u> <u>a lot of</u> <u>energy</u> to do <u>it</u> work.
            A   **B**   **C**   **D**

   Ⓐ   Ⓑ   Ⓒ   Ⓓ

9. <u>Will you</u> <u>please</u> explain <u>me</u> <u>the reason</u>?
    A   **B**   **C**   **D**

   Ⓐ   Ⓑ   Ⓒ   Ⓓ

10. Most supermarkets <u>give</u> <u>theirs</u> customers free
                     A   **B**

    grocery bags <u>for</u> <u>their</u> purchases.
              C **D**

    Ⓐ   Ⓑ   Ⓒ   Ⓓ

Unit 11
Modals

In Japan you **should** bow when you greet someone.

11A | *Can*

Form

Bears **can** climb trees.
Bears **can't** fly.

Affirmative and Negative Statements

Subject	Can	Base Verb	
I		ski.	
You		swim.	
He/She/It	**can** **cannot** **can't**	speak	French.
		cook	rice.
		drive	a car.
We		climb	trees.
They		sleep.	

Function

We use *can* to talk about ability in the present.

I come from Italy. I **can** speak Italian, but I **can't** speak Japanese.
Yuko comes from Japan. She **can't** speak Italian, but she **can** speak Japanese.
Ted **can** play the piano, but he **can't** play the guitar.

1 Practice

What do you know about animals? Look at the chart and write affirmative sentences and negative sentences about animals.

Animal		Verb
Animal		**Verb**
elephants		fly
birds		swim
chickens		make honey
bees	can/can't	climb trees
horses		sing
penguins		run
monkeys		see at night
dogs		lie down

Affirmative	**Negative**
1. *Elephants can swim* .	1. *Elephants can't fly* .
2. _____ .	2. _____ .
3. _____ .	3. _____ .
4. _____ .	4. _____ .
5. _____ .	5. _____ .
6. _____ .	6. _____ .
7. _____ .	7. _____ .
8. _____ .	8. _____ .

2 Your Turn

Work with a partner. Talk about things you can or can't do. Use these words and phrases or your own.

Example

I can write with my left hand.

cook pasta	ride a bicycle	sing	stand on my head
dance	run three miles	ski	type fast
paint pictures	see without glasses	speak Gaelic	write with both hands

Questions with *Can*

Form

Can they see us?
No, they **can't**.

Yes/No Questions			Short Answers
Can	**Subject**	**Base Verb**	
Can	you	**speak** English?	Yes, I/we **can**.
	he	**dance** the tango?	No, he **can't**.
	we	**go** outside?	Yes, you **can**.
	they	**see** us?	No, they **can't**.

Wh- Questions				
Wh- Word	**Can**	**Subject**	**Base Verb**	
Where		I	**buy**	this book?
When	can	you	**come?**	
What		she	**do?**	

Function

We use *can* in questions to ask about ability.

Can you study with me tomorrow?
When **can** you come to the library?

3 Practice

A Read the advertisement.

DAY CARE PROVIDER needed for 2 children, 4 and 7 years old.
Requirements: Drive, cook meals, tell stories, read music,
swim, draw, and have a lot of energy. Excellent pay.
Please call Monica 743-8995.

B Monica is talking to a job applicant. Complete her questions with *can* or other question forms.

1. ___*How old are*___ you?
2. _____ drive?
3. _____ meals?
4. _____ music?

5. _____ swim?
6. _____ stories?
7. _____ a lot of energy?
8. What other things _____ do?

4 Pair Up and Talk

A Practice the conversation with a partner.

A: Can you use a computer?
B: Yes, I can.   OR   No, I can't.

B Now practice the conversation with your partner again. Use these phrases or your own.

draw or paint	play a musical instrument	use a computer
drive a car	play chess	what/kind of food/cook
how many/languages/speak	ride a horse/a bicycle/a motorcycle	what/sports/play

Form

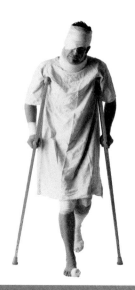

After the accident last week, he **couldn't see**, and he **couldn't walk**. He **could talk**.

Affirmative and Negative Statements

Subject	Could (Not)	Base Verb	
I		**come**	to class today.
You		**do**	the homework.
He/She	could could not couldn't	**find**	the store.
We			
They		**go**	to the concert.

Yes/No Questions / Short Answers

				Short Answers
	I	**run**	fast?	Yes, you **could**.
	you	**ride**	a bicycle?	Yes, I/we **could**.
Could	she/he	**finish**	the test?	No, she/he **couldn't**.
	we	**eat**	the food?	No, you/they **couldn't**.
	they	**play**	tennis?	Yes, they **could**.

Function

Could is the past form of *can*. We use *could* or *could not (couldn't)* to talk about ability in the past.

I **could** ride a bicycle when I was five.
I **couldn't** read.
Could you **read** when you were six?

5 Practice

A   Mary is 25 years old now. What couldn't she do when she was two years old that she can do now? Write sentences with these words and phrases.

1.   ride a bicycle *She couldn't ride a bicycle* .

2.   run fast _____ .

3.   drive a car _____ .

4.   ski _____ .

5.   take tests _____ .

6.   work _____ .

7.   write a letter _____ .

8.   read a book _____ .

B   Listen and check your answers. Then listen again and repeat each sentence.

DOWNLOAD
CD5, 18, 19

6 Your Turn

Write four things you couldn't do before that you can do now.

Example
Five years ago, I couldn't swim, but I can swim well now .

1.   _____ .

2.   _____ .

3.   _____ .

4.   _____ .

7 Practice

A Andy was at home last month with a broken leg. What could he do? What couldn't he do? Write sentences about Andy with these words and phrases.

1. go to school *He couldn't go to school* .
2. drive _____ .
3. play tennis _____ .
4. read magazines _____ .
5. swim _____ .
6. visit friends _____ .
7. watch TV _____ .
8. work online _____ .

B Listen and check your answers. Then listen again and repeat each sentence.

AUDIO
DOWNLOAD
CD5, 20, 21

8 Pair Up and Talk

A What could you do when you were six years old? Practice the conversation with a partner.

A: Could you play the piano?
B: Yes, I could. OR No, I couldn't.

B Now practice the conversation with your partner again. Use these words and phrases or your own.

brush your teeth	make a sandwich	ride a horse	tell the time
climb trees	paint pictures	sing	use a computer
count to a hundred	read	swim	use the telephone
eat with chopsticks	ride a bicycle	take photographs	write

11D | *Be Able To*

Form

Hercules Lewis is very strong. He **is able to** lift three people at the same time.

Present				Past			
Subject	Form of *Be*	*Able To*	Base Verb	Subject	Form of *Be*	*Able To*	Base Verb
I	am			I	was		
You	are			You	were		
He She It	is	able to	go.	He She It	was	able to	go.
We They	are			We They	were		

Future			
Subject	Form of *Be*	*Able To*	Base Verb
I You He She It We They	will be	able to	go.

Function

We can use *be able to* in place of *can* or *could* for ability in the present, future, and past.

Past

He **wasn't able to finish** the test yesterday.   OR   He **couldn't finish** the test yesterday.

Present

She **is able to run** five miles (8 kilometers).   OR   She **can run** five miles.*

Future

I'll **be able to go out** tomorrow.   OR   I **can go out** tomorrow.

Can is more common than *be able to* in the simple present.

9 Practice

A Read about Mozart.

Mozart was born in Austria in 1756. His father was a musician. At age three, he <u>could play</u> the piano. After he heard a piece of music one time, Mozart <u>could play</u> it. People <u>couldn't believe</u> it! At age five, he <u>could write</u> music for the piano. Soon his father <u>couldn't teach</u> him because little Mozart knew everything. At 12, he was famous and <u>could make</u> money for his family.

Mozart worked long hours and <u>could work</u> very fast. He <u>could write</u> an opera in just a few weeks. He <u>could work</u> better at night because it was quiet. He <u>could write</u> all kinds of music, even music for clocks. In all, he wrote over 600 pieces of music.

Mozart died at age 35. We still <u>cannot understand</u> why he died. Today, we still listen to Mozart at concerts. We <u>can buy</u> his music on tapes or CDs. Believe it or not, Mozart is still the world's best-selling composer!

B Change the underlined forms of *can/could* to forms of *be able to*. Write the new sentences on the lines.

1. <u>At age three, he was able to play the piano</u> .
2. _____ .
3. _____ .
4. _____ .
5. _____ .
6. _____ .
7. _____ .
8. _____ .
9. _____ .
10. _____ .
11. _____ .
12. _____ .

C Listen and check your answers. Then listen again and repeat each sentence.

 CD5, 22, 23

10 Practice

This is Tommy. He is nine years old now. Complete the sentences to say what he can do now, what he could do when he was a baby, and what he will be able to do when he is 16.

Baby	Now (age 9)	Age 16
cry	play football	dance
eat	ride a bike	drive a car
sleep	run	get a part-time job
smile	use a computer	sing in a group

Modals **305**

1. When he was a baby, _____ *he could cry* _____ .

2. Now, _____ *he can ride a bike* _____ .

3. When he is 16, _____ *he will be able to dance* _____ .

4. When he was a baby, _____ .

5. Now, _____ .

6. When he is 16, _____ .

7. When he was a baby, _____ .

8. Now, _____ .

9. When he is 16, _____ .

10. When he was a baby, _____ .

11. Now, _____ .

12. When he is 16, _____ .

11 Pair Up and Talk

A Practice the conversation with a partner.

A: What will you be able to do in the future?

B: I will be able to talk to people on the telephone in English.

B Now practice the conversation with your partner again. Use these words and phrases or your own.

pass all my tests

read English newspapers

talk to people on the telephone in English

travel in an English-speaking country

understand English grammar

watch movies in English

Form

In Japan, you **should** bow when you greet someone.

Affirmative and Negative Statements

Subject	*Should*	Base Verb
I You He/She/It We They	**should** **should not** **shouldn't**	go.

Yes/No Questions

Should	Subject	Base Verb	Short Answers
Should	I	go?	Yes, you **should**.
	you		No, I/we **shouldn't**.
	he/she/it		Yes, he/she/it **should**.
	we		No, you/they **shouldn't**.
	they		

Function

1. We use *should* to give advice. *Should* means it's a good idea to do something.

   Dick is very sick. He **should see** a doctor.

   It's 3:00 in the morning, and Nancy is still working. She **should go** to bed.

2. We use *shouldn't (should not)* when it's a bad idea to do something.

   You **shouldn't drive** in the storm. It's dangerous.

   Jimmy **shouldn't eat** the whole cake. He'll get sick.

12 Practice

Jim is going to Asia. Give him advice. Complete the sentences with *should* or *shouldn't*.

1. You _____*shouldn't*_____ speak fast. People may not understand you.

2. If you don't know what to do, you _____ ask someone.

3. You _____ blow your nose in front of other people at a meeting.

4. You _____ always be on time.

5. You _____ greet older people first.

6. You _____ use your hands too much when you speak. A hand sign may have a different meaning there.

7. You _____ take off your shoes before you go into someone's house.

8. You _____ leave your passport in your hotel room.

13 Practice

A Nick is a teenager. Say what Nick should or shouldn't do.

1. He skips school. *He shouldn't skip school* .

2. He comes home late. _____ .

3. He doesn't do his homework. _____ .

4. He doesn't listen to his parents. _____ .

5. He doesn't listen in class. _____ .

6. He doesn't clean up his room. _____ .

7. He always asks his parents for money.

   _____ .

8. He's not nice to his brother and sister.

   _____ .

CD5, 24, 25

B   **Listen and check your answers. Then listen again and repeat each sentence.**

AUDIO
DOWNLOAD

14   Practice
Give advice for these situations.

1. Ted has a very bad cold, and he is at work.

   He should go to bed .

2. You and your friend have a test tomorrow. You want to watch a long movie on television.

   _____ .

3. Tina goes to bed late and gets up late. She's often late for work.

   _____ .

4. When it's cold outside, Joe wears a T-shirt.

   _____ .

5. The coffee in the restaurant is cold. You cannot see the waiter.

   _____ .

6. Ken is overweight and has health problems because of his weight. He drives everywhere. He even drives to the corner store to get his cigarettes.

   _____ .

11F | *Must*

Form

You **must not** talk in class.

Affirmative and Negative Statements

Subject	Must (Not)	Base Verb	
I			
You			
He/She/It	**must** **must not**	**talk**	**in class.**
We			
They			

Note: Questions with *must* are formal and not very common. In American English, we usually use *have to* for questions.

What **do** I **have to** do?

Function

1. We use *must* to say that something is very important or necessary. We often use *must* for rules or strong advice. We use *must not* when something is against the law or rules or isn't right.

   I **must** go to the bank. I have no more money. (It's a necessity; there is no other choice.)

   You **must not** park there. (It is against the law or rules.)

2. *Must* is stronger than *should*. When we use *must*, we have no choice. When we use *should*, we have a choice.

   I **should** go to the bank. (It's a good idea, but not necessary.)

   You **shouldn't** park here. (It's not a good idea, but you can if you want.)

15 Practice

A Complete these class rules with *must* or *must not*.

1. _____You must_____ be quiet when someone else is speaking.
2. _____ listen to the teacher.
3. _____ arrive to class on time.
4. _____ eat in class.
5. _____ use a telephone in class.
6. _____ answer the teacher's questions.
7. _____ go to sleep.
8. _____ attend class every day.
9. _____ bring your books to class.
10. _____ do your homework.
11. _____ cheat or copy on a test.
12. _____ write letters to friends in class.

B Listen and check your answers. Then listen again and repeat each sentence.

AUDIO
DOWNLOAD
CD5, 26, 27

C Listen again. The teacher was angry at Jane today for breaking some of the class rules. Check all the things that Jane did wrong.

AUDIO
DOWNLOAD
CD5, 28

___ Jane came to class on time.   ___ She had all her books.

___ She wrote a note to Anita.   ___ She turned in her homework.

___ She ate potato chips.   ___ She couldn't stay awake.

Form

Bill **has to get up** at 5:00 A.M. to work in the garden.
Ken **doesn't have to get up** at 5:00 A.M., but he **has to wear** a suit to work.

Bill   Ken

Present Affirmative Statements			Present Negative Statements			
Subject	*Have To*	**Base Verb**	**Subject**	*Do/Does Not*	*Have To*	**Base Verb**
I You	**have to**		I You	**do not** **don't**		
He She It	**has to**	work.	He She It	**does not** **doesn't**	**have to**	work.
We They	**have to**		We They	**do not** **don't**		

Present Yes/No Questions				Present Short Answers
Do/Does	**Subject**	*Have To*	**Base Verb**	
Do	I you			Yes, you **do**. No, I/we **don't**.
Does	he/she/it	**have to**	work?	Yes, he/she/it **does**.
Do	we they			Yes, you **do**. No, they **don't**.

Past Affirmative Statements			Past Negative Statements			
Subject	*Had To*	**Base Verb**	**Subject**	*Did Not*	*Have To*	**Base Verb**
I You He She It We They	**had to**	work.	I You He She It We They	**did not didn't**	**have to**	work.

Past *Yes/No* Questions				Past Short Answers
Did	**Subject**	*Have To*	**Base Verb**	
Did	I you he/she/it we they	**have to**	work?	Yes, you **did**. No, I/we **didn't**. Yes, he/she/it **did**. Yes, you **did**. No, they **didn't**.

Function

1. We use *have to* for something that is necessary. *Have to* is not as strong as *must*. *Have to* means the same as *need to*:

   We **have to study** for the test. OR We **need to study** for the test.

   Joe **has to wear** a suit for his new job. OR Joe **needs to wear** a suit for his new job.

2. We use *don't have to* and *didn't have to* for the negative. *Don't/doesn't/didn't have to* means that something is not or was not necessary. There is a choice.

   Tomorrow is Saturday. We **don't have to** study tonight.

   Tim **didn't have to** wait at the airport yesterday.

3. We use *do/does ... have to ... ?* and *did ... have to ... ?* to ask if something is necessary.

   Do we **have to go** to school tomorrow?   Yes, you **do**.

   Did you **have to work** late yesterday?   No, I **didn't**.

16 Practice

What do you have to do in your English class? Make sentences with *have to* or *don't have to*.

1. _____We have to_____ learn grammar rules.
2. _____ write compositions.
3. _____ learn vocabulary.
4. _____ answer questions in English.
5. _____ read newspapers.
6. _____ sing songs.
7. _____ take tests.
8. _____ complete exercises.
9. _____ give speeches in English.
10. _____ dance.

17 Pair Up and Talk

A Practice the conversation with a partner.

A: Does a TV journalist have to have a degree?

B: No, he/she doesn't.

B Now practice the conversation with your partner again. Use these words and phrases or your own.

Qualities	TV Journalist	Fashion Model	Doctor
have a degree			x
be a good speaker	x		
be attractive		x	
be scientific			x

Complete the sentences with *must not* or *don't have to*.

1. You ___*don't have to*___ wash it by hand. You can wash it in a washing machine.

2. You _____ park here between 9:00 A.M. and 12:00 P.M. That is when the city cleans the street.

3. You _____ buy tickets at the box office. You can buy them online.

4. You _____ smoke in this restaurant. It is against the law.

5. You _____ turn onto this street. Traffic is going one-way in the opposite direction.

6. You _____ pay for children under the age of five. They get in free.

7. You _____ rollerblade on the sidewalk. It is against park regulations.

8. You _____ pay with cash. You can use a credit card.

19 Practice

A **This is Gloria Glamour. She was a famous movie star. She was also a millionaire. Complete the sentences with *had to* or *didn't have to*.**

1. She ___*had to*___ wear makeup.

2. She _____ drive her car. She had a chauffeur.

3. She _____ wait for the bus.

4. She _____ meet important people.

5. She _____ clean her house. She paid someone to clean it for her.

6. She _____ act in movies.

7. She _____ sing and dance.

8. She _____ look beautiful.

B   What do you think? What other things did Gloria have to do? Work with a partner. Make sentences about Gloria.

20   Pair Up and Talk

A   Work with a partner. Tell your partner five things you had to do as a child Tell your partner five things you didn't have to do as a child.

I had to go to bed at 8:00 P.M.

I didn't have to cook dinner.

B   Now write five sentences about what your partner had to do and didn't have to do as a child.

1. *Suzanne had to clean her room, but she didn't have to wash dishes.* .

2. _____ .

3. _____ .

4. _____ .

5. _____ .

6. _____ .

Form

TELLER: **May** I see your driver's license or a piece of identification?

WOMAN: Yes, of course. Here it is.

TELLER: Thanks.

Questions				Short Answers	
May/Can/Could	I	Base Verb		Affirmative	Negative
May Can Could	I	see	your license?	Of course. Certainly. Sure.* OK.* No problem.*	I'm sorry, no.
May Can Could	I	help	you?	Yes, please.	No, thanks.

*Use these expressions with friends or family members.

Function

HOTEL CLERK: **May** I help you?

GUEST: **Could I** have the key to Room 17, please?

1. We use *may I*, *can I*, and *could I* to ask for permission. We also use these expressions to offer to help someone else.

2. *May I*, *can I*, and *could I* have the same meaning, but *may I* is the most polite or formal. *Could I* is more polite than *can I*. *Could I* is appropriate in almost all situations.

21 Practice
Complete the conversations with *may I*, *can I*, or *could I*.

1. STUDENT: _____*May I*_____ go home early?

   TEACHER: No, you may not.

2. STUDENT: _____ borrow your dictionary?

   CLASSMATE: Sure.

3. BROTHER: _____ use your phone?

   SISTER: No, you can't.

4. CUSTOMER: _____ have another glass of water?

   WAITER: Certainly, sir.

5. EMPLOYEE: _____ ask a question, sir?

   DIRECTOR OF COMPANY: Yes, of course.

6. POLICE OFFICER: _____ see your driver's license?

   DRIVER: Yes. Here it is.

22 Pair Up and Talk

Work with a partner. Ask and answer questions with *may I*, *can I*, and *could I* for these situations.

You are a teenager. You want to go to a party tonight. Ask a parent.

TEENAGER: Can I go to a party tonight please, Dad?

FATHER: OK, you can go, but be back at 11:00.

1. You're an attendant at the theater. You want to see a person's ticket.

2. You are a customer in a restaurant. You do not have a fork to eat with. Ask the server.

3. You work in an office. You want to speak to your boss for a moment. Ask your boss.

4. Your teacher is carrying a lot of books. Ask if you can help.

5. Your friend is having trouble with her computer. You can fix it. Ask her.

6. You want to take next Monday off from school to go to the doctor. Ask your teacher.

7. You want to watch a movie on television tonight at 9:00. There is only one television in the house. Your sister is the only person who watches it. Ask your sister.

8. You are in a cafeteria with a tray of food. There is only one empty seat at a table, but there is someone sitting at the table. Ask if you can sit there.

9. Your roommate is coming home from the grocery store. She can't carry all of the bags. Ask if you can help with the bags.

10. You are working at the airport. You need to see a passenger's passport and airline ticket. Ask the passenger.

11. You are a waiter in a restaurant. You want to take the customer's order. Ask the customer.

12. You want to apply for a job in a music store. Ask for the manager.

23   Read
Read the story. Then write answers to the questions.

THE SMUGGLER

A clever smuggler brought a donkey to the border. The donkey's back was full of straw. The official at the border was suspicious and took all the straw down from the donkey's back. He searched it, but he couldn't find anything. "I'm sure you are smuggling something," the official said as the man crossed the border, "but I have to let you cross the border."

Each day for ten years the man came to the border with a donkey. The official searched and searched the straw on the donkey's back, but he could never find anything.

Many years later, after the official retired, he met the smuggler in a market and said, "Please, can you tell me what you were smuggling?"

"Donkeys," said the man.

1. What did the smuggler bring to the border?

_____ .

2. What was the official able to find after he took all the straw down?

_____ .

3. What did the official have to let the man do?

_____ .

4. What was the official able to find over ten years?

_____ .

5. What did the official want to know?

_____ .

6. What was the smuggler able to smuggle?

_____ .

Listening Puzzle

AUDIO DOWNLOAD   CD5, 29

A Listen and check the correct answer.

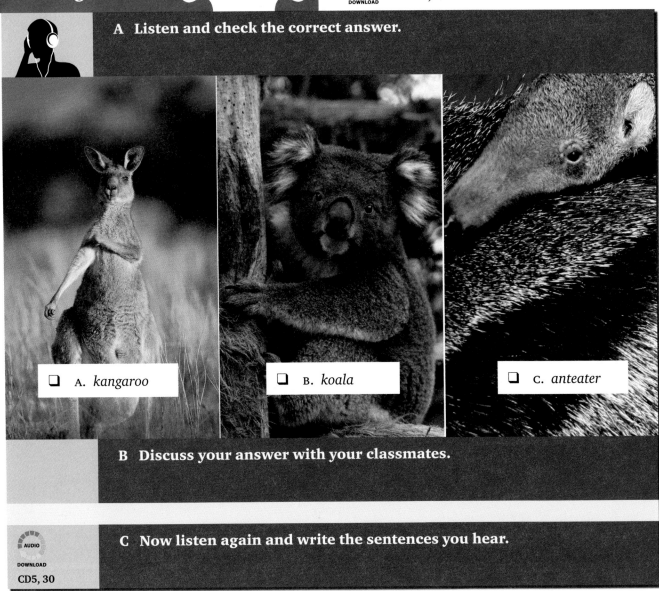

❑ A. *kangaroo*

❑ B. *koala*

❑ C. *anteater*

B Discuss your answer with your classmates.

AUDIO DOWNLOAD CD5, 30

C Now listen again and write the sentences you hear.

A Before You Read
Answer the questions.

1. What kinds of weather are dangerous?
2. What do tornadoes do?

B Read

TORNADOES

A tornado is a twisting storm. It's in the shape of a funnel, wide at the top and narrow at the bottom. The winds inside a tornado can

5 reach speeds of 300 miles (483 kilometers) an hour. These are the strongest winds in the world. Tornadoes can come from any direction.
They usually move in a
10 northeastern direction, but there's no guarantee. Tornadoes or twisters usually last about ten minutes.

The path of a tornado is narrow, but **it** is
15 very destructive. Can a tornado lift a house off the ground? Yes, it can. Tornadoes are like vacuum cleaners. They can suck up anything from farm animals to people and cars. They can
20 lift houses completely off the ground, and they can kill people, too.

Tornadoes can **occur** anywhere in the world, but about 800 of them pass through the U.S. That's more than any other country. If you live
25 in the state of Nebraska, Kansas, Oklahoma, Texas, or South Dakota, you'll know you're in Tornado Alley.

If you live in Tornado Alley, you have to be careful from late March to late June. If the sky
30 turns black, and it starts to rain heavily, run for the storm cellar[1] and hope for the best.

[1] storm cellar = a shelter under the ground to protect you from tornadoes

DID YOU KNOW … ?
Storm chasers get very close to tornadoes to take photos and do research. For them, it is exciting!

C Notice the Grammar
Underline all forms of modals.

When you come to a word you don't know, try to guess the meaning. Use clues from the words and sentences around it.

Choose the best answer.

D Look for Main Ideas

1. What is paragraph 2 mainly about?
   - (A) how tornadoes lift houses
   - (B) how a tornado is destructive
   - (C) how tornadoes lift up animals
   - (D) how a tornado moves

2. What is the main idea of paragraph 3?
   - (A) where tornadoes occur
   - (B) why tornadoes occur in the United States
   - (C) why Tornado Alley is dangerous
   - (D) how tornadoes occur in Tornado Alley

E Look for Details

3. The winds inside a tornado _____ .
   - (A) can come from any direction
   - (B) are like funnels
   - (C) are the strongest winds in the world
   - (D) move in a northeasterly direction

4. Tornado Alley _____ .
   - (A) is between Nebraska and Texas
   - (B) is where all tornadoes occur
   - (C) is dangerous from March to June
   - (D) has the most tornadoes in the world

5. Which of the following is NOT true about tornadoes?
   - (A) Tornadoes usually last ten minutes.
   - (B) Tornadoes can come from any direction.
   - (C) Tornadoes never kill people.
   - (D) Tornadoes can happen anywhere in the world.

F Make Inferences

6. We can infer from the reading that _____ .
   - (A) tornadoes occur every year in Tornado Alley
   - (B) tornadoes always kill people
   - (C) other countries get more tornadoes than the United States.
   - (D) tornadoes do not destroy anything

G Look for Vocabulary

7. The word *occur* in the reading is closest in meaning to _____ .
   - (A) move
   - (B) destroy
   - (C) show
   - (D) happen

H Reference the Text

8. The word *it* in the reading refers to _____ .
   - (A) narrow
   - (B) the path
   - (C) the tornado
   - (D) destructive

Writing: Write a Letter of Advice

Write a letter offering advice.

STEP 1

Read the situation and tell what your friend *should/shouldn't do, must/must not do,* and *has/doesn't have to do.*

A friend is coming to your country. The friend is going to dinner at an important person's house. Your friend writes you a letter and asks for your advice. Write six sentences.

1. take flowers/gift _____ .
2. wear nice/clean clothes _____ .
3. take shoes/coat off _____ .
4. be late/early arriving _____ .
5. bring a friend _____ .
6. say the food is good/bad _____ .

STEP 2

Rewrite your sentences as part of the letter below. Use a variety of modals.

May 1, 20XX

Dear Anita,

I'm so happy that you are coming for a visit. It's exciting that you are going to have dinner with the mayor of our city. You should ...

STEP 3

Evaluate your paragraph.
Checklist

_____ Did you use verb forms correctly?
_____ Did you give all the important information that your friend will need?
_____ Did you use modals correctly?

STEP 4

Work with a partner to edit your letter. Correct spelling, punctuation, vocabulary, and grammar.

STEP 5

Write your final copy.

Self-Test

1. When you were two years old, you _____ ride a bicycle.

   A. couldn't   Ⓐ Ⓑ Ⓒ Ⓓ
   B. can't
   C. must not
   D. have to

2. _____ answer the door, please?

   A. May you   Ⓐ Ⓑ Ⓒ Ⓓ
   B. Could you
   C. Have I
   D. You could

3. _____ to go there?

   A. Have we to   Ⓐ Ⓑ Ⓒ Ⓓ
   B. Had we
   C. Do we
   D. Do we have

4. He _____ to his parents.

   A. should listens   Ⓐ Ⓑ Ⓒ Ⓓ
   B. should listen
   C. have to listen
   D. must to listen

5. You _____ eat in class. Eat outside!

   A. haven't to   Ⓐ Ⓑ Ⓒ Ⓓ
   B. must not to
   C. mustn't
   D. don't have

6. You _____ ask for directions. I know how to get there.

   A. don't have to   Ⓐ Ⓑ Ⓒ Ⓓ
   B. must not
   C. should to
   D. do not have

7. Kathy _____ speak Japanese.

   A. is able   Ⓐ Ⓑ Ⓒ Ⓓ
   B. able to
   C. is able to
   D. can able to

8. I _____ to study tonight. There's no school tomorrow.

   A. haven't   Ⓐ Ⓑ Ⓒ Ⓓ
   B. don't have
   C. don't has
   D. must not

9. You _____ lose this key. This is the only one.

   A. haven't to   Ⓐ Ⓑ Ⓒ Ⓓ
   B. don't have
   C. don't has
   D. must not

10. I _____ study hard for my test yesterday.

   A. have to   Ⓐ Ⓑ Ⓒ Ⓓ
   B. had to
   C. must to
   D. should

1. We <u>able to</u> <u>go</u> <u>for</u> a vacation on the moon
      A   **B**   **C**
   <u>in the future</u>.
      D

   Ⓐ Ⓑ Ⓒ Ⓓ

2. You <u>must to</u> <u>use</u> a black <u>or</u> blue pen for the test.
        A   **B**   **C**
   You cannot <u>use</u> a pencil.
                  D

   Ⓐ Ⓑ Ⓒ Ⓓ

3. A camel <u>is able</u> live without <u>any</u> <u>water</u> for about
            A   **B** **C**
   <u>five days</u>.
      D

   Ⓐ Ⓑ Ⓒ Ⓓ

4. You must <u>have to</u> <u>a passport</u> to travel to
              A   **B**
   <u>another</u> <u>country</u>.
      C   **D**

   Ⓐ Ⓑ Ⓒ Ⓓ

5. The ostrich is <u>not able</u> to fly, <u>but</u> <u>it</u> can
                    A   **B** **C**
   <u>to run</u> fast.
      D

   Ⓐ Ⓑ Ⓒ Ⓓ

6. <u>Do</u> students <u>has to</u> wear <u>uniforms</u> in high
      A   **B**   **C**
   schools <u>in Japan</u>?
              D

   Ⓐ Ⓑ Ⓒ Ⓓ

7. You <u>can</u> live for a few days without <u>food</u>, but
        A   **B**
   you <u>mustn't</u> live without <u>air</u> for more than a
         C   **D**
   few minutes.

   Ⓐ Ⓑ Ⓒ Ⓓ

8. Mozart <u>was able</u> to work very fast, and <u>be able</u>
            A   **B**
   to write <u>an opera</u> in just a few <u>weeks</u>.
               C   **D**

   Ⓐ Ⓑ Ⓒ Ⓓ

9. <u>Penguins</u> <u>cannot</u> fly, but <u>they</u> <u>could</u> swim.
      A   **B**   **C**   **D**

   Ⓐ Ⓑ Ⓒ Ⓓ

10. "Walk in, no appointment necessary" <u>means</u>
                                            A
    you <u>haven't to</u> make <u>an</u> <u>appointment</u>.
          B   **C**   **D**

   Ⓐ Ⓑ Ⓒ Ⓓ

Unit 12

Special Expressions

Could you please look at this report again?

Form

BOY: Mom, I'm hungry.
MOTHER: OK, **let's** go home.

Let's	(Not)	Base Verb
Let's	(not)	wait. sit down. go. eat.

Let's is a contraction of *let + us*. We usually say and write *let's*.

Function

We use *let's* to make a suggestion for two or more people including the speaker.

It's cold. **Let's** close the window.
It's 12:30. **Let's** go to lunch.
Mother's birthday is next week. **Let's** not forget.

1 Practice
Respond to the statements with *let's* or *let's not* and one of these expressions.

clean up the apartment	make sandwiches	turn on the stereo
go to the beach	open the window	watch television

1. It's cold. We can't swim today.

   Let's not go to the beach   .

2. There's a football game on TV in half an hour.

   Great, _____ .

3. I'm hungry. There's some bread and cheese.

   _____ .

4. It's hot in here.

   _____ .

5. Our neighbors complained about the music last night.

   _____ .

6. Oh, no! My parents are coming.

   Quick! _____ .

2 Pair Up and Talk
A Practice the conversation with a partner.

A: Class starts in a few minutes.

B: Let's not be late.

B Now practice the conversation with your partner again. Take turns and give responses with *let's* or *let's not*. Use these phrases or your own.

beautiful day	next Monday/holiday	test tomorrow
birthday/next week	ten minutes before class	what/want to do/weekend

Form

WAITER: **Would you like** some cheese on your pasta?

MAN: No, thank you.

Statements

Subject	Would Like	Object
I You He She We They	**would like 'd like**	a cup of tea.

Yes/No Questions				Short Answers	
Would	**Subject**	*Like*	**Object**		
Would	you he/she they	**like**	a cup of tea?	Yes, I/we **would**. he/she **would**. they **would**.	No, I/we **wouldn't**. he/she **wouldn't**. they **wouldn't**.

When a verb follows *would like*, we use the base form of the verb with *to*.

I'd like to go to Italy.
Would you like to come?

Note: We rarely use *Would I like* … ? or *Would we like* … ?

Function

1. We use *would like* in place of *want*. *Would like* is more polite.

   I **want** a glass of water.   OR   I **would like** a glass of water. (polite)

2. *Would like* does not have the same meaning as *like*. Compare these sentences.

   I **would like** to go to the movies.   =   I want to go to the movies.

   I **like** to go to the movies.   =   I enjoy going to the movies.

3 Practice

A Complete the conversation with *would like*.

1. WAITER: _Would you like_ a salad with your pasta?

   MR. LU: No, thanks.

2. WAITER: _____ a bottle of mineral water?

   MR. LU: _____ two glasses of regular water, please.

3. WAITER: _____ some dessert?

   MR. LU: _____ the apple pie. My friend _____ ice cream.

4. WAITER: _____ some coffee?

   MR. LU: Yes, please. We both _____ coffee.

5. WAITER: _____ espresso, cappuccino, or regular coffee?

   MR. LU: Two espressos, please, and we _____ the check.

6. WAITER: _____ separate checks or one check?

   MR. LU: We _____ one check, please.

B Listen and check your answers. Then work with a partner. Listen again and repeat the conversation.

AUDIO
DOWNLOAD
CD5, 31, 32

C Listen again. Read the statements and circle *True* or *False*.

AUDIO

DOWNLOAD

CD5, 33

1. Mr. Lu ordered mineral water.   True   False
2. Mr. Lu's friend ate apple pie.   True   False
3. Mr. Lu and his friend paid for their own dinners. True   False

4 Practice

Write answers to these questions. Use either *Yes/No, I would/wouldn't* or *Yes/No, I do/don't.*

1. Do you like to dance?

    Yes, I do _____ .

2. Would you like to go dancing on Saturday?

    _____ .

3. Do you like ice cream?

    _____ .

4. Would you like to have ice cream after class?

    _____ .

5. Do you like coffee?

    _____ .

6. Would you like to have some coffee after class?

    _____ .

7. Do you like pizza?

    _____ .

8. Would you like to have pizza tonight?

    _____ .

9. Do you like to read?

    _____ .

10. Would you like more homework?

    _____ .

5 Pair Up and Talk

A Work with a partner. Ask and answer the questions.

A: What do you like to watch on television?

B: I like to watch mysteries and music videos.

1. Where would you like to go on vacation?

2. What would you like to be?

3. What do you like to eat?

4. What don't you like to eat?

5. Where would you like to live?

6. Where wouldn't you like to live?

7. What kind of car would you like to have?

8. What do you like to do in your free time?

9. What would you like to do after class?

10. Who would you like to meet one day?

B Work with another pair. Tell them about your partner.

Example

My partner would like to go to the beach on her vacation.

She likes to eat fish, but she doesn't like beef.

12c   *Could You* and *Would You*

Form

Could you call me back in a few minutes? My hands are full right now.

Would You/ Could You	Questions		Short Answers
	Base Verb		
Would you/ Could you	open	the door?	Certainly. Of course. Sure./OK. (informal)
	pass	me the salt?	
	stop	that noise?	

Function

Could you please look at this report again?

Would you (please) and *could you (please)* are two forms of requests. They are polite ways of asking someone to do something. They have the same meaning.

6 Practice

A Tom is picking up Mrs. Hardy at the airport. Use the phrases to write her requests.

1. carry my suitcase

   Could you please carry my suitcase _____?

2. open the car door

   _____?

3. turn off the car radio

   _____?

4. drive slowly

   _____?

5. turn on the heat

   _____?

6. speak louder/I can't hear you.

   _____?

7. repeat that/I didn't understand.

   _____?

8. close your window/There's too much noise.

   _____?

B Now work with a partner. Ask him or her the questions from Part A. Your partner will answer.

Form

Put your hands together above your head.
Bend to the right.
Keep your body straight.
Don't bend your knees.

Affirmative		Negative		
Base Verb		**Don't**	**Base Verb**	
Smile!			smile!	
Open	the door.	Don't	open	the door.
Answer	questions.		answer	questions.
Be	on time.		be	late!

Note: There is no subject in an imperative sentence. *You* is the understood subject.

Function

We use the imperative:
1. to give instructions;
   Turn right at the corner.   **Take** one tablet every four hours.
2. to give advice;
   Don't go there! It's dangerous.
   Get some rest.
3. to give orders or tell people what to do;
   Sit down!   **Stop!**   **Don't talk!**
4. to make requests (with *please*).
   Come in, please.   Please **close** the door.

1. Dial the number. Lift the telephone receiver. Wait for the dial tone.

    Lift the telephone receiver. Wait for the dial tone.

    Dial the number .

2. Write the letter. Mail it. Address the envelope. Put the letter in the envelope.
    Put a stamp on it. Sign your name.

    _____

    _____ .

3. Cut the oranges in half. Buy some fresh oranges. Throw away the seeds and pulp.
    Add a little sugar, if you wish. Drink. Squeeze the halves until all the juice is out.

    _____

    _____ .

B Now work with a partner. Use the imperative. Tell your partner how to do
these things. Then write what you told him or her to do.

Example

take care of a cold

Go home. Drink lots of warm liquids like tea and soup.

Take vitamin C or eat oranges. Take aspirin. Don't go to work .

1. lose weight

    _____

    _____ .

2. prepare for a test

    _____

    _____ .

3. prepare for a job interview

    _____

    _____ .

8 Read
Read the story. Then write answers to the questions.

HIS CLOTHES EAT

Once upon a time, there was a man who liked to travel. One day, he stopped at a farm and asked for food. The farmer looked at the man's dirty, old clothes and said, "You can't eat here."

So the man went to the next town and found a clothing store. He went in and said, "Give me your best coat." He then asked for the best pair of pants in the store. "Now I would like a hat." The store owner showed him his best hat, and the man bought it. He looked like a gentleman.

He went back to the same farm and asked for food. The same farmer said, "Come in, sir. Eat all you want."

The man ate. Then he put food into his pockets and his hat and said, "Eat all you want, beautiful clothes. The farmer likes you, not me!"

1. What did the man ask for at the farm?

   _____ .

2. What did he say first in the clothing store?

   _____ .

3. What did he say after he got the coat and the pair of pants?

   _____ .

4. Then where did he go?

   _____ .

5. What did the farmer say to him?

   _____ .

6. What did the man say to his clothes?

   _____ .

Listening Puzzle

CD5, 34

A Listen and check the correct answer.

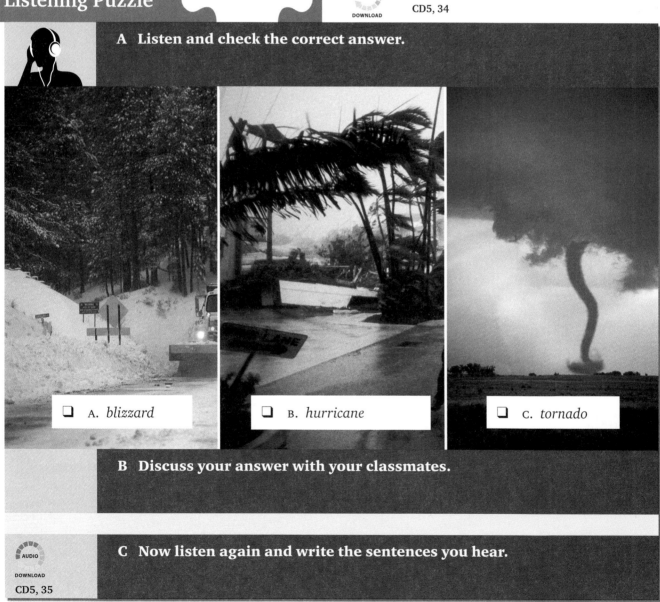

☐ A. *blizzard*   ☐ B. *hurricane*   ☐ C. *tornado*

B Discuss your answer with your classmates.

C Now listen again and write the sentences you hear.

CD5, 35

Reading Challenge

A Before You Read

Answer the questions.

1. What are the dangers of a lightning storm?
2. What are some things you can do to be safe?

B Read

WHEN LIGHTNING STRIKES

DID YOU KNOW ... ?
They say that lightning never strikes twice, but this isn't true. Roy Sullivan was struck by lightning seven times in his life. He died in 1983, but not from lightning.

There are about 6,000 flashes of lightning every minute in the world. Each flash of lightning is electricity. The electricity in lightning is 5 about 100 million volts. **This** is five times hotter than the sun. This heat makes the bright light we call lightning and the sudden loud noise 10 we call thunder. Lightning and thunder happen at the same time; however, we see lightning first because light travels faster than sound. 15 Lightning is dangerous. It starts fires and strikes people and animals. Many people die from

lightning strikes each year.

When lightning strikes, it's important to take the following **precautions**. When you 20 are inside your home, do not use electrical equipment. Especially avoid plug-in appliances such as hair dryers or telephones. Lightning can travel through the phone lines and into your ear. Keep away from metal inside the 25 home. When you are outside, avoid high places. Do not go to open areas such as sports fields. Avoid trees, especially tall trees because they attract lightning. Do not go near water such as swimming pools. Don't do activities in water 30 such as swimming or fishing. Find a shelter in a house or a cave.

C Notice the Grammar

Underline all forms of the imperative.

Choose the best answer.

READING SKILL:
Intensive Reading

Read as much as you can in English. Read shorter texts such as forms, recipes, or timetables. Read carefully. Look for specific information.

D Look for Main Ideas

1. What is paragraph 1 mainly about?
   - (A) the number of lightning flashes in the world
   - (B) what lightning is
   - (C) what thunder is
   - (D) what makes electricity

2. What is the main idea about lightning in paragraph 2?
   - (A) what to do inside your home
   - (B) what to do outside your home
   - (C) why electrical appliances are dangerous
   - (D) what actions we can take to protect ourselves

E Look for Details

3. A flash of lightning is _____ .
   - (A) fire
   - (B) electricity
   - (C) a big noise
   - (D) a volt

4. Thunder _____ .
   - (A) comes before lightning
   - (B) is a light
   - (C) happens at the same time as lightning
   - (D) comes after lightning

5. Which of the following is NOT safe during a lightning strike?
   - (A) to go under a tall tree
   - (B) to go inside a house
   - (C) to sit on a wooden chair inside a home
   - (D) to lie in bed

F Make Inferences

6. The writer seems to say that _____ .
   - (A) lightning is more dangerous than we think
   - (B) lightning is nothing to be afraid of
   - (C) there is nothing we can do to be safe from lightning
   - (D) lightning is only a problem in the United States

G Look for Vocabulary

7. The word **precautions** in the reading is closest in meaning to _____ .
   - (A) clues
   - (B) help you get from someone
   - (C) actions you take to prevent something dangerous
   - (D) positions

H Reference the Text

8. The word **This** in the reading refers to _____ .
   - (A) the sun
   - (B) trees
   - (C) the world
   - (D) electricity

Write instructions.

STEP 1   Put these sentences in the correct order.

How to make coffee

_____ Fill the coffee pot with boiling water.

_____ Pour the coffee into a cup.

___1___ Fill the kettle with water.

_____ Put some coffee in the coffee pot.

_____ Boil the water.

_____ Leave it for a few minutes.

STEP 2   Write the sentences from Step 1 in the correct order.

1. _____ .

2. _____ .

3. _____ .

4. _____ .

5. _____ .

6. _____ .

STEP 3   Write sentences to show how you make tea or another drink.

1. _____ .

2. _____ .

3. _____ .

4. _____ .

5. _____ .

6. _____ .

STEP 4   Rewrite your sentences from Step 3 in paragraph form. Check the order of your steps. Write a title in three or four words.

STEP 5   Work with a partner to evaluate and edit your paragraph. Check the order of your steps. Correct verb forms, spelling, punctuation, vocabulary, and grammar.

STEP 6   Write your final copy.

1. _____ go to a restaurant on your birthday.

   A. May   Ⓐ Ⓑ Ⓒ Ⓓ
   B. Could
   C. Let's to
   D. Let's

2. _____ a glass of water, please.

   A. I like   Ⓐ Ⓑ Ⓒ Ⓓ
   B. I would
   C. I'd like
   D. I would to like

3. A: Would you like a cup of coffee?
   B: Yes, I _____ .

   A. do   Ⓐ Ⓑ Ⓒ Ⓓ
   B. would
   C. would like
   D. like

4. _____ late!

   A. You no be   Ⓐ Ⓑ Ⓒ Ⓓ
   B. Don't be
   C. Not be
   D. Not to be

5. _____ , please?

   A. Can you me help   Ⓐ Ⓑ Ⓒ Ⓓ
   B. Could you help me
   C. May you help me
   D. Could you me help

6. _____ your passport!

   A. Forget not   Ⓐ Ⓑ Ⓒ Ⓓ
   B. Don't forget
   C. Don't forgetting
   D. Not forget

7. A: Would you give this to Mr. Black?
   B: _____ .

   A. Yes, I can   Ⓐ Ⓑ Ⓒ Ⓓ
   B. Yes, I would give
   C. Certainly
   D. I would

8. _____ speak English when you were ten?

   A. Could you   Ⓐ Ⓑ Ⓒ Ⓓ
   B. Would you
   C. Are you able to
   D. You could

9. _____ be quiet, please?

   A. Must you   Ⓐ Ⓑ Ⓒ Ⓓ
   B. Should you
   C. Could you
   D. Would

10. _____ the movie.

    A. I'd like to see   Ⓐ Ⓑ Ⓒ Ⓓ
    B. I would to see
    C. I'd like saw
    D. I'd like see

B Find the underlined word or phrase, A, B, C, or D, that is incorrect. Darken the oval with the same letter.

1. <u>Don't</u> <u>to breathe</u>. <u>Hold</u> <u>your</u> breath.
   A   **B**   **C** **D**

                  Ⓐ Ⓑ Ⓒ Ⓓ

2. <u>Could</u> you <u>to speak</u> English when you <u>were</u>
   A   **B**   **C**
<u>ten years old</u>?
   D

                  Ⓐ Ⓑ Ⓒ Ⓓ

3. <u>Would</u> <u>I</u> borrow <u>your</u> pen for <u>a moment</u>, please?
   A **B**   **C**   **D**

                  Ⓐ Ⓑ Ⓒ Ⓓ

4. <u>Could</u> you <u>please</u> <u>to repeat</u> that because I
   A   **B**   **C**
<u>didn't</u> hear you.
   D

                  Ⓐ Ⓑ Ⓒ Ⓓ

5. <u>May</u> you <u>please</u> <u>close</u> the window? <u>It's</u> cold here.
   A   **B**   **C**   **D**

                  Ⓐ Ⓑ Ⓒ Ⓓ

6. <u>Would</u> <u>you</u> <u>mailing</u> the letter <u>for me</u>?
   A   **B**   **C**   **D**

                  Ⓐ Ⓑ Ⓒ Ⓓ

7. <u>You</u> <u>look at</u> <u>that</u> airplane. <u>It's</u> flying very fast.
   A   **B**   **C**   **D**

                  Ⓐ Ⓑ Ⓒ Ⓓ

8. <u>I</u> <u>would</u> like <u>eat</u> <u>a sandwich</u> for lunch.
   A **B**   **C**   **D**

                  Ⓐ Ⓑ Ⓒ Ⓓ

9. <u>Could</u> <u>I</u> tell <u>me</u> <u>the time</u>?
   A **B**   **C**   **D**

                  Ⓐ Ⓑ Ⓒ Ⓓ

10. She <u>would</u> not <u>likes</u> <u>to be</u> <u>a movie star</u>.
      A   **B** **C**   **D**

                  Ⓐ Ⓑ Ⓒ Ⓓ

Unit 13

Adjectives and Adverbs

It's a **beautiful** day. The sky is **blue**. The air is **clean**.

Form

It is a **beautiful** day.
The sky is **blue**. The air is **clean**.
The **white** mountains are **beautiful**.

1. Adjectives come before nouns.
2. Adjectives can also come after the verb *be* and some other verbs such as *seem*.
3. Adjectives have the same form for singular and plural nouns.

Function

1. Adjectives describe nouns.
   Lee has a **big** smile.
2. Nouns can also describe other nouns.
   The noun that describes another noun is always singular, just like an adjective.
   She is holding a **coffee** cup.
   She is in the **student** cafeteria.

1 Practice
What are the underlined words? Put an *X* beside *Noun* or *Adjective*.

1.	Lin is a <u>good</u> student.	Noun _____	Adjective _X_
2.	She is going to a new <u>university</u>.	Noun _____	Adjective _____
3.	The university is <u>modern</u>.	Noun _____	Adjective _____
4.	Her <u>favorite</u> subject is biology.	Noun _____	Adjective _____
5.	She wants to be a <u>doctor</u>.	Noun _____	Adjective _____
6.	She is a <u>pretty</u> girl.	Noun _____	Adjective _____
7.	She has <u>black</u> hair.	Noun _____	Adjective _____
8.	She always helps her <u>friends</u>.	Noun _____	Adjective _____

2 Pair Up and Talk
A Practice the conversation with a partner.

A: What does the girl look like?

B: She seems sad. She has long hair.

B Now practice the conversation with your partner again. Describe each photo. Use these words or your own.

cute	happy	sad	thick
dark	long	short	young

3 Practice

A Read this paragraph. There are 12 more nouns used as adjectives. Underline them.

I went for a walk in the <u>city</u> center yesterday. There is a town hall in the center. On one side, there are office buildings and government offices. On the other side, there is a police station, a bus station, and a coffee shop. There is also a movie theater and an art gallery. In the center, there is a small park with big flowerpots and park benches. Yesterday, I saw a man near a telephone booth by one of the benches. He was waiting by the telephone. There was a cardboard box on the bench near him. I remember him because he looked very worried.

B What do you think? Why was the man waiting? Was the box his? What was in the box?

4 Practice
What are these items? Complete the names of the objects with these words.

coffee	light	paper	sun	tooth
key	note	perfume	tea	

1. ____*note*____ pad

2. _____ bulb

3. _____ ring

4. _____ pot

5. _____ cup

6. _____ bottle

7. _____ glasses   8. _____ clips   9. _____ brush

5 Practice

Work with a partner. Combine the word in capital letters with the words under it. Write the definition. Some combinations are two words; some are one. Check with your teacher or a dictionary.

1. SCHOOL

teacher   _____schoolteacher = a teacher at school_____

entrance   _____

adult   _____

2. MONEY

paper   _____

order   _____

box   _____

3. MUSIC

piano   _____

concert   _____

hall   _____

4. HOUSE

keeper   _____

work   _____

country   _____

5. BANK

account   _____

statement   _____

book   _____

Word Order of Adjectives

Form/Function

She has **beautiful brown** eyes.
She has **long brown curly** hair.

When we use two or more adjectives, we use this general order.

	1. Opinion	2. Size	3. Age	4. Color	5. Material	6. Nationality	
It's a	beautiful						box.
	beautiful	large					
	beautiful	large	old				
	beautiful	large	old	red			
	beautiful	large	old	red	wooden		
	beautiful	large	old	red	wooden	Chinese	

Note: We do not usually use more than two or three adjectives with one noun.

6 Practice

A Someone robbed Tina's apartment. Tina gave this list to the police. Underline *a* or *an* and put the adjectives in the correct order.

1. gold/new   a/an   _new gold_ credit card

2. diamond/interesting   a/an   _____ bracelet

3. beautiful/Chinese/old a/an   _____ plate

4. Japanese/new/small   a/an   _____ computer

5. leather/black/beautiful   a/an   _____ purse

6. gold/old/Swiss   a/an   _____ watch

7. expensive/big/blue   a/an   _____ ring

8. Persian/silk/old   a/an   _____ carpet

9. white/Japanese/pearl   a/an   _____ necklace

10. silver/antique/English   a/an   _____ jewelry box

B   **Listen and check your answers. Then listen again and repeat each phrase.**

CD6, 2, 3

7 Practice

A   **Complete the sentences. Use these words.**

| American | interesting | modern | quiet | rose |
| apple | leather | note | red | wood |

Fred is a _____quiet_____ young man. He lives alone in a _____
                       1   2

brick house. The house has one bedroom with a clean light _____ floor. It
                                                                         3

has a bright _____ kitchen. From the kitchen window, you can see a beautiful
                          4

_____ garden and an old _____ tree. In the office, there is a black
          5   6

_____ sofa and an _____ old desk. On the desk, there is a telephone, a
         7   8

small computer and a _____ pad. There are books everywhere. There are also old
                          9

_____ newspapers, mostly *The New York Times*.
      10

B   **Listen and check your answers. Then listen again and repeat each sentence.**

CD6, 4, 5

C Listen again. What does Fred like to do? Circle the letter of the correct answer.

AUDIO

DOWNLOAD

CD6, 6

A   have big parties

B   watch television

C   read

D   cook for friends

8 Your Turn

A Write sentences about these things. Use two adjectives or nouns used as adjectives.

Example

I'm wearing comfortable brown shoes.

1.   your shoes _____ .

2.   your house or apartment _____ .

3.   your camera _____ .

4.   your watch _____ .

5.   your eyes _____ .

6.   your hair _____ .

B Write a paragraph describing a person in your class. Use adjectives.

_____

_____

_____

_____

_____

_____

_____ .

The Same (As), Similar (To), and Different (From)

Form/Function

Photo A   **Photo B**

Photos A and B are **the same**.
A is **the same as** B.

Photo L   **Photo M**

Photos L and M are **similar**.
L is **similar to** M.

Photo X   **Photo Y**

Photos X and Y are **different**.
X is **different from** Y.

9 Practice

Which photos are the same, similar, or different?

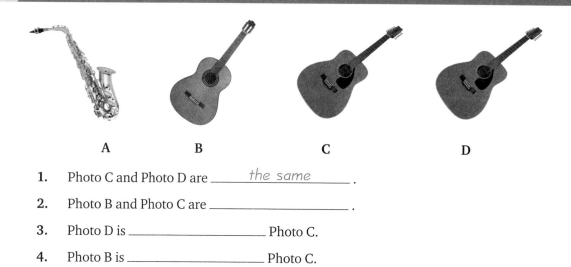

A   B   C   D

1. Photo C and Photo D are _____*the same*_____ .

2. Photo B and Photo C are _____ .

3. Photo D is _____ Photo C.

4. Photo B is _____ Photo C.

5. Photo A is _____ Photo C.

6. Photo A and Photo D are _____ .

10 Practice

Look at these lines of print. Which are the same, similar, or different?

Line 1: **To be or not to be**

Line 2: **To be or not to be**

Line 3: *To be or not to be*

Line 4: TO BE OR NOT TO BE

Line 5: TO BE OR NOT TO BE

Line 6: **TO BE OR NOT TO BE**

1. Line 1 is _____*the same as*_____ Line 2.

2. Line 2 and Line 1 are _____ .

3. Line 3 is _____ Line 2.

4. Line 3 is _____ Line 4.

5. Line 3 and Line 4 are _____ .

6. Line 4 and Line 5 are _____ .

7. Line 5 is _____ Line 4.

8. Line 5 is _____ Line 6.

11 Your Turn

Write about three people and three things in your classroom that are the same, similar, or different. Use complete sentences.

Example

X and I have the same book.
X and I have similar hair.
X and I have different eyes.   OR   *My eyes are different from X's.*

13D | *Like* and *Alike*

Form/Function

The daughter's eyes **are like** her mother's eyes.
The daughter's and mother's eyes **are alike**.

1. *Like* and *alike* have the same meaning.
2. *Like* is a preposition. It means "similar to."

Subject	Be	Like	Object
The daughter	is	like	the mother.

3. *Alike* is an adjective. It means "similar."

Subject	Be	Alike
The mother and daughter	are	alike.

12 Practice

Complete the sentences with *like* and *alike*.

Terry   **Jerry**

1. Terry and Jerry have similar faces. Their faces are _____ *alike* _____ .

2. Terry and Jerry have similar names. Terry's name is _____
   Jerry's name.

3. Terry and Jerry wear a similar style of clothes. Terry's clothes are
   _____ Jerry's clothes.

4. Terry and Jerry have similar cars. Their cars are _____ .

5. Terry and Jerry have similar jobs. Terry's job is _____ Jerry's job.

6. Terry and Jerry live in similar apartments. Jerry's apartment is _____
   Terry's apartment.

7. Terry and Jerry have similar friends. Their friends are _____ .

8. Terry and Jerry have similar lives. Terry's life is _____ Jerry's life.

13 Pair Up and Talk

A   Practice the conversation with a partner.

A: Which things are similar? Why?
B: A chicken is like a turkey. They are both birds.

B   Now practice the conversation with your partner again. Use these words.

blouse	guitar	shirt	turkey
chicken	New York	Tokyo	violin

13E | Comparative Form of Adjectives: *-er* and *More*

Form/Function

Monica's house is **bigger than** Olivia's house.
Olivia's house is **older than** Monica's house.
Monica's house is **more expensive than** Olivia's house.

Monica's house   **Olivia's house**

When we compare things, we use a comparative adjective + *than*.

1. Short adjectives (one syllable): Add *-er*.

Adjective	Comparative Adjective + *than*
long	long**er than**
old	old**er than**
hot	hot**ter* than**

* If an adjective ends in one vowel and one consonant, double the consonant.

2. One or two syllable adjectives ending in *y*: Change *y* to *i* and add *-er*.

Adjective	Comparative Adjective + *than*
happy	happ**ier than**
hungry	hungr**ier than**
friendly	friendl**ier than**

3. Long adjectives (two syllables or more): Use *more* before the adjective.

Adjective	Comparative Adjective + *than*
difficult	**more** difficult **than**
expensive	**more** expensive **than**
beautiful	**more** beautiful **than**

4. Irregular adjectives:

Adjective	Comparative Adjective + *than*
good	better than
bad	worse than
far	farther/further than

14 Practice

A Complete the sentences about Karen and Connie. Use the comparative form of the words in parentheses.

Connie

110 pounds (50 kilograms)

5 feet 2 inches

(157 centimeters)

quiet

28 years old

Karen

140 pounds (63.5 kilograms)

5 feet 5 inches

(165 centimeters)

friendly

34 years old

1. Karen is (old) _____*older than*_____ Connie.

2. Connie is (young) _____ Karen.

3. Karen is (tall) _____ Connie.

4. Connie is (small) _____ Karen.

5. Connie is (thin) _____ Karen.

6. Karen is (heavy) _____ Connie.

7. Karen is (friendly) _____ Connie.

8. Connie is (quiet) _____ Karen.

B Listen and check your answers. Then listen again and repeat each sentence.

AUDIO

DOWNLOAD

CD6, 7, 8

15 Practice

A Complete the sentences about London and New York. Use the comparative form of the words in parentheses.

London

Population:	6.7 million
Temperatures:	39-64°F/4-18°C
Rain:	24 inches/610mm

New York

Population:	8.0 million
Temperatures:	30-73°F/-1-23°C
Rain:	44 inches/1,123mm

1. London is (old) _____*older than*_____ New York.

2. New York is (crowded) _____ London.

3. London is (small) _____ New York in population.

4. The buildings in New York are (tall) _____ the buildings in London.

5. New York is (exciting) _____ London.

6. The buildings in New York are (modern) _____ the buildings in London.

7. Life in New York is (fast) _____ life in London.

8. The summer in New York is (hot) _____ the summer in London.

9. New York is (rainy) _____ London.

10. The museums in London are (interesting) _____ the museums in New York.

11. London is (expensive) _____ New York.

12. People in London are usually (polite) _____ people in New York.

B Listen and check your answers. Then listen again and repeat each sentence.

CD6, 9, 10

C What do you think? Do you prefer London or New York? Why?

As … As, Not As … As, and *Less … Than*

Form

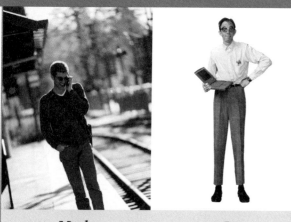

Mark

Joe

Mark is **as tall as** Joe. = Mark and Joe are the same height.

Mark is **as old as** Joe. = Mark and Joe are the same age.

Joe isn't **as trendy as** Mark. = Mark is more trendy. Joe is less trendy.

	As	Adjective	As	
Mark is	as	tall old	as	Joe.

	Not As	Adjective	As	
Joe is	not as	trendy casual	as	Mark.

	Less	Adjective	Than	
Joe is	less	trendy casual	than	Mark.

Function

1. We use *as … as* to show that two things or people are the same in some way.
2. We use *not as … as* to show that two things are different in some way.

   Mark isn't **as conservative as** Joe. = Mark is **less conservative than** Joe.

3. We can use *less … than* with a long adjective (two syllables or more), except for most adjectives ending in *y*.

This book is **less expensive than** that one.

CORRECT: This exercise isn't **as easy as** that one.

INCORRECT: This exercise ~~is less easy than that one~~.

4. We do not use *less … than* with one-syllable adjectives.

CORRECT: Mark isn't **as tall as** Joe.

INCORRECT: Mark ~~is less tall than Joe~~.

16   Practice

A   Complete the sentences with *as … as* and the adjectives in parentheses.

Mark's car

Joe's car

1.   Mark's car isn't (old) _____ *as old as* _____ Joe's car.

2.   Joe's car isn't (clean) _____ Mark's car.

3.   Mark's car isn't (small) _____ Joe's car.

4.   Joe's car isn't (luxurious) _____ Mark's car.

5.   Mark's car isn't (noisy) _____ Joe's car.

6.   Joe's car isn't (trendy) _____ Mark's car.

7.   Joe's car isn't (sporty) _____ Mark's car.

8.   Joe's car isn't (powerful) _____ Mark's car.

B   Listen and check your answers. Then listen again and repeat each sentence.

CD6, 11, 12

A   Rewrite the sentences to have the same meaning. Use *less than* where possible. Write "No change" if it isn't possible to use *less*.

1.   Joe's life isn't as fun as Mark's life.

      No change _____ .

2.   Joe's office isn't as luxurious as Mark's office.

      _____ .

3.   Joe's life isn't as complicated as Mark's life.

      _____ .

4.   Mark's life isn't as dull as Joe's life.

      _____ .

5.   Joe's clothes aren't as expensive as Mark's clothes.

      _____ .

6.   Joe's clothes aren't as fashionable as Mark's clothes.

      _____ .

7.   Joe's house isn't as sophisticated as Mark's house.

      _____ .

8.   Joe's house isn't as trendy as Mark's house.

      _____ .

B   **Mark is a musician. Joe is a banker. Write five sentences about Joe's life or Mark's life. Use *as … as* or *not as … as*.**

1.   _____ .

2.   _____ .

3.   _____ .

4.   _____ .

5.   _____ .

18   Practice

There are many expressions in English with *as … as* that make comparisons.
Work with a partner. Look at the pictures and complete the expressions.
Use the words and phrases.

a beet

a picture

ice

a bee

a bear   an ox

1.   Jamie is always working. She never stops. She is as busy as _____ *a bee* _____ .

2.   Tony can carry the suitcases for you. He is as strong as _____ .

3.   Bill didn't eat all day. He was very hungry. He was as hungry as _____ .

4.   Melanie looked pretty in her new dress. She was as pretty as _____ .

5.   Helen didn't look well. Her face was white, and her hands were as cold
     as _____ .

6.   Tina is very shy. She is in front of the class. Everyone is looking at her. Her face is as
     red as _____ .

19   Pair Up and Talk

Tell a classmate about the expressions in your language to make
comparisons. How are they similar to or different from the ones in this unit?

In my language, we make comparisons with …

20 Practice

Write sentences with the same meaning. Use *not as … as.*

The Victoria Hotel

The Hilton® Hotel

1. The room at the Victoria is smaller than the room at the Hilton.

   The room at the Victoria isn't as big as the room at the Hilton .

2. The Victoria is less expensive than the Hilton.

   _____ .

3. The bed in the Victoria is less comfortable than the bed in the Hilton.

   _____ .

4. The Victoria is farther away from the city center.

   _____ .

5. The hotel service at the Victoria is worse than at the Hilton.

   _____ .

6. The Victoria is less crowded than the Hilton.

   _____ .

7. The coffee at the Victoria is weaker than the coffee at the Hilton.

   _____ .

8. The Victoria is less modern than the Hilton.

   _____ .

9. The furniture at the Victoria is older than the furniture at the Hilton.

   _____ .

10. The restaurant at the Hilton is better than the restaurant at the Victoria.

    _____ .

21 Pair Up and Talk

A What can you say about the Hilton Hotel and the Victoria Hotel? Practice the conversation with a partner.

A: Which hotel is more comfortable?

B: The Hilton Hotel is more comfortable than the Victoria Hotel.

B Now practice the conversation with your partner again. Use comparative forms of these words or your own.

comfortable	good	new	quiet
expensive	modern	nice	spacious

22 Pair Up and Talk

A Look again at Monica's house and Olivia's house on page 357. Practice the conversation with a partner.

A: Monica's house is not as small as Olivia's house.

B: Olivia's house is less luxurious than Monica's house, too.

B Now practice the conversation with your partner again. Use *as ... as*, *not as ... as*, and *less than*. Use these words or your own.

big	expensive	modern	old
comfortable	luxurious	new	spacious

Form/Function

Beth is **the youngest of** the three women.
Lorraine has **the darkest** hair.
Kara is **the most** serious.

Kara   Lorraine   Beth

We form superlative adjectives with -*est* or *most*.

	Adjective	Comparative	Superlative
Short adjectives	long cheap	long**er** (than) cheap**er** (than)	**the** long**est** **the** cheap**est**
Two syllable adjectives ending in *y*	happy heavy	happ**ier** (than) heav**ier** (than)	**the** happ**iest** **the** heav**iest**
Two or more syllable adjectives	famous difficult	**more** famous (than) **more** difficult (than)	**the most** famous **the most** difficult
Irregular adjectives	good bad far	**better** (than) **worse** (than) **farther/further** (than)	**the best** **the worst** **the farthest/furthest**

We use *the* + the superlative form of an adjective (+ *of* or *in*) to compare three or more people or things.

Kara is **the most** talented **of** the three women.
Lorraine is **the funniest**.

23 Practice

A   Write the superlative forms of the adjectives.

1. cold _____the coldest_____
2. hungry _____
3. wet _____
4. useful _____
5. intelligent _____
6. easy _____
7. good _____
8. bad _____
9. far _____
10. boring _____
11. popular _____
12. friendly _____

B   Listen and check your answers. Then listen again and repeat each phrase.

CD6, 13, 14

24 Practice

Complete the geography facts with the correct form of the adjectives in parentheses.

1. Australia is (small) _____the smallest_____ continent in the world.
2. The Nile is (long) _____ river in the world.
3. Mount Everest is (high) _____ mountain in the world.
4. Antarctica is (cold) _____ continent in the world.
5. Asia is (big) _____ continent in the world.
6. The Dead Sea is (salty) _____ sea in the world.
7. The Pacific Ocean is (large) _____ ocean in the world.
8. The Sahara Desert is (hot) _____ desert in the world.

Adjectives and Adverbs   **367**

25 Practice

Complete the sentences about places with the correct form of the adjectives in parentheses.

1. The CN Tower in Canada was (tall) *the tallest* building in the world in 2004.

2. The Eiffel Tower in Paris is (famous) _____ building in France.

3. Mexico City is (crowded) _____ city in the world.

4. Urungu, a city in China, is (far) _____ city from the sea.

5. Jericho in Jordan is (old) _____ city in the world.

6. Hartsfield Airport in Atlanta is (busy) _____ airport in the world.

7. The White House in Washington, D.C., is (important) _____ house in the United States.

8. Los Angeles, California, has (good) _____ freeway system in the world.

26 Practice

Write true sentences. Use the comparative and superlative form of these adjectives. Use each word twice.

heavy   old   short   tall   thin   young

Ken   Paul   Brad

Ken
19 years old
6 feet 2 inches (1.9 meters)
190 lbs (86 kilos)

Paul
25 years old
5 feet 11 inches (1.5 meters)
175 lbs (79 kilos)

Brad
17 years old
5 feet 6 inches (1.7 meters)
158 lbs (72 kilos)

1. Ken is _____ younger than _____ Paul.

2. Ken is _____ of all.

3. Paul is _____ Brad.

4. Paul is _____ of all.

5. Ken is _____ Paul.

6. Ken is _____ of all.

7. Paul is _____ Ken.

8. Brad is _____ of all.

9. Paul is _____ Brad.

10. Brad is _____ of all.

11. Brad is _____ Ken.

12. Brad is _____ of all.

27 Pair Up and Talk

A **Practice the conversation with a partner.**

A: What is the biggest city in Japan?

B: Tokyo is the biggest city in Japan.

B **Now practice the conversation with your partner again. Ask and answer questions about your countries. Give complete answers. Use these phrases or your own.**

the biggest city	the largest airport
the busiest street	the most beautiful building
the coldest month	the oldest building
the hottest month	the wettest month

13H | *One Of The* + Superlative + Plural Noun

Form

Mona Lisa is **one of the most famous paintings** in the world.
It is in **one of the biggest museums** in the world, the Louvre, in Paris, France.

	One Of	Superlative	Plural Noun	
It is		**the biggest**	**stores**	in the city.
He is	**one of**	**the richest**	**men**	in the world.
They are		**the most powerful**	**families**	in the town.

28 Practice
Write sentences. Use the phrases and *one of the* + superlative + plural noun.

1. the Taj Mahal/beautiful building/in the world *The Taj Mahal is* *one of the most beautiful buildings in the world* .

2. the Beatles/successful rock band/in the world _____ _____ .

3. Siberia/cold place/in the world _____ _____ .

4. California/large state/in the United States _____ _____ .

5. Egypt/interesting country/to visit _____

    _____ .

6. the computer/great invention/of our time _____

    _____ .

7. New York/important city/in the United States _____

    _____ .

8. Mont Blanc/high mountain/in the world _____

    _____ .

9. the Sears Tower in Chicago/tall building/in the world _____

    _____ .

10. Tokyo/crowded city/in the world _____

    _____ .

11. a racehorse/fast animal/in the world _____

    _____ .

12. boxing/dangerous sport/in the world _____

    _____ .

29 Pair Up and Talk
A   Practice the conversation with a partner.

A: What is one of the most popular drinks in Asia?

B: Tea is one of the most popular drinks in Asia.

B   Now practice the conversation with your partner again. Use these phrases or your own to make questions and answers.

beautiful city/Paris	popular drink/tea
big city/Tokyo	popular food/pizza
cold place/the North Pole	popular sport/soccer
important university/Oxford University	strong animal/lion
long river/Amazon River	sweet food/honey

13ɪ Adjectives and Adverbs

Form

The ballerina danced **beautifully**.

Rules for Forming Adverbs	Adjective	Adverb
For most adverbs, we add *-ly* to an adjective.	slow quick beautiful bad	slow**ly** quick**ly** beautiful**ly** bad**ly**
If the adjective ends in *y*, we change the *y* to *i* and then add *-ly*.	happy easy	happ**ily** eas**ily**
Some adverbs are the same as the adjective.	hard fast late early	**hard** **fast** **late** **early**
The adverb form of *good* is *well*.	good	**well**

Function

Adjectives and adverbs look similar, but they do different things.

1. An adjective describes a noun and usually answers the question *what*.
   What color is the car? The car is **red**.
2. An adverb often answers the question *how*. Adverbs describe verbs, adjectives, and other adverbs.
   How does she dance? She dances **beautifully**. She dances **very beautifully**.

30 Practice
Put these words into the correct column.

carefully	early	fast	good	late	quietly
dangerous	easily	funny	hard	noisy	slowly

Adjective	Adverb	Adjective or Adverb
noisy		

31 Practice
A Read about Janet. Underline the adverbs. Then answer the questions.

Janet is a careful person. She gets to work on time and does everything <u>perfectly</u>. She works hard at home and at work. She drives her car to work. She drives carefully. She doesn't drive fast, and she stops at all the red lights. But, on her way home yesterday evening, she drove badly and almost had an accident.

1. How does Janet do everything at work?   *She does everything perfectly* .
2. Does she work hard?   _____ .
3. How does she get to work?   _____ .
4. How does she usually drive?   _____ .
5. How did she drive yesterday evening?   _____ .
6. What happened?   _____ .

B What do you think? Why did Janet drive badly yesterday?

32   Practice

A   Susan is the best person for this job. Here's why. Underline the correct form of the adjective or adverb.

1. She speaks English very (good/<u>well</u>).

2. She is very (polite/politely) to people.

3. She gets along with people (easy/easily).

4. She is a (hard/hardly) worker.

5. She is a (good/well) writer.

6. She types (fast/fastly) on the computer.

7. She is very (careful/carefully) with her work.

8. She keeps the office (clean/cleanly).

9. She is never (late/lately).

10. But you must pay her (generous/generously).

B   Listen and check your answers. Then listen again and repeat each sentence.

DOWNLOAD

CD6, 15, 16

33   Practice

English is very important for the speaker below. Underline the correct form of the adjective or adverb.

1. I want to have a (<u>good</u>/well) English accent.

2. I want to speak English (fluent/fluently).

3. I want to read an English newspaper (quick/quickly).

4. I want to understand people (good/well).

5. I want to be an (excellent/excellently) student in my English class.

6. I want to know my past participles (perfect/perfectly).

7. I want to spell words (correct/correctly).

8. I want to write English (easy/easily).

9. I want to understand English grammar (complete/completely).

10. I want to learn English (fast/fastly)!

Form/Function

snail

tortoise

A snail moves **more slowly** than a tortoise.
A snail moves **more silently** than a tortoise.
In fact, the snail moves **the most slowly** of all animals.

	Adverb	Comparative	Superlative
We compare adverbs ending in *ly* with *more* and *the most*.	easily slowly carefully	**more** easily **more** slowly **more** carefully	**the most** easily **the most** slowly **the most** carefully
For adverbs which have the same form as adjectives, we add *-er* and *-est*.	fast hard early	fast**er** hard**er** earli**er**	the fast**est** the hard**est** the earli**est**
Well is an irregular adverb.	well	**better**	**the best**

34 Practice

Complete the sentences. Use the comparative form of the adverbs in italics. Veronica thinks she is better at doing certain things than Karen. This is what Veronica thinks.

1. Karen learns English *easily*, but I learn it _____*more easily*_____ .

2. Karen dresses *fashionably*, but I dress _____ .

3. Karen runs *fast*, but I run _____ .

4. Karen works *hard*, but I work _____ .

5. Karen learns *quickly*, but I learn _____.

6. Karen speaks French *fluently*, but I speak French _____.

7. Karen cooks *well*, but I cook _____.

8. Karen speaks *carefully*, but I speak _____.

35 Practice

A Look at these descriptions of three women. Use these adjectives or adverbs. Write comparative and superlative sentences about the women.

careful/carefully	fast	hard	old/young
early/late	friendly*	longer	slower/slowly

* *Friendly* looks like an adverb, but it is really an adjective that ends in *-ly*.

Lydia

Sue

Age: 49

Experience: 20 years

- gets to work early
- works carefully
- writes reports a little late
- works fast
- works nine hours a day
- friendly at times

Age: 34

Experience: 2 years

- gets to work on time
- works very carefully
- writes reports on time
- works very fast
- works eight hours a day
- friendly all the time

Gina

Age: 29

Experience: 5 years

- gets to work late
- not careful
- writes reports late
- works slowly
- works six hours a day
- very friendly and happy person

1. *Sue is the most careful* _____ .

2. _____ .

3. _____ .

4. _____ .

5. _____ .

6. _____ .

7. _____ .

8. _____ .

B   **Talk with a partner. Who is going to be the new manager? Why?**

36   Pair Up and Talk
Work with a partner. Think about three bosses or teachers from your past.
Talk about them. Use superlative adverbs.

Example

Ms. Taheri was my best teacher. She taught us the most successfully of all the teachers.

13K   *As ... As* with Adverbs

Form/Function

Alex   Mike

Alex doesn't dress **as neatly as** Mike.

	As	Adverb	As	
Tony speaks English		**fluently**		John (does).
Karen runs	**as**	**fast**	**as**	Jan (does).
Mary and Jane work		**hard**		John and Pete (do).

1. When things are the same, we put *as ... as* around the adverb.
   She worked **as fast as** a machine.
2. We can also follow *as* + adverb + *as* with a subject and a form of the verb *do* or modals such as *can* or *could*.
   He worked **as fast as I did**.   He worked **as fast as he could**.
3. We use the negative form *not as ... as* to show things are not the same.
   Alex does**n't** study **as hard as** Mike.

37   Practice

A   Alex and Mike are friends, but they are different in many ways. Complete the sentences.

1. Alex doesn't work as hard _____*as*_____ Mike _____*does*_____ .
2. He doesn't get up as early _____ Mike _____ .
3. Mike doesn't go to bed as late _____ Alex _____ .
4. Alex doesn't work as quickly _____ Mike _____ .

5. Mike doesn't play sports as well _____ Alex and his friends _____ .

6. Alex doesn't talk as politely _____ Mike and his friends _____ .

7. Mike doesn't dress as casually _____ Alex and his friends _____ .

8. Alex doesn't drive as carefully _____ Mike _____ .

B   Listen and check your answers. Then listen again and repeat each sentence.

CD6, 17, 18

C   Listen again. Circle the letter of the correct answer.

CD6, 19

A   Who sleeps later in the morning?   Alex   Mike

B   Who is a better worker?   Alex   Mike

C   Who is a better driver?   Alex   Mike

D   Who is better at sports?   Alex   Mike

38   Practice

The students have a big test tomorrow. The teacher is giving advice to the students. Use the phrases. Write sentences with *as … as + can.*

1. get up/early   *Get up as early as you can* _____ .

2. study/hard   _____ .

3. come to school/early _____ .

4. be/relaxed   _____ .

5. read the instructions/carefully _____ .

6. answer the questions/completely _____ .

7. write/fast   _____ .

8. write/neatly   _____ .

9. take/much time   _____ .

10. check your work/carefully _____ .

39　Read

Read the story. Then write answers to the questions.

THE UNHAPPY MOUSE

Once upon a time, there was a little mouse. He wanted to be strong. He asked his friends, "What is the strongest thing in the world?"

His friends said, "The sun is." So the little mouse went to talk to the sun. The mouse asked the sun, "How can I be strong like you?"

The sun answered, "I am not so strong. The cloud is stronger. He can cover me and make the world cold."

The little mouse went to talk to the cloud, "How can I be strong like you?"

"I am not so strong," answered the cloud. "The wind can blow me away."

The little mouse went to talk to the wind.

The mouse asked the wind, "How can I be strong like you?"

"I am not so strong," answered the wind. "The wall can stop me."

The little mouse went to talk to the wall. The mouse asked the wall, "How can I be strong like you?"

The wall answered, "I am not so strong. A little mouse can eat holes in me, and I will fall down."

The little mouse was very happy.

1. What did the little mouse want to be?

   _____ .

2. Why did the mouse go to talk with the sun?

   _____ .

3. When the mouse talked to the sun, what did it want to be?

_____ .

4. What did the sun say?

_____ .

5. Why is the wall stronger than the wind?

_____ .

6. Why is the mouse stronger than the wall?

_____ .

Listening Puzzle

AUDIO DOWNLOAD   CD6, 20

A Listen and check the correct answer.

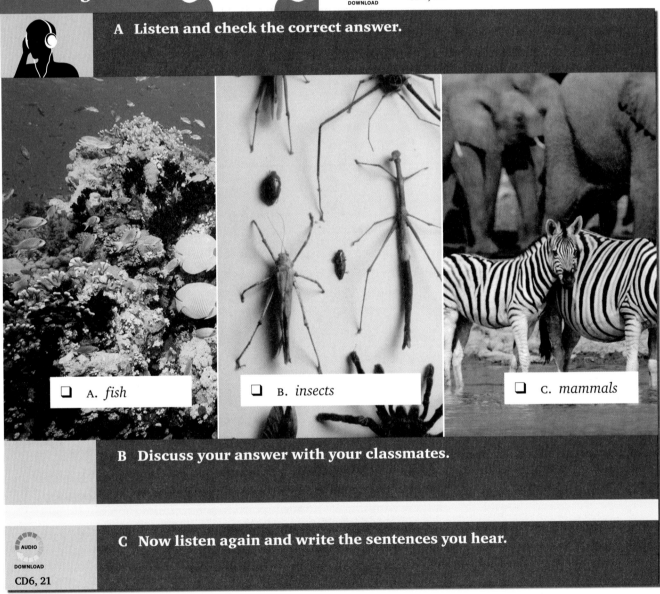

❑ A. _fish_   ❑ B. _insects_   ❑ C. _mammals_

B Discuss your answer with your classmates.

AUDIO DOWNLOAD CD6, 21

C Now listen again and write the sentences you hear.

A Before You Read

Answer the questions.

1. What do hummingbirds eat?
2. In which countries do you find hummingbirds?

B Read

HUMMINGBIRDS

DID YOU KNOW ... ?
To hover, one kind of hummingbird (the horned sungem) beats its wings 90 times per second.

Hummingbirds are the smallest birds. There are 325 species of hummingbirds. They all live in North, Central, and South America. In the wild, they can live from
5 five to six years.

Hummingbirds live a very fast life. Their hearts beat 500-600 times a minute at rest and up to 1,000 times
10 when they move. They move their wings so fast they can fly forwards, backwards, sideways, stop in mid air, and even fly upside down. When they **hover**, the sound they make with their wings
15 gives **them** their name.

Hummingbirds spend a lot of energy so they eat almost all the time. They eat about 50 percent of their weight in sugar every day. The hummingbird's food is the sweet nectar
20 of flowers. Hummingbirds have long, narrow beaks[1] and tongues to reach inside the flowers.

There are some special hummingbirds. The swordbill hummingbird has a beak that is three or four times the length of its body
25 so it can reach into the deepest flowers. The bee hummingbird from Cuba is the world's smallest bird. Its size, including its beak, is two inches or five centimeters. The ruby-throated hummingbird flies 600 miles (966 kilometers)
30 across the Gulf of Mexico every year.

[1]beak = the hard, curved, or pointed part of a bird's mouth

C Notice the Grammar

Underline all forms of adjectives. Include superlatives and names.

Reading aloud and reading silently are separate skills. Read aloud to report information or improve pronunciation. Read silently to improve concentration and comprehension.

Choose the best answer.

D   Look for Main Ideas

1. What is the main idea of paragraph 2?
   - (A) how hummingbirds move
   - (B) how the hummingbird got its name
   - (C) the speed of the hummingbird
   - (D) the heart of the hummingbird

2. The main idea of paragraph 3 is _____ .
   - (A) how the hummingbird gets its nutrition
   - (B) the beaks of hummingbirds
   - (C) the nectar of flowers
   - (D) when hummingbirds eat

E   Look for Details

3. Hummingbirds live in _____ .
   - (A) South and Central America
   - (B) North America
   - (C) the wild everywhere
   - (D) all the Americas

4. Which of the following is NOT true about hummingbirds?
   - (A) There are 325 kinds of hummingbirds.
   - (B) Hummingbirds fly the fastest of all birds.
   - (C) Hummingbirds can fly backwards.
   - (D) Hummingbirds eat nectar.

5. The swordbill hummingbird _____ .
   - (A) is the smallest hummingbird
   - (B) comes from Cuba
   - (C) flies 600 miles every year
   - (D) has a very long beak

F   Make Inferences

6. What can we infer about hummingbirds from the reading?
   - (A) Hummingbirds live longer in the wild.
   - (B) All hummingbirds fly across the Gulf of Mexico.
   - (C) Hummingbirds have short lives because they live fast.
   - (D) Hummingbirds look like bees.

G   Look for Vocabulary

7. The word *hover* in the reading is closest in meaning to _____ .
   - (A) stay in the air without moving backward or forward
   - (B) fly forward
   - (C) move forward or backward very fast
   - (D) turn

H   Reference the Text

8. The word *them* in the reading refers to _____ .
   - (A) hummingbirds
   - (B) their wings
   - (C) the sound
   - (D) their name

Writing: Make a Comparison

Write a paragraph of comparison.

STEP 1   A friend is coming to your city to study English. He/She wants you to find out about English schools. Your friend would like to be downtown. Cost is no problem. Read the information about the three language schools. With a partner, compare the three schools.

Name	Age of School	Price	Location	Test Pass Rate	Students in Class
Achieve Language Center	25 years	$1,200	Suburbs	75%	15
City School of English	2 years	$1,500	Downtown	40%	25
English Language Institute	15 years	$1,700	Downtown	60%	20

STEP 2   Write sentences that compare the schools.

STEP 3   Rewrite your sentences as a paragraph in the letter below. Be sure to use adjectives and adverbs correctly.

> Dear _____ ,
>
> It's great news that you're going to be here for a month.
> Here's what I found out about language schools. I'm enclosing
> information about each school so you can make a final decision.
> Achieve Language Center is the oldest of all the schools ...

STEP 4   Work with a partner to edit your paragraph. Correct spelling, punctuation, vocabulary, and grammar.

STEP 5   Write your final copy.

Self-Test

Choose the best answer, A, B, C, or D, to complete the sentence. Darken the oval with the same letter.

1. Tony's English _____ .

   A. like mine   Ⓐ Ⓑ Ⓒ Ⓓ
   B. like me
   C. is like mine
   D. alike mine

2. The new television show is _____ than the old show.

   A. more funny   Ⓐ Ⓑ Ⓒ Ⓓ
   B. funnier
   C. funniest
   D. the funnier

3. New York is _____ Tokyo.

   A. less crowded as   Ⓐ Ⓑ Ⓒ Ⓓ
   B. least crowded
   C. less crowded than
   D. less crowded then

4. It's _____ store in town.

   A. most expensive   Ⓐ Ⓑ Ⓒ Ⓓ
   B. the expensiviest
   C. the most expensive
   D. the more expensive

5. He ran _____ he could.

   A. as quicker as   Ⓐ Ⓑ Ⓒ Ⓓ
   B. as quickly as
   C. quickly as
   D. as quickest as

6. Your English is _____ mine.

   A. fluenter then   Ⓐ Ⓑ Ⓒ Ⓓ
   B. fluent than
   C. more fluenter than
   D. more fluent than

7. His car _____ my car.

   A. is the same as   Ⓐ Ⓑ Ⓒ Ⓓ
   B. is the same
   C. same
   D. is as same as

8. Ted's job is _____ my father's job.

   A. similar as   Ⓐ Ⓑ Ⓒ Ⓓ
   B. similar from
   C. the similar as
   D. similar to

9. He is a _____ man.

   A. Chinese, tall, young   Ⓐ Ⓑ Ⓒ Ⓓ
   B. young, tall, Chinese
   C. tall, young, Chinese
   D. Chinese, young, tall

10. I bought a pair of _____ shoes.

   A. black, leather, comfortable   Ⓐ Ⓑ Ⓒ Ⓓ
   B. leather, comfortable, black
   C. comfortable, black, leather
   D. comfortable, leather, black

B Find the underlined word or phrase, A, B, C, or D, that is incorrect. Darken the oval with the same letter.

1. Electricity is one of the most importanttest
   A   B   C
   inventions in the world.
   D

   Ⓐ Ⓑ Ⓒ Ⓓ

2. The elephant is bigger land animal in the world.
   A   B   C   D

   Ⓐ Ⓑ Ⓒ Ⓓ

3. The Forbidden City in China is the most largest
                          A   B   C
   palace in the world.
         D

   Ⓐ Ⓑ Ⓒ Ⓓ

4. The CN Tower in Toronto, Canada, is more taller
             A   B   C
   than the Sears Tower in Chicago.
   D

   Ⓐ Ⓑ Ⓒ Ⓓ

5. The Louvre Museum in Paris is one of the
                        A   B
   famousest museums in the world.
   C   D

   Ⓐ Ⓑ Ⓒ Ⓓ

6. A cup of Italian espresso coffee is more stronger
                          A B   C
   than a cup of American coffee.
   D

   Ⓐ Ⓑ Ⓒ Ⓓ

7. The world's tallest and most shortest people live
            A   B C   D
   in Africa.

   Ⓐ Ⓑ Ⓒ Ⓓ

8. The blue whale is the largest animal in the world
                A B
   and it is as heavy than about 1,800 people.
         C   D

   Ⓐ Ⓑ Ⓒ Ⓓ

9. A newborn African elephant is two times as
                     A   B
   heavy than an adult human.
   C D

   Ⓐ Ⓑ Ⓒ Ⓓ

10. The most fastest animals in the world are birds.
       A   B   C   D

    Ⓐ Ⓑ Ⓒ Ⓓ

Unit 14

The Present Perfect

Carlos **has been** a waiter **for** six months.

14A The Present Perfect of *Be*: *For* and *Since*

Form

Carlos **has been** a waiter **for** six months.

We form the present perfect of *be* with *have* or *has* and the past participle of the verb *be*.

<table>
<tr><th colspan="4">Affirmative Statements</th></tr>
<tr><th>Subject</th><th>Have/Has</th><th>Past Participle of Be</th><th></th></tr>
<tr><td>I
You</td><td>have</td><td rowspan="3">been</td><td rowspan="3">here for two hours.
here since 10 o'clock.</td></tr>
<tr><td>He
She
It</td><td>has</td></tr>
<tr><td>We
You
They</td><td>have</td></tr>
</table>

388   Unit 14

e-Workbook 14A

Yes/No Questions			Short Answers	
Have/Has	**Subject**	**Past Participle of *Be***	**Affirmative**	**Negative**
Have	I	**been** here?	Yes, you **have**.	No, you **haven't**.
	you		I/we **have**.	I/we **haven't**.
	we		you **have**.	you **haven't**.
	they		they **have**.	they **haven't**.
Has	he		he **has**.	he **hasn't**.
	she		she **has**.	she **hasn't**.
	it		it **has**.	it **hasn't**.

Contractions			
Subject Pronoun + *Have/Has*		**Have/Has + Not**	
I have	I**'ve**	I **haven't**	
you have	you**'ve**	you **haven't**	
he has	he**'s**	he **hasn't**	
she has	she**'s**	she **hasn't**	
it has	it**'s**	it **hasn't**	
we have	we**'ve**	we **haven't**	
they have	they**'ve**	they **haven't**	

Note: In the contractions *he's*, *she's*, and *it's*, the *'s* can take the place of either *has* or *is*. The sentence structure tells which one it is.

Function

Lin and Sue **have been** friends **for** four years.

1. We can use the present perfect to talk about an action or situation that started in the past and continues up to the present.
2. We often use the present perfect with *for* and *since*.
3. We use *for* and *since* with the present perfect to talk about how long the action or situation existed from the past to the present. We use *for* to talk about a length of time. We use *since* to talk about when a period of time began.

For		Since	
for	four years	since	1990
	six months		last year
	five weeks		(last) June
	four days		(last) Friday
	three hours		yesterday
	20 minutes		this morning
	a minute		nine o'clock this morning
	a long time		I moved to Tokyo

1 Practice

A Complete the sentences with the present perfect of the verb *be*.

1. Sue and Lin met at the university four years ago. They _____*have been*_____ friends for four years.

2. Lin married Steve last April. She _____ married since April.

3. Lin and Steve bought a new home last June. They _____ in the new house since June.

4. Life _____ very good for them since they got married.

5. Sue works part-time in a lab. She _____ a chemist for ten months now.

6. Sue also moved to a new apartment with her sister this month. They _____ in the apartment for only three weeks.

B Listen and check your answers. Then listen again and repeat each sentence.

AUDIO DOWNLOAD CD6, 22, 23

C Listen again. Read the statements and circle *True* or *False*.

 AUDIO DOWNLOAD CD6, 24

1. Sue and Lin have lived together since June.   True   False
2. Sue is moving to a new apartment.   True   False
3. Sue has worked as a chemist for ten months.   True   False

2 Practice

A Complete the sentences with *for* or *since*.

1. Mark and Yolanda have been married _____*for*_____ 22 years.

2. They have been at the same address _____ 1992.

3. Yolanda has been a teacher _____ 1990.

4. Mark has been a salesman _____ 25 years.

5. He has been with the same company _____ 1995.

6. Now Mark is in Texas on a business trip. He has been there _____ last Monday.

7. Mark has been on four business trips _____ last June.

8. It's Saturday. Yolanda is at the shopping center. She has been there _____ 10:00 this morning. She wants to get a birthday present for her son, Clark. He is 16 today.

9. Yolanda has been busy _____ yesterday. She wants to prepare for Clark's birthday.

10. Right now Clark is at the school gym. He has been there _____ 9:00 this morning.

11. Clark has been at the gym _____ three hours now.

12. He has been on the school basketball team _____ a year.

B Listen and check your answers. Then listen again and repeat each sentence.

 AUDIO DOWNLOAD CD6, 25, 26

C Listen again. Why is Yolanda busy? Circle the letter of the correct answer.

AUDIO

DOWNLOAD

CD6, 27

A   because Mark is away on business

B   because it is Clark's birthday today

C   because she is a teacher

3 Practice

A Work with a partner. Talk about yourself. Complete the following.

1.   I came to this school in (month, year) _____September 2002_____ .

2.   I have been here since _____ .

3.   I have been here for _____ .

B Write about your partner. Complete the sentences.

1.   My partner's name is _____ .

2.   He/She came to this school in (month, year) _____ .

3.   He/She has been here since _____ .

4.   He/She has been here for _____ .

5.   We have been in this class since _____ .

6.   We have been in this class for _____ .

C Tell the class about yourself and your partner.

Example

I have been in this school since September.

My partner has been here for three months.

14B | The Present Perfect: Regular and Irregular Verbs

Form

I **have owned** a grammar book.

1. We form the present perfect with *have/has* and the past participle of the verb.
2. We form the past participle of regular verbs by adding *-ed* to the verb. This is the same form as the simple past:

   play/play**ed**   finish/finish**ed**   work/work**ed**   live/liv**ed**
3. Irregular verbs have irregular past participles:

   know/**known**   write/**written**

Regular Verbs	Simple Past	Past Participle*
own	owned	**owned**
study	studied	**studied**

*Use the same spelling rules for the simple past and for the past participle.

Irregular Verbs	Simple Past	Past Participle
be	was/were	**been**
have	had	**had**
know	knew	**known**
go	went	**gone**

Affirmative Statements				
Subject	*Have/Has*	**Past Participle**		*For/Since*
I You	**have**	**had owned studied**	a grammar book	**for** six months. **since** June.
He/She/It	**has**			
We They	**have**			

4 Practice

A Complete the sentences with the present perfect of the verbs in parentheses.

Belton is a small town. Brad Peltry (live) ___*has lived*___ in Belton all
   1

his life. Brad is 58 years old. Brad is married. He (be) _____
                                                              2

married to Dora for 25 years. They (know) _____ each other since
                                              3

high school. Brad and Dora have a son. He is a student at a university in

Atlanta. He (study) _____ medicine for three years now.
                        4

Brad owns the grocery store in town. He (own) _____ the store
                                                    5

for 22 years. He (work) _____ in the store for 22 years, too.
                           6

   Something strange happened this week. Nobody (see) _____
                                                            7

Brad for four days. His truck (disappear) _____ . Dora doesn't
                                              8

know where he is. Dora (be) _____ worried. Brad (have)
                                9

_____ money problems lately.
   10

B Listen and check your answers. Then listen again and repeat each sentence.

CD6, 28, 29

C What do you think? What has happened to Brad?

THE POOR BROTHER AND THE RICH BROTHER

Bob and Jim are brothers. They both grew up on a farm in Texas, in the United States. Bob is 75, and Jim is 73. When Bob was 16, he left school. He worked on his father's farm. When his father died, Bob took over the farm. Bob has lived on the farm all his life. When Bob was 20, he married Brenda. Brenda was another farmer's daughter. Bob and Brenda have been married for 55 years. They have been very happy. They have three children and 12 grandchildren. Bob says he has had a good life.

Jim didn't like life on the farm. When he was 16, he left the farm. He went to New York. Jim has had an interesting life. He has made a lot of money in business. At age 24, he was a very rich man. He has been married three times and divorced three times. His family life has been unhappy. He has two children, but his children don't love him. They haven't spoken to their father for many years. Jim has lived alone in his luxury villa in the south of France for ten years. Jim has visited many countries since he was 24, and he has made a lot of money, but is he happy? Jim thinks about his brother. He has not seen him since he was 16, but Bob has written to him every Thanksgiving. He has sent him pictures of his family for 30 years. Jim has decided to visit his brother in Texas this Thanksgiving.

Write complete sentences about the story. Use the present perfect forms of these verbs.

be – was/were – been	make – made – made	speak – spoke – spoken
have – had – had	see – saw – seen	visit – visited – visited
live – lived – lived	send – sent – sent	write – wrote – written

1. Bob/live/on the farm all his life

   Bob has lived on the farm all his life .

2. Bob and Brenda/be/married for 55 years

   _____ .

3. Bob and Brenda/be/happy

   _____ .

4. Bob/have/a good life

   _____ .

5. Jim/have/an interesting life

   _____ .

6. Jim and his children/not speak/for many years

   _____ .

7. Jim/visit/many countries

   _____ .

8. Jim/make/a lot of money

   _____ .

9. Jim/live/alone for ten years

   _____ .

10. Bob/write to/Jim every Thanksgiving

    _____ .

11. Bob/send/pictures of his family/to Jim

    _____ .

12. Bob/not see/Jim/for a long time

    _____ .

The Present Perfect: Negative Statements and Questions

Form

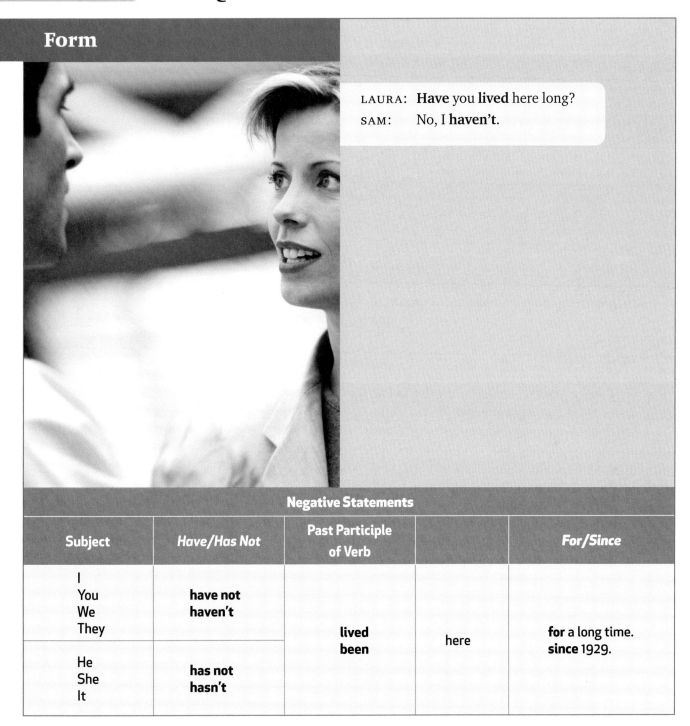

LAURA: **Have** you **lived** here long?

SAM: No, I **haven't**.

		Negative Statements		
Subject	**Have/Has Not**	**Past Participle of Verb**		**For/Since**
I You We They	**have not** **haven't**	**lived** **been**	here	**for** a long time. **since** 1929.
He She It	**has not** **hasn't**			

Yes/No Questions				Short Answers	
Have/Has	Subject	Past Participle of Verb		Affirmative	Negative
Have	I			Yes, you **have**.	No, you **haven't**.
	you			I/we **have**.	I/we **haven't**.
	we	**been** **lived**	here long?	you **have**.	you **haven't**.
	they			they **have**.	they **haven't**.
Has	he			he **has**.	he **hasn't**.
	she			she **has**.	she **hasn't**.
	it			it **has**.	it **hasn't**.

Wh- Questions			
Wh- Word	*Have/Has*	Subject	Past Participle of Verb
How long	**have**	I you we they	**lived** **been** here?
	has	he she it	

6 Practice

A Complete the sentences. Use the present perfect of the verbs in parentheses.

A

ALEX: How long (be) ____<u>have</u>____ you ____<u>been</u>____ in this class?
                                       1   2

PETER: Since February.

ALEX: (make) _____ you _____ any friends?
                                  3   **4**

PETER: Yes, I (make) _____ a lot of friends in this class, but my
                               5

       English (not, improve) _____ .
                                    6

B

JOHN: How long (have) _____ you _____ your
                                  1   **2**

       driver's license?

BOB: For two years.

JOHN: (have) _____ you _____ any accidents?
                          3   **4**

BOB: No, I _____ .
                5

C

SUE: How long (work) _____ you _____ here?
                                1   **2**

DON: Since May. But I (be) _____ a computer programmer for
                              3

       four years.

SUE: (work) _____ you _____ for other companies?
                         4   **5**

DON: Yes, I _____ . I (work) _____ for three
                 6   **7**

       companies since the year 2000.

SUE: (live) _____ you _____ in Boston since 2000?
                      8   **9**

DON: Yes, I _____ . I like Boston. How long (live)
                  10

       _____ you _____ in Boston?
                   11   **12**

SUE: For three months now, and the weather (not,be) _____
                                                               13

       good for the last three months. It (be) _____ so cold.
                                            14

B Listen and check your answers. Then work with a partner. Listen again and repeat each conversation.

CD6, 30, 31

Form/Function

KEN: **Have** you **ever been** to Hawaii?
BRENDA: No, I'**ve never been** to Hawaii.

1. We often use *ever* with the present perfect to ask questions. *Ever* means "at any time up to now."
2. We use *never* to answer in the negative. *Never* means "at no time up to now."

KEN: Have you **ever** visited Australia?
BRENDA: No, I haven't.   OR   No, I've **never** visited Australia.

Have/Has	Subject	Ever/Never	Past Participle	
Have	you	ever	been	to Bangkok?

Subject	Have/Has	Ever/Never	Past Participle	
I	have	never	been	to Bangkok.
I	have	not ever	been	to Bangkok.

7 Read

A Do you remember Bob from Practice 5 on page 395? Read some more about Bob.

Bob has lived on the farm all his life. Bob loves the simple farm life. He loves nature and animals. He is not interested in city life, expensive restaurants, expensive clothes, or cars. He spends his vacations camping and fishing near his home with his family. He has not gone outside his small town, and he doesn't want to. Bob doesn't want to be a millionaire. He just wants to stay on his farm and enjoy his family.

B Work with a partner. Make questions with the words. Your partner answers.

Example

Bob/ever/be/to Europe

A: Has Bob ever been to Europe?

B: No, he hasn't./No, he has never been to Europe./No, he has not ever been to Europe.

1. Bob/ever/take/a plane

2. Bob/ever/visit/New York

3. Bob/ever/eat/sushi

4. Bob/ever/wear/expensive clothes

5. Bob/ever/drink/champagne

6. Bob/ever/drive/expensive cars

7. Bob/ever/want/to be a millionaire

8. Bob/ever/work/in the city

C Now write four more questions about Bob and answer them.

1. _____ ?

    _____ .

2. _____ ?

    _____ .

3. _____ ?

    _____ .

4. _____ ?

    _____ .

8 Read
Read the story. Then write answers to the questions.

COOKING BY CANDLE

Mula bet some friends he could survive one night on an icy mountain with nothing to warm him. He took a book and a candle for some light and sat through the freezing night on the mountain. When he came down to claim his winnings, his friends asked, "Did you take anything up there to keep you warm?"

"No," said Mula, "just a small candle to read by."

"Aha!" they exclaimed, "then you have lost the bet!"

A week later, he invited the same friends to dinner at his house. They waited and waited for food. "Dinner's not ready," said Mula. "Come and see why!"

In the kitchen, they saw a huge pot of water. Under the pot a small candle was burning. Mula said, "Does this remind you of our bet? The pot has been over this candle since yesterday, and it hasn't warmed it yet!"

1. What did Mula bet some friends?

   _____ .

2. What did Mula take with him on the mountain? Did he win the bet?

   _____ .

3. What did Mula do a week later?

_____ .

4. What did his friends see in the kitchen?

_____ .

5. According to Mula, how long has the pot been over the candle?

_____ .

6. From what Mula says, has the candle warmed the pot yet?

_____ .

Listening Puzzle

AUDIO DOWNLOAD   CD6, 32

A Listen and check the correct answer.

❏ A. *corn*

❏ B. *wheat*

❏ C. *potatoes*

B Discuss your answer with your classmates.

AUDIO DOWNLOAD CD6, 33

C Now listen again and write the sentences you hear.

A Before You Read

Answer the questions.

1. Where is Mount Everest?
2. How many people have been to the top of Mount Everest?

B Read

EVEREST AND HILLARY

Edmund Hillary was born in 1919 in New Zealand. He worked as a beekeeper, but he also liked to climb mountains. He climbed mountains in New Zealand 5 and the Alps. He climbed 11 mountains in the Himalayas. Hillary wanted to be the first to climb the highest mountain in the 10 world—Mount Everest.

Hillary joined a team to climb Mount Everest. They set off in May 1953. When **they** got near the summit, only Hillary and Tenzing Norgay, 15 a native Sherpa[1] from Nepal were left. All the others went back because of **exhaustion**. Hillary

and Tenzing set off for the summit on May 29th, and they reached it at 11:30 A.M. Hillary took a photo of Tenzing, but Tenzing did not 20 know how to use a camera, so there were no pictures of Hillary.

When they returned, they became world famous. Hillary continued to climb ten more 25 mountains in the Himalayas. He went to the North Pole and the South Pole. He was the first person to reach the top of the highest mountain, the North Pole, and the South Pole. Tenzing became a hero for his people. Since 30 that time, about 3,000 people have been to the top of Mount Everest.

[1.]Sherpa = name of the people who live in the Himalayas

> **DID YOU KNOW ... ?**
> Mount Everest was named after Sir George Everest, a British surveyor general of India. He pronounced his last name EEV-rest.

C Notice the Grammar

Underline all forms of the simple past and present perfect.

Choose the best answer.

D Look for Main Ideas

1. What is the main idea of paragraph 1?
   - Ⓐ what Hillary did before he climbed Mount Everest
   - Ⓑ Hillary's life in New Zealand
   - Ⓒ the mountains Hillary climbed
   - Ⓓ Hillary's life as a beekeeper

2. What is paragraph 2 mainly about?
   - Ⓐ how Tenzing Norgay reached the summit
   - Ⓑ how Hillary became world famous
   - Ⓒ why there are no pictures of Hillary
   - Ⓓ the first people to reach the summit

E Look for Details

3. Edmund Hillary _____ .
   - Ⓐ climbed many mountains before Mount Everest
   - Ⓑ wanted to reach the summit alone
   - Ⓒ did not like the rest of the team
   - Ⓓ never climbed mountains in the Himalayas before Everest

4. Hillary and Tenzing _____ .
   - Ⓐ reached the summit on the morning of May 29, 1953
   - Ⓑ left with the rest of the team for the summit on the morning of May 29th
   - Ⓒ took photos of each other at the summit
   - Ⓓ were afraid to reach the summit

Read English for pleasure. Read a magazine article or a short novel. Don't worry if you don't understand every word. Read for a general understanding. If you are taking the TOEFL™, read academic texts.

5. Which of the following is NOT true about Tenzing Norgay?
   - Ⓐ He was from Nepal.
   - Ⓑ He was at the summit of Everest with Hillary.
   - Ⓒ He loved to take photos.
   - Ⓓ He became a hero for his people.

F Make Inferences

6. What can we infer from the reading?
   - Ⓐ Hillary is a man of strength and courage.
   - Ⓑ Hillary didn't like to share his fame.
   - Ⓒ Native people are better climbers.
   - Ⓓ Everyone who has been to the top of Everest is famous.

G Look for Vocabulary

7. The word *exhaustion* in the reading is closest in meaning to _____ .
   - Ⓐ sickness
   - Ⓑ lack of air
   - Ⓒ tiredness
   - Ⓓ lack of water

H Reference the Text

8. The word *they* in the reading refers to
   _____ .
   - Ⓐ Hillary, Tenzing, and the Sherpa
   - Ⓑ all the climbers except Hillary
   - Ⓒ Hillary and Tenzing
   - Ⓓ the team of climbers

Writing: Describe Experiences

Write a paragraph about your experiences in a class.

STEP 1   Think about your English class. Ask yourself these questions. Write your answers in sentences.

1. How long have you studied English?

2. When did this English class start?

3. Who is your teacher?

4. How many students are there in your class? How many of them do you know?

5. What grammar structures have you studied since the class started? (simple present, simple past, etc.)

6. What grammar structures have been the hardest?

7. How long did you study the simple past?

8. How long have you studied the present perfect?

9. How many tests have you had since the class started?

10. When was the last test? How did you do on it?

STEP 2   Rewrite your sentences in paragraph form. Be sure you have used the present perfect correctly.

STEP 3   Evaluate your paragraph.

Checklist

_____ Did you use the verb forms correctly?

_____ Did you answer all the questions?

_____ Did you organize your answers into paragraphs?

STEP 4   Work with a partner to edit your paragraph. Correct spelling, punctuation, vocabulary, and grammar.

STEP 5   Write your final copy.

Self-Test

Choose the best answer, A, B, C, or D, to complete the sentence. Darken the oval with the same letter.

1. _____ to Europe?

   A. Have you ever been   Ⓐ Ⓑ Ⓒ Ⓓ
   B. Ever been you
   C. Been ever
   D. Were have you ever

2. Danny's not here. He _____ to the office an hour ago.

   A. went   Ⓐ Ⓑ Ⓒ Ⓓ
   B. was going
   C. has gone
   D. has went

3. We _____ to India.

   A. ever have been   Ⓐ Ⓑ Ⓒ Ⓓ
   B. been never have
   C. have never been
   D. have been never

4. We _____ grammar since early this morning.

   A. studied   Ⓐ Ⓑ Ⓒ Ⓓ
   B. have to study
   C. have study
   D. have studied

5. A: Have you ever had a dog?
   B: Yes, I _____ .

   A. have had   Ⓐ Ⓑ Ⓒ Ⓓ
   B. have
   C. had
   D. do

6. Nick _____ since yesterday.

   A. have not called   Ⓐ Ⓑ Ⓒ Ⓓ
   B. hasn't call
   C. did not call
   D. hasn't called

7. We _____ to a movie for a long time.

   A. haven't been   Ⓐ Ⓑ Ⓒ Ⓓ
   B. weren't
   C. haven't be
   D. haven't go

8. When _____ ?

   A. the movie starts   Ⓐ Ⓑ Ⓒ Ⓓ
   B. has the movie starts
   C. did the movie start
   D. the movie has started

9. I _____ my mother yesterday.

   A. have called   Ⓐ Ⓑ Ⓒ Ⓓ
   B. was calling
   C. called
   D. have call

10. How long _____ ?

    A. have been married John   Ⓐ Ⓑ Ⓒ Ⓓ
    B. married John
    C. has John been married
    D. did marry John

1. <u>Humans</u> <u>lived</u> on Earth <u>for millions</u> of <u>years</u>.
   A   B   C   D

   Ⓐ Ⓑ Ⓒ Ⓓ

2. The weather <u>has</u> <u>change</u> <u>in</u> the last ten <u>years</u>.
                A   B   C   D

   Ⓐ Ⓑ Ⓒ Ⓓ

3. <u>There</u> <u>were</u> many <u>earthquakes</u> <u>in</u> California
   A   B   C   D
   since 1914.

   Ⓐ Ⓑ Ⓒ Ⓓ

4. The president <u>is</u> not <u>been</u> in the country <u>since</u>
                  A   B   C
   <u>last Wednesday</u>.
   D

   Ⓐ Ⓑ Ⓒ Ⓓ

5. <u>Students</u> <u>did had</u> problems <u>with English spelling</u>
   A   B   C
   <u>for</u> a long time.
   D

   Ⓐ Ⓑ Ⓒ Ⓓ

6. This <u>was been</u> the <u>hottest</u> <u>summer</u> <u>since</u> 1964.
         A   B   C   D

   Ⓐ Ⓑ Ⓒ Ⓓ

7. People <u>have played</u> soccer <u>since</u> four <u>hundred</u>
           A   B   C
   <u>years</u>.
   D

   Ⓐ Ⓑ Ⓒ Ⓓ

8. Mozart <u>has written</u> 600 <u>pieces</u> of <u>music</u> before
           A   B   C
   he died <u>in</u> 1791.
           D

   Ⓐ Ⓑ Ⓒ Ⓓ

9. <u>Did</u> you <u>gone</u> to Singapore when you <u>lived</u> <u>in</u>
   A   B   C   D
   Asia?

   Ⓐ Ⓑ Ⓒ Ⓓ

10. <u>Since</u> 1990, scientists <u>found</u> many <u>new drugs</u> to
    A   B   C
    help <u>us</u> fight diseases.
         D

   Ⓐ Ⓑ Ⓒ Ⓓ

Audio Script

Unit 1, Practice 1B, Page 3 (CD1, 2, 3)

1. a table
2. an ear
3. an animal
4. a hotel
5. an eye
6. an armchair
7. a question
8. an uncle
9. a city
10. a house
11. a bed
12. an exercise
13. a university
14. an elephant
15. an office
16. an hourglass

Unit 1, Practice 7B, Page 9 (CD1, 4, 5)

1. It's a passport.
2. They're keys.
3. We're from Canada.
4. He's a doctor.
5. She's a teacher.
6. I'm Italian.
7. You're late.
8. We're from Brazil.
9. It's a book.
10. He's from Spain.

Unit 1, Practice 9B and 9C, Page 11 (CD1, 6-8)

1. I'm not in class 1A. I'm in class 2A.
2. The class isn't at 10:00. It's at 9:00.
3. The students aren't in the classroom. They're outside.
4. The book isn't black. It's white.
5. The exercises aren't long. They're short.
6. The questions aren't difficult. They're easy.
7. She isn't in class today. She's sick. She's not in class today. She's sick.
8. The food in the cafeteria isn't bad. It's good.
9. I'm not ready. Please wait.
10. We're students. We aren't teachers. We're students. We're not teachers.

Unit 1, Practice 15B, Page 16 (CD1, 9, 10)

1. She isn't Chinese. She's American.
2. She isn't short. She's tall.
3. She isn't lazy. She's hardworking.
4. She isn't heavy. She's thin.
5. She isn't old. She's young.
6. She isn't married. She's single.

Unit 1, Practice 19B, Page 20 (CD1, 11, 12)

Give me the English names for the things you can see.
1. This is a table.
2. This is a newspaper.
3. This is a dictionary.
4. This is a pen.
5. This is a cup.
6. Those are sandwiches.

7. This is a napkin.
8. These are my books.

Unit 1, Practice 21B, Page 22 (CD1, 13, 14)

1. Is she a teacher?   No, she isn't.
2. Is she young?   Yes, she is.
3. Is she Brazilian?   No, she isn't.
4. Is she Colombian?   Yes, she is.
5. Is she 18 years old?   Yes, she is.
6. Is she a student?   Yes, she is.
7. Is he 19 years old?   No, he isn't.
8. Is he Malaysian?   Yes, he is.
9. Is he a doctor?   No, he isn't.
10. Is he single?   Yes, he is.
11. Are they students?   Yes, they are.
12. Are they young?   Yes, they are.
13. Are they single?   Yes, they are.
14. Are they American?   No, they aren't.

Unit 1, Listening Puzzle, Page 29 (CD1, 15-16)

This country is in South America. It is a long country. The ocean is on one side of this country. The language of this country is Spanish. The Andes Mountains are in this country. This country is famous for its beef or red meat. Beef is from cattle. These animals are on big ranches. The tango is a popular dance in this country. What is the name of this country?

Unit 2, Practice 1B, Page 37 (CD1, 17, 18)

1. What's the weather like in New York City?
   It's cloudy.
2. How's the weather in Houston?
   It's sunny.
3. What's the weather like in Los Angeles?
   It's sunny.
4. Is it rainy or windy in Chicago today?
   It's windy.
5. Is it hot or cold in Miami?
   It's hot.
6. What's the weather like in Boston?
   It's rainy.
7. How's the weather in San Francisco?
   It's windy.
8. Is it cloudy or windy in Denver?
   It's cloudy.

Unit 2, Practice 3B, Page 39 (CD1, 19, 20)

1. It's six o' five. OR It's five past six.
2. It's twelve forty-five. OR It's a quarter to one.
3. It's five fifteen. OR It's a quarter past five.
4. It's one o'clock.
5. It's ten o' five. OR It's five past ten.
6. It's three forty. OR It's twenty to four.

Unit 2, Practice 9B, Page 44 (CD1, 21, 22)

1. There is a table in the kitchen. There are two chairs.
2. There are plates and pots on the table.
3. There are cups on the floor. There is a telephone on the floor, too.
4. There is a pot on the stove.
5. There are pots and dishes in the sink.

6. There is a backpack under the table. There is a jacket on the floor.

Unit 2, Practice 12C, Page 47 (CD1, 23, 24)
1. Is there a view from the hotel?
   Yes, there is.
2. Are there mountains near the hotel?
   Yes, there are.
3. Is there an exercise center?
   Yes, there is.
4. Is there train service to the town?
   Yes, there is.
5. Is there an underground parking lot?
   Yes, there is.
6. Is there a town near the hotel?
   No, there isn't.
7. Is there a movie theater?
   Yes, there is.
8. How many swimming pools are there?
   There are two swimming pools.
9. How many restaurants are there?
   There are three restaurants.
10. How many shops are there?
    There are over twenty shops.

Unit 2, Practice 16B and 16C, Page 50 (CD1, 25-27)
1. Our school is old, but it is clean.
2. The classrooms are sunny and bright.
3. There are old tables and chairs in our classroom.
4. The chairs are old, but they are strong.
5. There are two cafeterias. There is a cafeteria for the students, and there is a cafeteria for the teachers.
6. We sell two kinds of food: hot food like pizza and cold food like sandwiches.
7. In my class, there are students from Mexico, and there are students from Japan.
8. Is your teacher funny or serious?
9. My English class is great, but I have a lot of homework.
10. Is your book blue, or is it green?

Unit 2, Practice 19B and 19C, Page 53 (CD1, 28-30)
1. Today, Bertie is 80 years old.
2. Fifty years ago, Bertie was an engineer.
3. Brenda was a secretary 50 years ago.
4. Brenda is 75 years old today.
5. Fifty years ago, they were in the city most of the time.
6. Today, they are on their farm.
7. Bertie and Brenda were happy 50 years ago.
8. Bertie and Brenda are happy today.

Unit 2, Practice 21B, Page 56 (CD1, 31, 32)
1. Was the food good?
2. Was the food expensive?
3. Were the servers polite?
4. Was the restaurant clean?
5. Was the place busy?
6. Was the restaurant convenient?
7. Were the plates full?
8. Was the service good?
9. Was the restaurant big?
10. Was the food tasty?

Unit 2, Listening Puzzle, Page 59 (CD1 33-34)
This city is in the United States. It is near the ocean. It is a very big city, but it isn't the capital of the United States. There is a big park in the center of this city. Its name is Central Park. There are many tall buildings, restaurants, and museums. This city is famous for its theaters on Broadway. The Empire State Building is in this city, too.
What is the name of this city?

Unit 3, Practice 1B, Page 67 (CD1, 35, 36)
1. The alarm clock rings at 7:00 every morning.
2. She gets up.
3. She takes a shower.
4. Janet says, "I brush my teeth every morning."
5. She puts on her clothes.
6. Janet eats breakfast with her sister Meg.
7. They watch the news on television.
8. Meg stays home.
9. They say good bye.
10. Janet locks the door.
11. She waits for the bus.
12. She gets on the bus.

Unit 3, Practice 7B, Page 73 (CD1, 37, 38)
Dan Thomas comes from Canada, but he lives in New York. He teaches English. He likes to walk, so he walks to school every day. He sometimes arrives late for class. He enjoys his job and loves his students, but he sometimes forgets their names. He usually gives a lot of homework.

Unit 3, Practice 12B, Page 76 (CD1, 39, 40)
Sam has a good job. He has a wife, Kate. They have two children. Kate has a good job, too. She is a teacher. They have one car, and they have a small house. The house has two bedrooms. It has a garden, too. The garden has trees and flowers. Sam and his family are happy. They have a good life.

Unit 3, Practice 15B, Page 78 (CD1, 41, 42)
1. Birds don't give milk.
2. Fish swim.
3. A chicken comes from an egg.
4. Plants need water to grow.
5. Penguins don't live in Italy.
6. Elephants don't eat chickens.
7. Rice doesn't grow on trees.
8. The Chinese drink tea.

Unit 3, Practice 16B, Page 79 (CD1, 43, 44)
It is August. The sun is hot. There aren't any clouds in the sky. Tony is in Hawaii. He doesn't get up early. He gets up at 11:00 o'clock. He doesn't put on his shirt and tie. He puts on his shorts. He doesn't go to work. He goes to the beach. He doesn't wait for the bus. He waits for his friends. Tony and his friends don't sit in front of computers. They sit at a table in a café on the beach. They don't talk about work. They talk about fun things to do. They don't eat sandwiches. They eat delicious food. They don't look at computers. They look at the blue sea. Tony doesn't worry about his work. He is happy and relaxed. But Tony isn't on vacation. He is in his office. It's just a dream.

Unit 3, Practice 18B and 18C, Page 81 (CD1, 45-47)

1. Do you love him?	Yes, I do.
2. Do you know his family?	Yes, I do.
3. Does he have a good job?	Yes, he does.
4. Does he live in a nice apartment?	Yes, he does.
5. Does he drive a nice car?	Yes, he does.
6. Does he wear nice clothes?	Yes, he does.
7. Does he smoke?	Yes, he does.
8. Does he buy you nice gifts?	Yes, he does.
9. Does he take you out?	Yes, he does.
10. Does he want to marry you?	No, he doesn't.

Unit 3, Practice 23B, Page 86 (CD1, 48, 49)

1. What is the largest animal on land?
   It's the elephant.
2. Where does it live?
   It lives in Africa and Asia.
3. What does it eat?
   It eats plants.
4. How long does it live?
   It lives about 70 years.
5. Are elephants intelligent?
   Yes, they are. Elephants are intelligent.
6. Do elephants live alone?
   No, they don't. They live in groups.
7. How many kinds of elephants are there?
   There are two kinds of elephants.
8. What are they?
   They are the African elephant and the Indian elephant.
9. Does an elephant cry?
   Yes, it does. An elephant cries.
10. Do elephants laugh?
    Yes, they do. Elephants laugh.

Unit 3, Listening Puzzle, Page 89 (CD1 50-51)

This animal is not a fish but likes to be in water. It is a good swimmer. We find this animal in the sea, river, or ocean. It usually eats fish. This animal doesn't lay eggs. It has babies. This animal usually lives with a group. It is a very intelligent animal. It is also very friendly. We see this animal in water shows. This animal uses sound to find things. This animal is part of the whale family. What is the name of this animal?

Unit 4, Practice 1B, Page 97 (CD2, 2, 3)

1. The birds are singing.
2. Tony is working in the yard.
3. Fred and Tom are talking in the street.
4. A child is eating ice cream.
5. Children are playing in the park.
6. Bob is washing his car.
7. Mike and Linda are going to the car.
8. Alex is fixing his motorbike.
9. Carol is reading the newspaper.
10. A man is waiting for the bus.
11. An airplane is flying in the sky.
12. Two girls are watching the airplane.

Unit 4, Practice 6B, Page 102 (CD2, 4, 5)

1. saving – save
2. making – make
3. typing – type
4. studying – study
5. hoping – hope
6. planning – plan
7. adding – add
8. smiling – smile
9. hurrying – hurry
10. driving – drive
11. agreeing – agree
12. giving – give

Unit 4, Practice 8B and 8C, Page 103 (CD2, 6-8)

Dear Elsie,
It's Monday evening, and it is raining outside. I am sitting at my desk in my room. I am watching the rain from my window, and I am thinking of you. I really miss you! All the family is at home this evening. My father is reading a book and eating popcorn. My brother is playing video games in his room. My mother is in the kitchen. She is making a cake because it's my sister's birthday tomorrow. Right now my sister is in her room. She is doing her homework, and she is listening to music at the same time. The telephone is ringing, and my mother is calling me. I must go now.
Write soon,
Magda

Unit 4, Practice 9B, Page 105 (CD2, 9, 10)

1. The man and the woman aren't standing in an office. They are standing in the street.
2. The man isn't talking on the phone. The woman is talking on the phone.
3. The man isn't holding a book. He's holding an umbrella.
4. The man isn't looking at cars. He's looking at the woman.
5. The man isn't wearing a raincoat. He's wearing a jacket.
6. The woman isn't holding her handbag. She's holding a telephone.
7. It isn't sunny. It's raining.
8. The woman isn't working on her computer. She's talking on the phone.

Unit 4, Practice 10B, Page 107 (CD2, 11, 12)

1. Is your sister studying?
   d. No, she isn't. She's watching TV.
2. Is the sun shining?
   f. No, it's not. It's cloudy.
3. Am I taking your seat?
   a. No, you're not. That seat is free.
4. Are you studying?
   e. Yes, we are. We're learning grammar.
5. Is David cooking?
   c. Yes, he is. He's making rice.
6. Are the children sleeping?
   b. Yes, they are. They're in their beds.

Unit 4, Practice 12B, Page 109 (CD2, 13, 14)

1. What is she watching?
   She's watching a movie.
2. What are you drinking?
   I am drinking tea.
3. When is Sandra coming?
   Sandra is coming at six.
4. Why are you taking an umbrella?
   I am taking an umbrella because it's raining.
5. Who is Peter talking to?
   Peter is talking to his father.
6. How is Linda feeling?

Linda is feeling fine.
7. Where are the children playing?
The children are playing in the park.
8. Who are you talking to?
I am talking to Bill on the telephone.

Unit 4, Practice 13B, Page 110 (CD2,15, 16)
1- b. Mary has a lot of work right now.
2 - a. Susan needs a new coat.
3 - b. Look! That man is taking a photo of us.
4 - b. Please be quiet. I am studying.
5 - b. This cup of coffee smells good.
6 - b. I'm looking for a new apartment.
7 - b. The children love ice cream.
8 - b. He doesn't understand Japanese.

Unit 4, Practice 14B and 14C, Page 111 (CD2, 17-19)
The woman in the picture has long hair. She is wearing a white blouse and a skirt. In the picture, she is sitting at a table in a restaurant. She is reading a book. She has some flowers. She loves flowers, so she buys flowers from the market every week

Unit 4, Practice 15B, Page 115 (CD2,20, 21)
A
A: What are you doing? Are you studying?
B: No, I'm not studying. I'm cleaning my car.
A: Do you wash your car every week?
B: Yes, I like a clean car.
B
A: Why are you sitting in front of the class? You usually sit at the back.
B: I know. I don't have my glasses with me today.
C
A: Do you speak Japanese?
B: Yes, I speak a little.
A: What does "moshi moshi" mean?
B: It means "hello."
D
A: How often do you write to your family?
B: I don't like to write letters. I call them every week.
E
A: Are you going out now?
B: Yes, I'm going to the store. Do you need anything?
F
A: Are you working at the moment?
B: Yes, I'm sitting at my desk right now.
A: Do you like it?
B: Yes, I love it. I write for five hours every day.
G
A: Why are you putting on your coat?
B: I'm going for a walk. Do you want to come?
H
A: What are you waiting for?
B: I'm waiting for the store to open.
A: But it opens at ten every day.
B: I know. I want to be early. The sales start today.
I
A: Why are you walking so fast? You usually don't walk fast.
B: I am hurrying because my father is waiting for me.

J
A: Do you usually take the bus to school?
B: Yes, I always take the bus. I like it. I don't have a problem with parking.
K
A: Do you remember Joanne?
B: Yes. Is she still studying?
A: No. She's working now. She has a very good job in a hospital.

Unit 4, Listening Puzzle, Page 117 (CD2, 22-23)
This is a traditional holiday in North America. It isn't a religious holiday. Everybody celebrates this day. People are traveling to be with their families. Families are getting together, talking, and eating. They are having a big meal. They always have turkey on this day. They also have pumpkin pie. On this holiday people do not give gifts to each other. This holiday is in October in Canada. There are no fireworks or parades in the street on this day.
What is the name of this holiday?

Unit 5, Practice 4B and 4C, Page 126 (CD2, 24-26)
He has some coffee. He puts some milk in his coffee. He also puts in some sugar. He has some bread. He puts some butter on the bread. Sometimes he has some cheese. He likes some fruit in the morning. He has an orange every morning. And he has a banana with a cookie at 10:30.

Unit 5, Practice 5B, Page 128 (CD2, 27, 28)
A
I live in an apartment in the city. The apartment is in a big building. The building is old, but it is near transportation and stores. I usually take a bus or a tram to work. The bus stops in front of the apartment building, and the tram is just a hundred yards, 91 meters, from the building.

B
Don: What do you want to do today?
Kate: I want to see a movie.
Don: Which movie?
Kate: There's a movie I want to see at the movie theater near my house. I don't know the name of the movie. It's about a man with a dog. The dog has a special ability. It speaks like a person.
Don: That sounds like a silly movie.
C
Dave: Do you live in a house or an apartment?
James: Well, I have a house in the country and an apartment in the city. The house was my mother's, and I rent the apartment.
Dave: Oh. I guess you have a car and a motorbike, too.

Unit 5, Practice 9B, Page 133 (CD2, 29, 30)
1. a bar of soap
2. a roll of toilet paper
3. a can of tomatoes
4. a carton of milk
5. a loaf of bread
6. a box of cereal
7. a bag of sugar
8. a bottle of shampoo
9. a pack of batteries
10. a tube of toothpaste
11. a jar of mayonnaise

12. a bottle of oil
13. a piece of cheese
14. a bottle of juice

Unit 5, Practice 11B, Page 135 (CD2, 31, 32)
1. David doesn't eat much meat.
2. He doesn't eat much bread.
3. He eats many kinds of cereal.
4. He doesn't eat many eggs.
5. He doesn't drink much milk.
6. He doesn't eat much cheese.
7. He doesn't eat much food at meals.
8. He doesn't spend much money on food.

Unit 5, Practice 12B and 12C, Page 135 (CD2, 33-35)
1. He drinks a few glasses of juice every day.
2. When he is hungry, he eats a few nuts.
3. He exercises for a few hours every day.
4. He only uses a little salt on his food.
5. He also uses a little oil.
6. He eats a little fish.
7. He eats a few oranges every morning.
8. He eats a few kinds of fruit every day.

Unit 5, Practice 14B, Page 138 (CD2, 36,37)
1. Whose bicycle is this? It's Mike's.
2. Whose sneakers are these? They're Ted's.
3. Whose hat is this? It's Jane's.
4. Whose house is this? It's Sandra's.
5. Whose ball is this? It's Timmy's.
6. Whose car is this? It's my parents'.

Unit 5, Listening Puzzle, Page 141 (CD2, 38-39)
This is a food. We need flour, water, and salt to make it. Then we bake it in an oven. We also buy this food ready in stores. We put cheese and vegetables such as tomatoes, mushrooms, and peppers on it. We also put meat like sausage or ham on it. This food is usually round. We cut it into slices. It is a popular food around the world. We think it comes from Italy.
What is the name of this food?

Unit 6, Practice 4B, Page 153 (CD3, 2, 3)
Pamela: Where were you? I called you four times last week.
Meg: I was in New York. I was there for a conference. It started last Monday and ended yesterday.
Pamela: Lucky you. I love New York in the fall. I was there two years ago in October. The weather was beautiful!
Meg: Well, this October was terrible. The rain started two weeks ago and stopped last week for just two days. Then it started to rain again yesterday afternoon just as I arrived at the airport.
Pamela: Yesterday afternoon? Were you in that traffic jam at the airport?
Meg: Yes, I was. I was really tired last night when I got home. I was in bed by nine and opened my eyes only an hour ago.
Pamela: Oh, I called you ten minutes ago, but your phone was busy.
Meg: That was my brother. He called me about 20 minutes ago. He called me yesterday evening too, but I was asleep.
Pamela: By the way, Mary Jane called me last Friday. She's getting married!
Meg: Really! Who's the lucky man?

Pamela: His name is Tony Bradson. She started to work with him three years ago, and they decided to get married last year. So they saved some money and decided the wedding date last month.
Meg: Tony Bradson? Are you sure?
Pamela: Yes, why?

Unit 6, Practice 6B, Page 155 (CD3, 4, 5)
1. add - added
2. carry - carried
3. allow - allowed
4. show - showed
5. count - counted
6. erase - erased
7. fit - fitted
8. marry - married
9. die - died
10. fail - failed
11. stop - stopped
12. hurry - hurried
13. wait - waited
14. stay - stayed
15. cry - cried
16. drop - dropped
17. study - studied
18. taste - tasted
19. cook - cooked
20. worry - worried

Unit 6, Practice 10B, Page 157 (CD3,6, 7)
Dear Mom and Dad,
Greetings from New York! We arrived last Friday. It rained all weekend, so we carried umbrellas.
We shopped in the big stores on Fifth Avenue, but I preferred the small shops in the East Village. We visited the Statue of Liberty. We entered at her feet and climbed up to her head. That was great! We walked around Central Park and even watched a parade in the streets. Last night, we decided to go to Little Italy to have dinner. The food was delicious, and we enjoyed the lovely Italian music.
See you soon!
Susan

Unit 6, Practice 11B and 11C, Page 159 (CD3, 8-10)
Jennifer: Hello, Brad. It's Jennifer. How are you?
Brad: I'm fine, Jennifer. I arrived in Hawaii yesterday morning, and right now I'm walking on the beach, and I'm talking to you.
Jennifer: It sounds wonderful! Are you thinking about me?
Brad: Of course, I'm thinking about all the work you have in the office.
Jennifer: Yes, I have so much work. By the way, Tommy Jones called you at the office yesterday. He asked about you and wanted to speak to you. I said you are out of town.
Brad: Good.
Jennifer: By the way, where are you staying?
Brad: I'm staying at the Sands Hotel on Waikiki Beach. I have a beautiful room.
Jennifer: Does it have a view?
Brad: Yes, it has a beautiful view of the ocean.
Jennifer: How was the meeting yesterday?
Brad: The meeting was fine. After the meeting, we all walked

to a restaurant on the beach. The waiter offered us a table under the stars and allowed us to choose the music. And we danced all night. I really enjoyed it.

Jennifer: Oh, really? You danced! Who with?

Unit 6, Practice 12B, Page 161 (CD3, 11, 12)

Luis opened his eyes. The hands on the clock pointed to 9:20. He yawned and stayed in bed until 10:30. Then he showered and shaved. He dressed at 12:00 o'clock and finished at around 1:00 o'clock. Then he walked to the café on the corner and ordered breakfast. He enjoyed it as usual. It started to rain, so he called his friend and invited him to his apartment to watch videos. His friend arrived at 6:00 P.M., and they watched videos and they laughed a lot. At 10:00 P.M. the rain stopped and his friend wanted to go back home. It was then 11:00 P.M., and Luis returned to his favorite place — his bed!

Unit 6, Practice 13B, Page 162 (CD3, 13, 14)

At 8:30 A.M. yesterday, Ann played tennis with a friend. At 10:00 o'clock, she washed her clothes. Then she dried her clothes in the dryer and folded them. At 12:00 o'clock, she cooked lunch. After lunch, she turned on her computer and answered her email. Then she talked on the telephone with her friends. She needed to buy a birthday gift for a friend. So she shopped in the stores and picked out a gift. By 9:00 P.M., she was at home and tired, so she watched television.

Unit 6, Practice 15B and 15C, Page 165 (CD3, 15-17)

A Trip to Paris

Last April, Pete and Paula flew to Paris from New York. They found a small hotel in the center of town. The hotel wasn't expensive, and it was clean. Every morning, they ate French bread and drank strong French coffee. They took the Metro all the time. They heard people sing in the subway.

One day, they made friends with a French person. They were lucky because he spoke English. He told them all the interesting places to visit. He also taught them two French words, *bonjour* and *merci*. They took a trip on the river Seine, and they saw a lot of interesting places. One day, they went shopping.

They bought French perfume for gifts. Then they sat outside in a café and had an expensive lunch. They spent a lot of money that day. Pete and Paula thought Paris was a very romantic city.

Unit 6, Practice 16B, Page 166 (CD3, 18, 19)

Jane Goodall was born in London, England, in 1934. As a child, she loved stories about Africa. She finished school and worked for a film company. One day, a friend invited her to Kenya, in Africa. She saved money for the trip, and she went there. Jane was 23 years old.

In Kenya, she met Louis Leakey. He was a famous anthropologist (a person who studies humans and where they come from). Jane Goodall became his assistant. She traveled with Louis Leakey and his wife in Africa.

In 1960, she began to study chimpanzees. She lived alone in the forest in Africa. Every morning, she went to the same place in the forest. The chimpanzees saw her, but they stood far away. After about six months, the chimpanzees came near her. Jane Goodall began to know each chimpanzee. She gave each chimpanzee a name.

After years of work, she discovered many things about the chimpanzees. For example, chimpanzees eat meat.

Today, sadly, there are fewer chimpanzees. People are killing the chimpanzees or cutting down the forests where they live. Jane studied chimpanzees for over 40 years. Now she is traveling around the world and talking about how to save chimpanzees.

Unit 6, Practice 22B, Page 171 (CD3, 20, 21)

Billy: Did you enjoy your vacation, Dolores?
Dolores: No, I didn't.
Billy: Why not?
Dolores: Well, I didn't like the food.
Billy: Did you like the city?
Dolores: No, I didn't.
Billy: What about the weather? Did you like it?
Dolores: No, I didn't. It rained every day.
Billy: Was the hotel good?
Dolores: No, it wasn't. Every time I called the reception desk, nobody answered.
Billy: Did you visit any museums?
Dolores: No, I didn't. They were all closed. It was a holiday.
Billy: That's terrible. Did you go shopping at least?
Dolores: Yes, I did, but I didn't buy anything. It was very expensive.
Billy: Well, did you have a good flight?
Dolores: No, I didn't. The flight was five hours late and the service was terrible.
Billy: So, it wasn't a good vacation, I guess.
Dolores: No, it was NOT!

Unit 6, Practice 27B, Page 176 (CD3, 22, 23)

1. Who did you see?
   I saw Karen.
2. When did you see her?
   I saw her yesterday morning.
3. Where did you see her?
   I saw her in a café.
4. How did she look?
   She looked happy.
5. What did she find?
   She found an apartment.
6. How did she find it?
   She looked in the newspaper.
7. Who had a bad day yesterday?
   Dave had a bad day yesterday.
8. When did he come home?
   He came home at 10 P.M.
9. How did he feel?
   He felt tired.
10. Why did he come home so late?
    Because he had a lot of work to do.
11. Who did you see yesterday?
    I saw Tina yesterday.
12. Where was she?
    She was in the street.
13. When did you see her?
    I saw her in the afternoon.
14. How did she look?
    She looked happy.
15. What did she say?
    She said hello.

Unit 6, Listening Puzzle, Page 183 (CD3, 24-25)

It was 1945. Percy Spencer was an engineer. He worked for a company in the United States. His company made this machine. One day Spencer stopped in front of this machine. He had

some chocolate in his pocket. The chocolate melted! He didn't understand this. Then he put popcorn next to this machine. This time the popcorn popped all over the room. Spencer had a new idea for this machine. Today two out of three homes in the United States have this machine.
What is the name of this machine?

Unit 7, Practice 3B, Page 194 (CD3, 26, 27)

1. Was Sue doing her homework when I called?
   No, she wasn't doing her homework. She was cleaning the apartment.
2. Were Dave and Bob talking about the basketball game?
   No, they weren't talking about the basketball game. They were talking about the soccer game.
3. Were you trying to reach me?
   No, I wasn't trying to reach you. I was trying to reach your brother.
4. Was I speaking too loudly?
   No, you weren't speaking too loudly. You were speaking too softly.
5. Were you reading the *New York Times*?
   No, I wasn't reading the *New York Times*. I was reading the *Los Angeles Times*.
6. Was Mr. Black explaining the present progressive?
   No, he wasn't explaining the present progressive. He was explaining the past progressive.

Unit 7, Practice 5B and 5C, Page 197 (CD3, 28-30)

We were talking about the questions on the test when the teacher walked into the classroom. While she was giving out the tests, we sat in silence. We started the test at 9:15. While we were taking the test, the teacher watched us. While Leo was taking the test, he talked to himself. He was talking to himself when the teacher told him, "Be quiet, Leo." His face became red. I was finishing my last answer when the teacher said, "STOP." I was smiling when I left the classroom. While I was walking home, I said to myself, "I did a great job on that test."

Unit 7, Practice 6B, Page 199 (CD3, 31, 32)

A
One day, I was studying in the library when I saw her. She came towards me and sat down in the chair next to me. Then she put on her glasses and started to read a book. While she was reading, I looked at her quickly for a moment. Suddenly our eyes met. I smiled, and then she smiled.

B
I had a bad dream last night. In my dream it was Sunday morning. It was ten o'clock, and I was reading a book in the yard in front of the house. Suddenly the sky became dark. It started to rain, so I went inside the house. I closed the windows and turned on the television to listen to the news and weather. I was watching the news when the storm began. I remember that the wind was blowing and the windows were shaking when I heard a terrible noise like a big bang. Then I woke up on the floor.

C
It was getting dark when I got off the train. There was no one in the street. While I was walking down the street, I heard footsteps behind me. When I began to walk fast, the footsteps got fast. When I began to run, the footsteps got faster. Finally, I got to my house. I

was shaking when I put the key in the door. Just then I heard a man's voice behind me. "Is this your purse? You left it on the train."

Unit 7, Listening Puzzle, Page 203 (CD3, 33-34)

Two American brothers worked in a clinic. One brother was a doctor. The other brother did other jobs in this clinic. People went to this clinic to get healthy. The brothers tried to make healthy foods for their patients. One day, one brother was cooking a special food when he left and forgot about the food. When he came back, he discovered a new kind of food. The brothers started to make this food and sell it in 1906. Today, many people like to eat this with milk and sugar in the morning.
What is the name of this food?

Unit 8, Practice 2B and 2C, Page 213 (CD4, 2-4)

Yuko:	Guess what! I am going to go to London next week!
Meg:	Lucky you! You're not going to work! How long are you going to stay?
Yuko:	I'm going to stay for five days.
Meg:	What are you going to do?
Yuko:	On Monday, I'm going to see St. Paul's, and then I'm going to walk in the parks. On Tuesday, I'm going to visit the Houses of Parliament. On Wednesday, I'm going to go to some museums. On Thursday, I'm going to shop on Oxford Street. I'm going to buy some English tea.
Meg:	Are you going to eat fish and chips? English people eat fish and chips, you know.
Yuko:	That's one thing I'm not going to do. I don't like fish. I'm going to eat hamburgers as usual.

Unit 8, Practice 3B, Page 214 (CD4, 5, 6)

1. When are you going to have the party?
2. What kind of food are you going to have?
3. What food are you going to make?
4. What are you going to wear?
5. How many people are you going to invite?
6. Where are you going to have the party?
7. What time is the party going to start?
8. What kind of music are you going to have?

Unit 8, Practice 8B, Page 224 (CD4, 7, 8)

A
Julia:	I am going to the supermarket right now. Do you want anything?
Leyla:	Yes. Can you get some orange juice?
Julia:	Sure. It's on my list, so I'll get it.
Leyla:	I also wanted to pick up my photos today, but I don't have time to do it.
Julia:	Don't worry. I'll pick them up for you. I'll be back soon. Will you be here?
Leyla:	I'm going to work now.
Julia:	OK. I'll see you later. Remember Tony and Suzy are coming by tonight.

B
Steve:	Hi, Dave. Are you going to the picnic on Saturday?
Dave:	I don't think I can. I'm helping Joanne move from her apartment.
Steve:	Oh, no! I forgot she's moving this weekend.
Dave:	Well, are you coming to help?
Steve:	Sure. What time are you going to go to Joanne's apartment?
Dave:	I don't know right now. I'll call you tomorrow night,

and I'll tell you.

Steve: OK. Someone is knocking on the door right now. I'm going to see who it is. I'll call you right back. Bye.

Dave: OK. Bye.

Unit 8, Practice 9B, Page 226 (CD4, 9, 10)

1.
Friend: I'm going to Boston this winter.
You: Take warm clothes. It will be cold. It's always cold there in winter.

2.
Friend: I'm going to Los Angeles in the summer.
You: Take your shorts and light clothes. It will be hot. It's always hot there in the summer.

3.
Friend: I want to walk around New York at night.
You: Be careful. It may be dangerous. People sometimes get hurt.

4.
Friend: In June, I'm going to Bangkok, in Thailand.
You: Take an umbrella. It will be rainy. It always rains there in June.

5.
Friend: I'm going to stay in Tokyo for a month.
You: Take a lot of money. It will be expensive. Tokyo is always expensive.

6.
Friend: I'm flying from New York to Sydney, Australia.
You: It's a long trip. Take a book with you. You might get bored.

7.
Friend: I want to go to Rio de Janeiro for the Carnival.
You: Make a hotel reservation. It will be crowded. It's always crowded then.

8.
Friend: I'm going to Africa to see wild animals.
You: Take some medicine with you. You might get sick. People sometimes get sick when they travel there.

Unit 8, Practice 12B, Page 229 (CD4, 11, 12)

1. We'll change some money before we leave.
2. We'll make a list of all the interesting places before we leave.
3. When we get there, we'll stay at the Hilton® hotel.
4. After we see the city, we'll visit museums.
5. When we stay in Istanbul, we won't go to other cities.
6. We won't have time to see everything before we leave.
7. We'll go to the bazaar after we visit the museums.
8. When we go to the bazaar, we'll buy a rug.
9. When we walk around the bazaar, we'll take photos.
10. When we stay in Istanbul, we won't need a car.
11. We'll take a taxi when we want to go somewhere.
12. Before we leave Istanbul, we'll get lots of souvenirs.

Unit 8, Practice 15B, Page 232 (CD4, 13, 14)

1 -c. If you go out without a coat, you'll catch a cold.
2 -f. If you lie in the sun, you'll get sunburned.
3 -a. If you don't eat breakfast, you'll be hungry.
4 -h. If you eat too many french fries, you'll get fat.
5 -b. If you don't study hard, you won't pass your exam.
6 -d. If you don't call home, you'll be lonely.
7 -e. If you go to bed late, you'll be tired the next day.
8 -g. If you get sick, you'll miss class.

Unit 8, Practice 19B and 19C, Page 235 (CD4, 15-17)

1. Julia works in an office from 9:00 to 5:00. When she has some extra work, she stays until 6:00.
2. If she has a lot of work tomorrow, she'll stay until 8:00.
3. If she's at the office, she usually sees Terry at lunchtime.
4. If the weather is nice, they usually go out for lunch.
5. Julia usually gets tired when she works on the computer all day.
6. Tomorrow, she'll go to meetings before she works on the computer.
7. When she comes home tomorrow, it will be about 8:30.
8. If she is tired tomorrow, she won't make dinner.
9. She'll buy a sandwich before she comes home from work tomorrow.
10. Tomorrow, Julia won't turn on her computer after she has dinner.
11. After she has dinner tomorrow, she'll go to bed.
12. If she works like this all year, Julia will ask for more money from her boss.

Unit 8, Listening Puzzle, Page 237 (CD4, 18-19)

A British scientist gave the money for this museum. The museum is named after him. The museum opened in 1846. It is in the nation's capital city. If you go there, you will see the first flag of this country. You will also see many interesting things. You will learn about the country's history and art. You will also learn about technology. This museum is very popular, and about eight million people visit it every year. It will take you a long time to see everything in this museum. It has 140 million objects. What is the name of this museum?

Unit 9, Practice 3B, Page 246 (CD4,20, 21)

1. All of the food is delicious.
2. All of the dishes come with a salad.
3. Most of the wines are Italian.
4. None of the dishes are expensive.
5. Almost all of the dishes have pasta with them.
6. Some of the servers are Italian.
7. All of the music is Italian.
8. Almost all of the furniture is Italian.
9. All of the fish is very fresh.
10. Some of the pizzas are wonderful.

Unit 9, Practice 4B, Page 248 (CD4,22, 23)

1. Every classroom has a number.
2. Every person in this school is from my country.
3. Every teacher speaks excellent English.
4. Every teacher gives a lot of homework.
5. Every student in this class is learning English.
6. Every student has a grammar book.
7. Every unit in the book has a test.
8. Every test has 20 questions.
9. Every question has four answers.
10. Every question is interesting.

Unit 9, Practice 8B, Page 251 (CD4, 24, 25)

1.
Julia: That jacket is beautiful, and it's very expensive.
Pam: Are you going to buy it?
Julia: Yes, I am.

2.
Berta: Do you like our new teacher?
Mario: Yes, I do. She's an excellent teacher, and she's very intelligent.

3.
Sue: I didn't like that cake.
Pam: What was wrong?
Sue: It was too sweet.
4.
Louis: Does your sister drive?
Maria: No, she doesn't. She's only 13. She's too young.
5.
Jo: Do you want to play tennis with us this afternoon?
Karen: I'm very tired, but I think I will. Thanks.
6.
Mel: Can you read this tiny writing?
Jim: Sorry, I can't read it without my glasses. It's too small.
7.
Chris: Can you help me with this statistics problem?
Jan: Sorry, I can't. It's too difficult.
8.
Lisa: Did you like the new fish restaurant yesterday?
Mike: Yes, I did. The fish was very fresh.

Unit 9, Practice 9B, Page 252 (CD4, 26, 27)
1. There is too much crime.
2. There are too many cars.
3. There is too much traffic.
4. There are too many people.
5. There is too much pollution.
6. There is too much noise.
7. There are too many buildings.

Unit 9, Practice 10B, Page 253 (CD4, 28, 29)
1. Mr. Lang spent too much money.
2. There were too many guests and too much food.
3. There were too many flowers everywhere.
4. There were too many drinks.
5. There were too many sandwiches.
6. There was too much fruit.
7. There was too much meat.
8. There was too much fish.
9. There were too many cakes.
10. There were too many waiters.

Unit 9, Practice 12B, Page 255 (CD4, 30, 31)
1. I am too tired to drive.
2. This room is too small to be comfortable.
3. This computer is too old to work well.
4. Peter is too sleepy to study.
5. Janet is too busy to go.
6. The children are too excited to sleep.

Unit 9, Practice 14B, Page 257 (CD4, 32, 33)
1. The chair is too uncomfortable. It is not comfortable enough.
2. The water is too hot. It is not cold enough.
3. The soup is too warm. It is not cool enough.
4. The server is too slow. He is not fast enough.
5. The bread is too old. It is not fresh enough.
6. The portion is too small. It is not large enough.
7. The coffee is too weak. It is not strong enough.
8. The table is too small. It is not big enough.
9. The meat is too tough. It is not tender enough.
10. The meal is too expensive. It is not cheap enough.

Unit 9, Practice 16B, Page 259 (CD4, 34, 35)
1. Did I invite enough people?
2. Do I have enough food for people to eat?
3. Do I have enough time to get ready?
4. Is there enough soda to drink?
5. Are there enough CDs to listen to?
6. Are there enough chairs to sit on?

Unit 9, Listening Puzzle, Page 261 (CD4, 36-37)
This is a very beautiful mountain, especially when you look at it from far. It is in a country in Asia. It is the tallest mountain of this country. A long time ago this mountain was a volcano. In winter, the mountain has snow on top. Many people climb this mountain every year. The official time to climb the mountain is in July and August. During the other months of the year, there is too much snow and the weather is very bad. But, in the middle of August there are too many people on the mountain. They sometimes wait in lines to get to the top.
What is the name of this mountain?

Unit 10, Practice 1B, Page 269 (CD5, 2, 3)
1. We study English at the same school.
2. He is our teacher.
3. He teaches us English grammar.
4. He uses it to teach grammar.
5. The students like him.
6. They ask John Blackie questions.
7. He answers them.
8. Linda is a student in our class. She always asks questions.
9. We don't like to listen to her, but Mr. Blackie is very patient.
10. He always answers her questions.

Unit 10, Practice 2B, Page 271 (CD5, 4, 5)
A
At the moment, I am studying English. It is a difficult language. Most of my friends are in the school with me. Our teachers are good, but they give us a lot of homework. We are having a test next week, and I want to pass it. Then my parents will not worry about me so much.
B
John: Do you know that woman?
Pete: Yes, I work with her.
John: Is she nice?
Pete: Yes, she is very nice. We work in the same office. Come with me to the office, and I will introduce you to her. Her husband is my boss. He is a great boss. Do you want me to introduce you to him, too?
John: No. That's OK.
C
Nick: My father bought me a new computer, but I don't know how to use it. Can you help me?
Dave: Sure, I'll show you how it works. When do you want me to teach you?
Nick: Can you come tomorrow?
Dave: OK. I'll see you at ten tomorrow. You need to learn some basic steps. You can learn them in a few hours.

Unit 10, Practice 5B, Page 273 (CD5, 6, 7)
1. The teacher handed me the paper.
2. He sends my parents newspapers.
3. She showed us the photos.
4. My grandfather told us stories.

5. I write my brother letters.
6. John passed Maria the book.
7. We lent Kim ten dollars.
8. My father gave me a watch.
9. His parents gave him an old computer.
10. Her brother gave her the message.

Unit 10, Practice 6B, Page 274 (CD5, 8, 9)

1.
Jim: I gave my mother the house.
Tom: Who did you give it to?
Jim: I gave it to my mother.
2.
Tom: I sold Mr. Black my car.
Jim: Who did you sell it to?
Tom: I sold it to Mr. Black.
3.
Jim: I offered my neighbor the television.
Tom: Who did you offer it to?
Jim: I offered it to my neighbor.
4.
Tom: I sent my friends an email.
Jim: Who did you send it to?
Tom: I sent it to my friends.
5.
Jim: I told my boss the news.
Tom: Who did you tell it to?
Jim: I told it to my boss.
6.
Tom: I showed my friends the photos.
Jim: Who did you show them to?
Tom: I showed them to my friends.
7.
Jim: I gave my roommate a birthday gift.
Tom: Who did you give it to?
Jim: I gave it to my roommate.

8.
Tom: I handed my sister a theater ticket.
Jim: Who did you hand it to?
Tom: I handed it to my sister.

Unit 10, Practice 7B, Page 276 (CD5, 10, 11)

1. A teacher answers questions for the students.
2. A server shows the menu to you in a restaurant.
3. A teacher pronounces words for the students.
4. A comedian tells jokes to you.
5. A teller in a bank cashes checks for its customers.
6. A customer hands money to a salesperson.
7. A mechanic fixes cars for customers.
8. A teacher gives tests to the students.

Unit 10, Practice 11B, Page 279 (CD5, 12, 13)

1. The teacher explained the answer to us.
2. The teacher introduced indirect objects to us.
3. The teacher repeated the questions for us.
4. The teacher explained the meaning of the word to me.
5. The student repeated the sentence for her.
6. The teacher introduced the new student to us.
7. The student explained her problem to the teacher.
8. The teacher introduced the speaker to the class.

Unit 10, Practice 15B, Page 284 (CD5, 14, 15)

1.
Karen: Don't forget your umbrella!
Jamie: That's not my umbrella. Mine is black.
2.
Jim: Do the Petersons live there?
Dave: Yes, they do.
Jim: Is that their house?
Dave: No, it isn't. Theirs is around the corner.
3.
Bobby: That's my teddy bear!
Jenny: No, it isn't! It's my teddy bear.
Mother: Stop it children! Jenny, give Bobby his teddy bear.
Jenny: It isn't his. It's mine.
4.
Larry: My brother rents his apartment, and I rent my apartment.
Sherry: My roommate and I rent ours, too. Our apartment is small, but it's big enough for us.
5.
Tony: Where is their car parked?
Pete: Theirs is on the street.
Tony: Is Maria's car on the street, too?
Pete: No, hers is in the driveway.
6.
Ben: Shall we take your car or my car?
Jerry: Let's take mine. It's faster than yours.
Ben: Yes, but my car is more comfortable.
7.
Suzy: Is that your bag over there?
Laura: No, it isn't mine. I thought it was yours.
8.
Ben: Our classroom is very neat and organized.
Jerry: That's true. The teacher has her table and chair, and we have ours.

Unit 10, Listening Puzzle, Page 289 (CD5, 16-17)

As a boy, he was not a good student. The teacher told him to leave school because he was not intelligent. His mother taught him at home. Later, at age twelve he sold newspapers. One day he saved someone's life. For this he got a job as a telegraph operator. He liked this and studied electricity at work. After a few years, he started to invent many important things for us. No one invented as many things as this person. He also started his own laboratory and paid people to work for him. He was the first person to do this. What is the name of this inventor?

Unit 11, Practice 5B, Page 301 (CD5, 18, 19)

1. She couldn't ride a bicycle.
2. She couldn't run fast.
3. She couldn't drive a car.
4. She couldn't ski.
5. She couldn't take tests.
6. She couldn't work.
7. She couldn't write a letter.
8. She couldn't read a book.

Unit 11, Practice 7B, Page 302 (CD5, 20, 21)

1. He couldn't go to school.
2. He couldn't drive.
3. He couldn't play tennis.
4. He could read magazines.
5. He couldn't swim.

6. He couldn't visit friends.
7. He could watch TV.
8. He could work online.

Unit 11, Practice 9C, Page 305 (CD5, 22, 23)
1. At age three, he was able to play the piano.
2. After he heard a piece of music one time, Mozart was able to play it.
3. People were not able to believe it.
4. At age five, he was able to write music for the piano.
5. Soon his father wasn't able to teach him because little Mozart knew everything.
6. At 12, he was famous and was able to make money for his family.
7. Mozart worked long hours and was able to work very fast.
8. He was able to write an opera in just a few weeks.
9. He was able to work better at night because it was quiet.
10. He was able to write all kinds of music, even music for clocks.
11. We are still not able to understand why he died.
12. We are able to buy his music on tapes or CDs.

Unit 11, Practice 13B, Page 309 (CD5, 24, 25)
1. He shouldn't skip school.
2. He shouldn't come home late.
3. He should do his homework.
4. He should listen to his parents.
5. He should listen in class.
6. He should clean up his room.
7. He shouldn't always ask his parents for money.
8. He should be nice to his brother and sister.

Unit 11, Practice 15B and 15C, Page 311 (CD5, 26-28)
1. You must be quiet when someone else is speaking.
2. You must listen to the teacher.
3. You must arrive to class on time.
4. You must not eat in class.
5. You must not use a telephone in class.
6. You must answer the teacher's questions.
7. You must not go to sleep.
8. You must attend class every day.
9. You must bring your books to class.
10. You must do your homework.
11. You must not cheat or copy on a test.
12. You must not write letters to friends in class.

Unit 11, Listening Puzzle, Page 321 (CD5, 29-30)
This animal only lives in Australia. It eats plants. It cannot walk or jump backwards, and has a long tail. The tail can be over five feet, 1.5 meters, long. The baby animal has to live in its mother's pouch on her stomach for six months. When the English first arrived in Australia, they saw this strange animal. They asked some aborigines in English, "What is the name of that animal?" The aborigines couldn't speak English and answered in their own language, "I don't understand you." The English thought this was the animal's name. It is still the same name.

What is the name of this animal?

Unit 12, Practice 3B and 3C, Page 331-332 (CD5, 31-33)
1.
Waiter: Would you like a salad with your pasta?
Mr. Lu: No, thanks.

2.
Waiter: Would you like a bottle of mineral water?
Mr. Lu: I'd like two glasses of regular water, please.
3.
Waiter: Would you like some dessert?
Mr. Lu: I'd like the apple pie. My friend would like ice cream.
4.
Waiter: Would you like some coffee?
Mr. Lu: Yes, please. We both would like coffee.
5.
Waiter: Would you like espresso, cappuccino, or regular coffee?
Mr. Lu: Two espressos, please, and we'd like the check.
6.
Waiter: Would you like separate checks or one check?
Mr. Lu: We'd like one check, please.

Unit 12, Listening Puzzle, Page 339 (CD5, 34-35)
When you see dark clouds and rain far away, you know there is danger. Listen to the radio for the latest news. If there is a warning, follow the instructions. Leave everything. Do not stay in your house or your car. Run to the storm shelter under the ground. Make sure your family members are with you. Go inside and shut the door tightly. When you hear a loud sound like a train, you know the storm is over you. Stay in the shelter until there is no more noise outside. Now you can come out and look at the damage.
What kind of storm is this?

Unit 13, Practice 6B, Page 351 (CD6, 2, 3)
1. a new gold credit card
2. an interesting diamond bracelet
3. a beautiful old Chinese plate
4. a small new Japanese computer
5. a beautiful black leather purse
6. an old gold Swiss watch
7. an expensive big blue ring
8. an old silk Persian carpet
9. a white pearl Japanese necklace
10. an antique silver English jewelry box

Unit 13, Practice 7B and 7C, Page 351-352 (CD6, 4-6)
Fred is a quiet young man. He lives alone in a red brick house. The house has one bedroom with a clean light wood floor. It has a bright modern kitchen. From the kitchen window, you can see a beautiful rose garden and an old apple tree. In the office, there is a black leather sofa and an interesting old desk. On the desk, there is a telephone, a small computer and a note pad. There are books everywhere. There are also old American newspapers, mostly *The New York Times*.

Unit 13, Practice 14B, Page 358 (CD6, 7, 8)
1. Karen is older than Connie.
2. Connie is younger than Karen.
3. Karen is taller than Connie.
4. Connie is smaller than Karen.
5. Connie is thinner than Karen.
6. Karen is heavier than Connie.
7. Karen is friendlier than Connie.
8. Connie is quieter than Karen.

Unit 13, Practice 15B, Page 359 (CD6, 9, 10)
1. London is older than New York.
2. New York is more crowded than London.

3. London is smaller than New York in population.
4. The buildings in New York are taller than the buildings in London.
5. New York is more exciting than London.
6. The buildings in New York are more modern than the buildings in London.
7. Life in New York is faster than life in London.
8. The summer in New York is hotter than the summer in London.
9. New York is rainier than London.
10. The museums in London are more interesting than the museums in New York.
11. London is more expensive than New York.
12. People in London are usually more polite than people in New York.

Unit 13, Practice 16B, Page 361 (CD6, 11, 12)
1. Mark's car isn't as old as Joe's car.
2. Joe's car isn't as clean as Mark's car.
3. Mark's car isn't as small as Joes's car.
4. Joe's car isn't as luxurious as Mark's car.
5. Mark's car isn't as noisy as Joe's car.
6. Joe's car isn't as trendy as Mark's car.
7. Joe's car isn't as sporty as Mark's car.
8. Joe's car isn't as powerful as Mark's car.

Unit 13, Practice 23B, Page 367 (CD6, 13, 14)
1. cold - the coldest
2. hungry - the hungriest
3. wet - the wettest
4. useful - the most useful
5. intelligent - the most intelligent
6. easy - the easiest
7. good - the best
8. bad - the worst
9. far - the farthest, the furthest
10. boring - the most boring
11. popular - the most popular
12. friendly - the friendliest

Unit 13, Practice 32B, Page 374 (CD6, 15, 16)
1. She speaks English very well.
2. She is very polite to people.
3. She gets along with people easily.
4. She is a hard worker.
5. She is a good writer.
6. She types fast on the computer.
7. She is very careful with her work.
8. She keeps the office clean.
9. She is never late.
10. But you must pay her generously.

Unit 13, Practice 37B and 37C, Page 379 (CD6, 17-19)
1. Alex doesn't work as hard as Mike does.
2. He doesn't get up as early as Mike does.
3. Mike doesn't go to bed as late as Alex does.
4. Alex doesn't work as quickly as Mike does.
5. Mike doesn't play sports as well as Alex and his friends do.
6. Alex doesn't talk as politely as Mike and his friends do.
7. Mike doesn't dress as casually as Alex and his friends do.
8. Alex doesn't drive as carefully as Mike does.

Unit 13, Listening Puzzle, Page 381 (CD6, 20-21)
There are several classes of animals such as mammals, fish, and insects. This group is the biggest group. Up to this time, we know of about one million species or kinds, but scientists discover thousands of new species each year. Scientists believe there are about 30 million in this group. There are more species of these than any other group. The animals in this group make up 90 percent of all animals. If you weigh them, they will be heavier than all of the other animals in the world. These animals all have three parts to their body.
What is the name of this species or group?

Unit 14, Practice 1B and 1C, Page 391 (CD6, 22-24)
1. Sue and Lin met at the university four years ago. They have been friends for four years.
2. Lin married Steve last April. She has been married since April.
3. Lin and Steve bought a new home last June. They have been in the new house since June.
4. Life has been very good for them since they got married.
5. Sue works part-time in a lab. She has been a chemist for ten months now.
6. Sue also moved to a new apartment with her sister this month. They have been in the apartment for only three weeks.

Unit 14, Practice 2B and 2C, Page 391-392 (CD6, 25-27)
1. Mark and Yolanda have been married for 22 years.
2. They have been at the same address since 1992.
3. Yolanda has been a teacher since 1990.
4. Mark has been a salesman for 25 years.
5. He has been with the same company since 1995.
6. Now Mark is in Texas on a business trip. He has been there since last Monday.
7. Mark has been on four business trips since last June.
8. It's Saturday. Yolanda is at the shopping center. She has been there since 10:00 this morning. She wants to get a birthday present for her son, Clark. He is 16 today.
9. Yolanda has been busy since yesterday. She wants to prepare for Clark's birthday.
10. Right now Clark is at the school gym. He has been there since 9:00 this morning.
11. Clark has been at the gym for three hours now.
12. He has been on the school basketball team for a year.

Unit 14, Practice 4B, Page 394 (CD6, 28, 29)
Belton is a small town. Brad Peltry has lived in Belton all his life. Brad is 58 years old. Brad is married. He has been married to Dora for 25 years. They have known each other since high school. Brad and Dora have a son. He is a student at a university in Atlanta. He has studied medicine for three years now. Brad owns the grocery store in town. He has owned the store for 22 years. He has worked in the store for 22 years, too. Something strange happened this week. Nobody has seen Brad for four days. His truck has disappeared. Dora doesn't know where he is. Dora has been worried. Brad has had money problems lately.

Unit 14, Practice 6B, Page 399 (CD6, 30, 31)
A
Alex: How long have you been in this class?
Peter: Since February.
Alex: Have you made any friends?
Peter: Yes, I have made a lot of friends in this class, but my English has not improved.

B
John: How long have you had your driver's license?
Bob: For two years.
John: Have you had any accidents?
Bob: No, I haven't.
C
Sue: How long have you worked here?
Don: Since May. But I have been a computer programmer for four years.
Sue: Have you worked for other companies?
Don: Yes, I have. I have worked for three companies since the year 2000.
Sue: Have you lived in Boston since 2000?
Don: Yes, I have. I like Boston. How long have you lived in Boston?
Sue: For three months now, and the weather has not been good for the last three months. It has been so cold.

Unit 14, Listening Puzzle, Page 403 (CD6, 32-33)

This plant comes from South America. It grew in the mountains there about 7,000 years ago. The Spanish brought it to Europe about two hundred years ago. People in Europe didn't know what to do with it. At first they refused to eat it because it was ugly. The plant is easy to grow and later became a main food for a lot of people. This food has been especially important in Ireland. In the United States, they use this plant to make a tasty food. It has been a favorite menu item at MacDonald's.

What is the name of this plant?

Index

Photo Credits

Page xii: © BananaStock/JupiterImages; xiii: © image 100 Ltd.; 1: © Barbara Penoyar/Getty Images; 2 (left to right): © Ryan McVay/Getty Images, © Royalty-Free/Corbis, © MedioImages; 3 (left to right): © MedioImages, © Stockdisc/PunchStock, © Joshua Ets-Hokin/Getty Images, © PhotoLink/Getty Images, 6 (top left): © Michael Matisse/Getty Images; 6 (top right): © Scott T. Baxter/Getty Images; 6 (2nd row left): © Ryan McVay/Getty Images; 6 (2nd row right): © ImageState/PunchStock; 6 (3rd row left): © Brand X Pictures/PunchStock; 6 (3rd row right): © Ryan McVay/Getty Images; 6 (bottom left): © Brand X Pictures/JupiterImages; 6 (bottom right): © Siede Preis/Getty Images; 7 (top row left to right): © F. Schussler/PhotoLink/Getty Images, © PhotoLink/Photodisc/Getty Images, © Anthony Saint James/Getty Images; 7 (middle row left to right): © Stockdisc/PunchStock, © Photodisc/PunchStock, © Amos Morgan/Getty Images; 7 (bottom row left to right): © Siede Preis/Getty Images, © S. Meltzer/PhotoLink/Getty Images, © Barbara Penoyar/Getty Images; 8: © Barbara Penoyar/Getty Images; 10: © Ingram Publishing/AGE Fotostock; 12: © Brand X Pictures/PunchStock; 14 (top left): © Kevin Peterson/Getty Images; 14 (top right): © Kevin Peterson/Getty Images; 14 (middle left): © Kevin Peterson/Getty Images; 14 (middle right): © liquidlibrary/PictureQuest; 14 (bottom left): © PhotoLink/Getty Images; 14 (bottom right): © Royalty-Free/Corbis; 15: © Royalty-Free/Corbis; 16: © BananaStock/PictureQuest; 17: © Digital Vision/Getty Images; 19: © Neil Beer/Getty Images; 20: © Hyphen-Engineering Education; 21: © Barbara Penoyar/Getty Images; 22 (left): © Digital Vision; 22 (right): © Ryan McVay/Getty Images; 23 (top row left): © Stockbyte/PunchStock; 23 (top row right): © Brand X Pictures/PunchStock; 23 (2nd row left): © PhotoAlto/PunchStock; 23 (2nd row right): © Photodisc/Getty Images; 23 (3rd row left): © Jules Frazier/Getty Images; 23 (3rd row right): © Jules Frazier/Getty Images; 23 (bottom row left): © Royalty-Free/Corbis; 23 (bottom row right): © PhotoLink/Getty Images; 24: © Barbara Penoyar/Getty Images; 25 (top): © Eric Audras/Photoalto/PictureQuest; 25 (center): © BananaStock/PictureQuest; 25 (bottom): © Digital Vision; 26 (all): © Hyphen-Engineering Education; 27: © Hyphen-Engineering Education; 28: © Hyphen-Engineering Education (Thanos Tsilis); 29 (all): © Hyphen-Engineering Education; 30: © Royalty-Free/Corbis; 32: © Getty Images/Digital Vision; 35: © Ryan McVay/Getty Images; 36: © Eyewire (Photodisc)/PunchStock; 37: © Hyphen-Engineering Education; 38: © PhotoDisc/Getty Images; 39: (top row all) : © Edgewater Pictures; 39 (second row left to right): © Edgewater Pictures, © Lawrence Lawry/Getty Images, © Photodisc; 40: © Emanuele Taroni/Getty Images; 41: © Getty Images/Digital Vision; 43: © Mel Curtis/Getty Images; 44: © Hyphen-Engineering Education; 45: © Ryan McVay/Getty Images; 46: © Lynn Betts/USDA Natural Resources Conservation Service; 47: © Russell Illig/Getty Images; 49: © Philip & Karen Smith/Getty Images; 52 (left): © Index Stock Photography Inc./Photodisc/Getty Images; 52 (right): © Image Source/Getty Images; 54 (left): © Pixtal/age Fotostock; 54 (right): © Stefano Bianchetti/Corbis; 55: © Bettmann/Corbis; 57: © Index Stock/Getty Images; 58: © Hyphen-Engineering Education (Thanos Tsilis); 59 (left to right): © Photodisc/Getty Images, © Royalty-Free/Corbis, © John A. Karachewski; 60: © Robert Glusic/Getty Images; 65: © Doug Menuez/Getty Images; 66 (both): © Brand X Pictures/PunchStock; 68 (top): © PhotoLink/Getty Images; 68 (bottom): © Doug Menuez/Getty Images; 69: © Doug Menuez/Getty Images; 71: © McGraw-Hill Companies, Inc./Gary He, photographer; 73: © image 100, Ltd; 74: © Royalty-Free/Corbis; 77: © Ryan McVay/Getty Images; 80: © Amos Morgan/Getty Images; 82: © Digital Vision, Ltd; 83: © C Squared Studios/Getty Images; 84: © image100/PunchStock; 85: © Royalty-Free/Corbis; 86 (left): © Digital Vision; 86 (right): © Michael Matisse/Getty Images; 88: © Hyphen-Engineering Education (Thanos Tsilis); 89 (left to right): © Creatas/PunchStock, © Getty Images, © Creatas/PunchStock; 90: © Royalty-Free/Corbis; 95: © Digital Vision/Getty Images; 96: © Joaquin Palting/Getty Images; 97 (left): © BananaStock/PictureQuest; 97 (right): © Royalty-Free/Corbis; 98 (top left): © C Squared Studios/Getty Images; 98 (top right): © Photodisc; 98 (bottom left): © Digital Vision/Getty Images; 98 (bottom right): © BananaStock/Alamy; 99 (top left): © Photomondo/Getty Images; 99 (top right): © C Squared Studios/Getty Images; 99 (bottom left): © Index Stock/Getty Images; 99 (bottom right): © Index Stock Photography, Inc./Photodisc/Getty Images; 101: © Steve Mason/Getty Images; 104: © image100/PunchStock; 105: © Kaz Chiba/Getty Images; 106: © Jules Frazier/Getty Images; 107: © Buccina Studios/Getty Images; 108: © Ryan McVay/Getty Images; 109: © IMS Communications Ltd/Capstone Design/FlatEarth Images; 111: © John A. Rizzo/Getty Images; 112 (left): © Stockbyte; 112 (right): © Stockbyte; 116: © Hyphen-Engineering Education (Thanos Tsilis); 117 (left to right): © Liquidlibrary/Jupiterimages © Ryan McVay/Getty Images, © Royalty-Free/Corbis; 118: © Alison Wright/Corbis; 123: © Royalty-Free/Corbis; 124: © C Squared Studios/Getty Images; 125: © Michael Lamotte/Cole Group/Getty Images; 127: © Goodshoot/PunchStock; 129: © Anthony Saint James/Getty Images; 130: © Brand X Pictures/PunchStock; 131 (top): © Andrew Ward/Life File/Getty Images; 131 (bottom): © Dennis Gray/Cole Group/Getty Images; 132: © John A. Rizzo/Getty Images; 134: © Royalty-Free/Corbis; 136: © PhotoAlto/PunchStock; 137: © PhotoDisc/Getty Images; 138 (top left): © Doug Menuez/Getty Images; 138 (top right): © Doug Menuez/Getty Images; 138 (center left): © Royalty-Free/Corbis; 138 (center right): © David Bugginton/Getty Images; 138 (bottom left): © Stockdisc/PunchStock; 138 (bottom right): © McGraw-Hill Companies, Inc./Gary He, photographer; 140: © Hyphen-Engineering Education (Thanos Tsilis); 141 (left to right): © John A. Rizzo/Getty Images, © Royalty-Free/Corbis, © Bob Montesclaros/Cole Group/Getty Images; 142: © Royalty-Free/Corbis; 144: © Ed Carey/Cole Group/Getty Images; 147: © Creatas/PunchStock; 148 (top): © Steve Cole/Getty Images; 148 (bottom): © BrandX/JupiterImages/Getty Images; 149: © Photodisc Collection/Getty Images; 151: © Donovan Reese/Getty Images; 154: © Creats/PictureQuest; 158 (left): © Imagesource/PicturesQuest; 158 (right): © Jeff Maloney/Getty Images; 160: © Comstock Images/JupiterImages; 163: © Creatas/PunchStock; 164: © Creatas/PunchStock; 165: © Karl Ammann/Corbis; 167: © Index Stock/Getty Images; 168: © Index Stock

Photography Inc./Photodisc/Getty Images; 170: © Royalty-Free/Corbis; 173: © Doug Menuez/Getty Images; 174: © Monica Lau/Getty Images; 175 (top): © fStop; 175 (bottom): © Photodisc Collection/Getty Images; 176: © The McGraw-Hill Companies, Inc./Lars A. Niki; 177 (both): © Hyphen-Engineering Education (Thanos Tsilis); 179 (left): © Jonnie Miles/Getty Images; 179 (right): © BananaStock/PictureQuest; 181 (top left): © Buccina Studios/Getty Images; 181 (top right): © Bananastock/PictureQuest; 181 (center left): © Digital Vision; 181 (center right): © Dynamic Graphics/JupiterImages; 181 (bottom left): © image100 Ltd; 181 (bottom right): © Brand X/JupiterImages/Getty Images; 182: © PhotoLink/Photodisc/Getty Images; 183 (left to right): © Royalty-Free/ Corbis, © Burke/Triolo Productions/Getty Images, © CMCD/Getty Images; 184: © Royalty-Free/Corbis; 189: © BananaStock/JupiterImages; 190: © BananaStock/JupiterImages; 191: © Photodisc; 192 (top left): © Photodisc; 192 (top right): © Mel Curtis/Getty Images; 192 (center left): © Jonnie Miles/ Getty Images; 192 (center right): © Liquidlibrary/Dynamic Graphics/JupiterImages; 192 (bottom left): © Getty Images/Steve Allen; 192 (bottom right): © PhotoAlto/PunchStock; 193 (top left): © Creatas/PunchStock; 193 (top right): © Photodisc Collection/Getty Images; 193 (center left): © Photodisc; 193 (center right): © The McGraw-Hill Companies, Inc./Ken Cavanagh, photographer; 193 (bottom left): © Digital Vision/Getty Images; 193 (bottom right): © Jeff Maloney/Getty Images; 195: © Ryan McVay/Getty Images; 198: © MichelTouraine/pixland/Corbis; 202: © Hyphen-Engineering Education (Thanos Tsilis); 203 (left to right): © Comstock/Jupiter Images, © Greg Kuchik/Getty Images, © The McGraw-Hill Companies, Inc./Ken Cavanagh, photographer; 204: © Bettmann/Corbis; 209: © MedioImages/Getty Images; 210: © Brand X Pictures/PunchStock; 211: © Royalty-Free/Corbis; 212 (top row left): © Andersen Ross/Getty Images; 212 (top row right): © C. Borland/PhotoLink/Getty Images; 212 (middle row left): © C. Borland/PhotoLink/Getty Images; 212 (middle row right): © Royalty-Free/Corbis; 212 (bottom row left): © PhotoLink/Getty Images; 212 (bottom row right): © Photodisc; 215: © BananaStock/PunchStock; 217: © Getty Images; 218: © Ryan McVay/Getty Images; 220: © Royalty-Free/Corbis; 221 (top): © Getty Images; 221 (bottom): © Imagesource/PictureQuest; 224: © Keith Brofsky/Getty Images; 227: © Ryan McVay/Getty Images; 228: © John A. Rizzo/Getty Images; 230: © Steve Mason/Getty Images; 231: © Dynamic Graphics/JupiterImages; 233 (top): © C. Borland/PhotoLink/Getty Images; 233 (bottom): © MedioImages/Getty Images; 236: © Hyphen-Engineering Education (Thanos Tsilis); 237 (left to right): © Andrew Ward/Life File/Getty Images, © Charles Bowman/Robert Harding World Imagery/Corbis, © The McGraw-Hill Companies, Inc./Jill Braaten, photographer; 238: © Austin Post, U.S. Geological Survey, Tacoma, WA; 243: © The McGraw-Hill Companies, Inc./ Ken Cavanagh Photographer; 244: © Library of Congress; 245 (top): © Library of Congress; 245: (bottom): © Library of Congress Prints and Photographs Division {LC-USZ662-117580}; 246: © Philip Coblentz/Brand X Pictures/PictureQuest; 247: © Comstock/JupiterImages; 249: © The McGraw-Hill Companies, Inc./Ken Cavanagh Photographer; 250 (top): © Karl Weatherly/Getty Images; 250 (left): © Dynamic Graphics/Creatas/PictureQuest; 250 (right): © Stockbyte/Getty Images; 250 (bottom): © Spencer Jones/Getty Images; 252: © Andrew Ward/Life File/Getty Images; 254: © C Squared Studios/Getty Images; 256: © Mel Curtis/Getty Images; 258: © fStop; 260: © Hyphen-Engineering Education (Thanos Tsilis); 261 (left to right): © Royalty-Free/Corbis, © Imageshop/Alamy, © PhotoLink/Getty Images; 262: © Stockbyte/PunchStock; 267: © Andersen Ross/Getty Images; 268: © BananaStock/PunchStock; 272: © Royalty-Free/Corbis; 275: © Ryan McVay/Getty Images; 277: © Royalty-Free/Corbis; 280: © Royalty-Free/Corbis; 281 (top row left to right): © Ryan McVay/Getty Images, © Comstock/PictureQuest, © Flat Earth Images; 281 (2nd row left): © Royalty-Free/Corbis; 281 (2nd row right): © Andersen Ross/ Getty Images; 281 (middle): © Royalty-Free/Corbis; 281 (bottom): © Photodisc Collection/Getty Images; 282 (top): © Jules-Frazier/Getty Images; 282 (middle): © Royalty-Free/Corbis; 282 (bottom): © The McGraw-Hill Companies, Inc./Ken Cavanagh Photographer; 286: © IMS Communications Ltd/ Capstone Design/FlatEarth Images; 288: © Hyphen-Engineering Education (Thanos Tsilis); 289 (all): © Library of Congress; 290: © Library of Congress; 295: © Digital Vision; 296: © Don Farrall/Getty Images; 298: © Design Pics Inc./Alamy; 300: © Joshua Ets-Hokin/Getty Images; 303: © Royalty-Free/Corbis; 305: © Comstock/PictureQuest; 307: © Digital Vision; 308: © BananaStock/JupiterImages; 310: © Doug Menuez/Getty Images; 312 (left): © Doug Menuez/ Getty Images; 312 (right): © Keith Brofsky/Getty Images; 315: © Royalty-Free/Corbis; 317: © Keith Brofsky/Getty Images; 318: © Skip Nail/Getty Images; 320: © Hyphen-Engineering Education (Thanos Tsilis); 321 (left to right): © Digital Vision Ltd, © Royalty-Free/Corbis, © Federico Gambarini/epa/Corbis; 322: © Chet Phillips/Getty Images; 327: © Creatas/PictureQuest; 328: © Royalty-Free/Corbis; 330: © Steve Mason/Getty Images; 334 (top): © Steve Cole/ Getty Images; 334 (bottom): © Creatas/PictureQuest; 335: © Royalty-Free/Corbis; 336: © Corbis/PunchStock; 338: © Hyphen-Engineering Education (Thanos Tsilis); 339 (all): © Royalty-Free/Corbis; 340: © Don Farrall/Getty Images; 342: © Royalty-Free/Corbis; 345: © Brand X Pictures/PunchStock; 346 (top): © Brand X Pictures/PunchStock; 346 (bottom): © Creatas/PictureQuest; 347 (left): © The McGraw-Hill Companies, Inc./Lars A. Niki, photographer; 347 (right): © Photodisc Collection/Getty Images; 348 (top row left to right): © Photodisc/Getty Images, © C Squared Studios/Getty Images, © C Squared Studio/Getty Images; 348 (bottom row left to right): © C Squared Studio/Getty Images, © The McGraw-Hill Companies, Inc./Dot Box Inc. photographer, © C Squared Studios/Getty Images; 349 (left to right): © C Squared Studios/Getty Images, © The McGraw-Hill Companies, Inc./Ken Cavanagh Photographer, © David Buffington/Getty Images; 350: © Barbara Penoyar/Getty Images; 353 (top row both): © Sandra Ivany/Brand X Pictures/Getty Images; 353 (middle row left): © Medioimages/PunchStock; 353 (middle row right): © Sandra Ivany/Brand X Pictures/Getty Images; 353 (bottom row left) © Sandra Ivany / Brand X Pictures / Getty Images; 353 (bottom row right): © James Gritz/Getty Images; 354 (all): © C Squared Studios/Getty Images; 355: © Liquidlibrary/ Dynamic Graphics/JupiterImages; 356: © Kim Steele/Getty Images; 357 (left): © C. Borland/PhotoLink/Getty Images; 357 (right): © Royalty-Free/Corbis; 358: © The McGraw-Hill Companies, Inc/Andrew Resek, photographer; 359 (left): © Michael Evans/Life File/Getty Images; 359 (right): © Donovan Reese/ Getty Images; 360 (left): © Patagonik Works/Getty Images; 360 (right): © Royalty-Free/Corbis; 361 (left): © McGraw-Hill Companies, Inc./Gary He, photographer; 361 (right): © Copyright 1997 IMS Communications Ltd/Capstone Design. All Rights Reserved; 363 (top row left to right): © Stockdisc/ PunchStock, © The McGraw-Hill Companies, Inc/Ken Karp, photographer, © Glen Allison/Getty Images; 363 (bottom row left to right): © Courtesy of The National Human Genome Research Institute, © Digital Vision/PunchStock, © PhotoLink/Getty Images; 364 (left): © Royalty-Free/Corbis; 364 (right): © The McGraw-Hill Companies, Inc/Andrew Resek, photographer; (Hilton is a registered trademark of Hilton Hospitailty, Inc., which was not involved in the production of and does not endorse this product.); 366: © Royalty-Free/Corbis; 368: © Bloom Productions/Getty Images; 370: © Gianni Dagli Orti/Corbis; 372: © Digital Vision; 375 (left): © G.K. & Vikki Hart/Getty Images; 375 (right): © IT Stock/PunchStock; 376 (left): © PhotoLink/Photodisc/Getty Images; 376 (right): © PhotoLink/Getty Images; 377: © Creatas/PictureQuest; 378: © Big Cheese Photo/JupiterImages; 380: © Hyphen-Engineering Education (Thanos Tsilis); 381 (left to right): © Digital Vision/Getty Images, © CMCD/Getty Images, © Jeremy Woodhouse/Getty Images; 382: © Royalty-Free/Corbis; 387: © Royalty-Free/Corbis; 388: © Royalty-Free/Corbis; 389: © Dynamic Graphics/JupiterImages; 393: © IT Stock Free; 395 (left): © Don Tremain/Getty Images; 395 (right): © Stockbyte/Punchstock Images; 397: © Eric Audras/Photoalto/PictureQuest; 400: © C. Borland/PhotoLink/Getty Images; 402: © Hyphen-Engineering Education (Thanos Tsilis); 403 (left to right): © Photolink/Getty Images, © Pixtal/age footstock, © BananaStock/PunchStock; 404: © Imageshop/Alamy; back cover (top to bottom): © The McGraw-Hill Companies Inc./Ken Cavanagh, Photographer, © Andrew Ward/Life File/Getty Images, ©Library of Congress Prints and Photographs Division (LC-USZ662-117580), ©Getty Images, © Comstock/Jupiter Images.

430